Advances in Cross-Cultural Assessment

Advances in Cross-Cultural Assessment

Ronald J. Samuda
Reuven Feuerstein
Alan S. Kaufman
John E. Lewis
Robert J. Sternberg
and Associates

SAGE Publications
International Educational and Professional Publisher
Thousand Oaks London New Delhi

For information:

SAGE Publications, Inc.
2455 Teller Road
Thousand Oaks, California 91320
E-mail: order@sagepub.com

SAGE Publications Ltd.
6 Bonhill Street
London EC2A 4PU
United Kingdom

SAGE Publications India Pvt. Ltd.
M-32 Market
Greater Kailash I
New Delhi 110 048 India

Printed in the United States of America

Library of Congress Cataloging-in-Publication Data

Main entry under title:

Advances in cross-cultural assessment / by Ronald J. Samuda . . . [et al.].
   p. cm.
  Includes bibliographical references and index.
  ISBN 0-7619-1212-6 (cloth: acid-free paper) ISBN 0-7619-1213-4
(pbk.: acid-free paper)
   1. Educational tests and measurements—Social aspects—United States.
  2. Intelligence tests—Social aspects—United States. 3. Minority students—
Rating of—United States. 4. Psychometrics. 5. Test bias—United States.
  6. Kaufman Assessment Battery for Children. I. Samuda, Ronald J.
LB3051 .A538 1998
371.26′01′3—ddc21   98-8891

98 99 00 01 02 03 10 9 8 7 6 5 4 3 2 1

Acquiring Editor:	Jim Nageotte
Editorial Assistant:	Fiona Lyon
Production Editor:	Diana E. Axelsen
Editorial Assistant:	Denise Santoyo
Typesetter:	Marion Warren
Indexer:	Mary Mortensen
Cover Designer:	Ravi Balasuriya
Print Buyer:	Anna Chin

Contents

1. Cross-Cultural Assessment: Issues and Alternatives　　　**1**
RONALD J. SAMUDA

　　Problems in Cross-Cultural Assessment　　　3
　　What Is Intelligence?　　　7
　　The Goals and Purposes of This Book　　　8
　　Intelligence in Historical Context　　　9
　　Cattell's Model of Fluid and Crystallized Intelligence　　　11
　　Organization and Structure of the Book　　　12
　　Conclusions　　　18

2. Kaufman Assessment Battery for Children:
Theory and Application　　　**20**
ELIZABETH O. LICHTENBERGER, ALAN S. KAUFMAN, AND
NADEEN L. KAUFMAN

　　K-ABC Theory　　　21
　　Minority Group Assessment　　　24
　　Standardization and Properties of the Scale　　　26
　　Overview　　　28
　　Practical Application of the K-ABC　　　29
　　Case Study: John V.　　　29
　　Case Study: Roberto G.　　　39

3. Kaufman Assessment Battery for Children (K-ABC):
Recent Research　　　**56**
ELIZABETH O. LICHTENBERGER AND ALAN S. KAUFMAN

　　Introduction　　　56

African American–White Group Differences on the
    K-ABC   58
Native American–White Group Differences on the
    K-ABC   65
Hispanic–White Group Differences on the K-ABC   68
Content Validity   70
Construct Validity   75
Criterion-Related Validity: Predictive Validity   86
Criterion-Related Validity: Concurrent Validity   95
Summary   99

**4. The Learning Potential Assessment Device:
An Alternative Approach to the Assessment
of Learning Potential**   **100**
*REUVEN FEUERSTEIN, LOUIS H. FALIK,
AND RAFI FEUERSTEIN*

The LPAD Process of Dynamic Assessment   102
The Instruments of the LPAD   116
The Structure of the LPAD   126
Group LPAD Assessment   146
Differentiating LPAD From Other Dynamic
    Assessment Methods   150
Current and Future Problems for Study   157
Summary and Conclusions   159

**5. Linking Assessment to Intervention With
Instrumental Enrichment**   **162**
*YVETTE JACKSON, JOHN E. LEWIS, REUVEN FEUERSTEIN, AND
RONALD J. SAMUDA*

Instrumental Enrichment   164
Using the Instruments   188
The Atlanta Project   190
Refocusing the Goal for Assessment and Instruction   194
Applying IE Dimensions for Reforming Assessment and
    Instruction   195
Summary   196

6. All Intelligence Testing Is "Cross-Cultural":
   Constructing Intelligence Tests to Meet the
   Demands of Person × Task × Situation Interactions   197
   ROBERT STERNBERG

     The Thesis   199
     The Prototype-Based Test of Intelligence   200
     The Sternberg Triarchic Intelligence Test   202
     Tests of Analytical Intelligence   204
     Tests of Creative Intelligence   206
     Tests of Practical Intelligence   209
     Tests of Social Intelligence   211
     Survey Tests of Intelligence   212
     A Levels-of-Processing Intelligence Test   213
     Some Current Testing Projects   215
     Conclusion   215

7. Nontraditional Uses of Traditional Aptitude Tests   218
   JOHN E. LEWIS

     Preassessment Issues   219
     Culture-Free and Culture-Fair Tests   221
     Translated Measures   225
     System of Multicultural Pluralistic Assessment (SOMPA)   227
     Comprehensive Assessment   229
     Dynamic Assessment Approaches   230
     Post-Assessment Considerations   235
     Recommended Assessment Practices   235
     Conclusion   239

8. Multicultural Assessment and the Buros Institute
   of Mental Measurements: On the Cutting Edge of
   Measurement Concerns   242
   GARGI ROYSIRCAR SODOWSKY, JORGE E. GONZALEZ, AND
   PHOEBE Y. KUO-JACKSON

     Section 1: The 1993 Buros-Nebraska Symposium on
        Testing and Measurement: Multicultural Assessment   243

Section 2: Evaluation of Multicultural Ability,
    Achievement, and Language Tests   253
Section 3: Evaluation of Select Personality Tests   266
Conclusion   272

References   274

Index   287

About the Authors   299

1 Cross-Cultural Assessment

Issues and Alternatives

RONALD J. SAMUDA

Assessing intelligence and the special abilities and propensities of individuals is an essential fact of modern society. The need for testing and evaluating potential and achievement is particularly necessary within school systems. Without a systematic testing procedure, the educational enterprise would return to a time when the subjective judgment of teachers formed the basis for finding the best accommodation for students within the schools, classifying and promoting individual students, and predicting the potential for successful completion of training programs. Tests are indispensable when selecting college candidates, training recruits for the professions and vocations, and placing individuals within the occupational structure of industry.

Testing is an inescapable reality of the educational, social, and economic enterprise of any modern society. It began in an effort to help rather than limit the prospects of those who were different and especially of those children who had difficulty learning in the normal classroom. That was the original purpose of the pioneer work of Alfred Binet (see Binet & Simon, 1916). Even now, the search for intellectual deficiencies is still a primary application of psychological tests. Schools are the largest test users. At regular intervals, students are classified with regard to their ability to profit from various types of school instruction and identified as intellectually retarded or gifted. Routinely, tests are used to diagnose academic failures and to aid in educational and vocational counseling at high schools and colleges. Without some kind of objective measure, we cannot calibrate an individual's level or rate of learning nor can we discover the reasons why the individual does not achieve. Psychological testing plays a vital role in education and in establishing the level of developed abilities in various spheres of training and on-the-job expertise.

Given the immense importance of testing and its contribution to educational practice and significance in the social, industrial, and economic systems of many countries, why has it fallen into disrepute? Why has testing come under the critical scrutiny of minorities? Why has testing been brought before the courts, beginning in the latter part of the 20th century and continuing even today? Why has testing divided the ranks of social scientists and psychologists into those who assert the fairness of traditional tests and those who hurl accusations of discrimination, social injustice, and even racial genocide?

To illustrate the problem, it would seem appropriate to recall the words of Ernest Hemingway, who once told a group of journalists, "The writer's dilemma is to write what is true and to communicate that truth so that it becomes useful and part of the reader's experience." There exists a parallel enigma for social scientists in assessing human subjects—that is, to find and state what is true and to communicate that truth so that it can be understood and useful to those for whom it is intended. But that has not always been the case in the assessment of intelligence, especially when applied across cultures. Despite the many benefits deriving from psychological tests, ethnic minorities, as well as culturally different and socioeconomically disadvantaged groups, have suffered indignity and harm from the use of tests and the interpretation of their results. Indeed, the nature/nurture debate and the IQ controversy have been central issues in the history of psychology. Arguments are still being proposed today to justify ethnic and class differences and to link test results with genetic endowment of intellectual potential.

In the fall of 1994, the IQ controversy gathered new momentum with the publication of Herrnstein and Murray's *The Bell Curve*. The book not only stirred up new disputations with far-reaching scientific ramifications, but it also provoked political outcomes and impassioned feelings. As the authors of a February 1996 article published in the *American Psychologist* maintained, "Herrnstein and Murray have gone well beyond the scientific findings, making explicit recommendations on various aspects of public policy" (Neisser et al., 1996, p. 78). The implications of

Herrnstein and Murray's (1994) book are reminiscent of the early part of the 20th century, when tests and their interpretation had a massive impact on the politics of immigration, for they provided the rationale to determine who would be the preferred immigrant. In a similar vein, *The Bell Curve*, if it were absorbed into public policy, could have devastating social and educational consequences in the new century.

Problems in Cross-Cultural Assessment

Too often, the main use of testing has been to serve a sorting and labeling function. Concomitantly, minority children have been placed into programs of minimal curriculum content on the basis of spurious results. Well-meaning teachers, counselors, and administrators often administer tests and evaluate the results, believing that they are doing a worthy and professional job by sticking closely to the protocol of standard instructions for administering the instruments and interpreting the results. No doubt, the vast majority of professionals in the business of education and psychology are imbued with the sincere desire to be helpful and effective in enhancing the education of students. However, too often those results are the very means by which the school system can become the unwitting agent in blaming the victim and providing a crutch that excuses the system for its failure to create the appropriate learning environment for the atypical individual. The issue of test results and their interpretation extends beyond concerns that relate to their use in the school systems. Tests can have dire social and economic consequences for those individuals who are labeled and placed in minimal curricular programs, and thus curtailed from further secondary or tertiary education. Tests and their results, therefore, can bring disastrous outcomes affecting the lives and aspirations of minorities in any society.

Minority children, as a group, have always scored lower on standardized tests. That statement holds good regardless of the ethnicity of the group: the Irish of the 1900s, the southern and eastern Europeans of the 1910s and '20s; the Blacks and Spanish-speaking groups of the mid-century. In fact, the use of standard ability and achievement tests in schools was primarily motivated by liberal views that translated equal opportunity into identical treatment. However, as Professor Sandra Scarr

(1977, p. 73) has so cogently contended, equal opportunity does not always ensue from identical treatment. In fact, equality of opportunity is more likely to result from a "different strokes for different folks" approach where individuals are treated according to the advantages or idiosyncrasies of their environmental, linguistic, cultural, and ethnic background.

Assessment issues necessarily embrace legal, technical, scientific, political, and philosophical implications. Psychometricians and social scientists face the dilemma of making ethical and moral choices to determine the purposes for testing intelligence. One African American activist put the question squarely: Why test at all? What is the purpose of the psychometric enterprise? If its purpose is to establish the scientific basis for comparing social, cultural, or ethnic groups on a particular trait, then the use of testing can be rationalized, provided the methodology can be justified and the limitations of the tests are taken into account when interpreting the results (Berry, Poortinga, Segall, & Dasen, 1994). But if the purpose of assessment is to use psychological tests to help in the educational process, then standardized norm-referenced tests of intelligence represent merely culture-specific devices that can tell no more than the extent to which a particular individual veers from the mainstream norm.

Opponents of the use of standardized tests with minority children contend that the results have very negative social outcomes; they blame biases in the tests and in the procedures of testing. Some argue for the elimination of testing for minorities, whereas others envision culturally relative measures that would discard mean group differences. On the other hand, representatives of the testing establishment warn that such changes would lead to subjective and potentially more biased assessments with no potential for predictive use for ethnically adjusted scores. Psychometricians also point to the fact that tests have equal predictive validity for all groups. Scoring low on a test of mental aptitude will, in all probability, indicate low performance in school; and, a low score on the SAT will generally predict a low grade point average in college or, in extreme cases, the actual failure to function adequately in the college program.

Some social scientists claim that traditional assessment measures cannot indicate the true potential of minorities because those instruments are geared to the values, information, learning styles, environmental influences, and cognitive structures that are common to the middle-class lifestyle. Many ethnic minorities and socioeconomically disadvantaged mainstream individuals do not share these amenities. Many subscribe to an entirely different pattern of values; some are raised in environments of poverty, high crime rates, or other social ills typically not experienced by the mainstream middle class. Thus, tests cannot be universally applied, and their results should not be used to label and place minority students in programs and classes for the subnormal. Moreover, technical flaws in the validity and reliability of the instruments occur when traditional Eurocentric tests are used with culturally different individuals.

In a chapter entitled "Heredity, Intelligence, Politics, and Psychology: II," Professor Leon Kamin (1976) cited certain quotations from the writings of pioneers in the U.S. testing movement to demonstrate its sociopolitical consequences. The following serves to illustrate the point concerning the consequences of test results even when interpreted by the most illustrious psychometrician:

> Their dullness seems to be racial, or at least inherent in the family stocks from which they come. The fact that one meets this type with such extraordinary frequencies among Indians, Mexicans, and Negroes suggests quite forcibly that the whole question of racial differences in mental traits will have to be taken up anew. . . . there will be discovered enormously significant racial differences . . . which cannot be wiped out by any scheme of mental culture. (Terman, 1916, as cited in Kamin, p. 374)

As Kamin (1976) points out, Professor Terman should not be thought of merely as a racist. Rather, he was a man who had a very definite point of view that he applied even-handedly to poor people of all colors. He sincerely believed that he was making an important contribution to the cause of education and, indeed, to the cause of the betterment of the American nation in his way of dealing with a situation he deplored:

> How serious a menace it is to the social, economic and moral welfare of the state. . . . If we would preserve our state for a class of people worthy to possess it, we must prevent, as far as possible, the propagation of mental degenerates . . . the increasing spawn of degeneracy. (Terman, 1917, cited in Kamin, p. 375)

Professor Terman's statements represent an extreme point of view today. The drive toward the cleansing of the state through the links between psychometrics and eugenics, although still discernable in some degree, is not a widespread philosophy of testing. There can be, however, no denying that the system of education, whether at the elementary, secondary, or tertiary level, is heavily weighed in terms of middle-class Eurocentric values, emphasizing the Puritan ethic. Professor Scarr's address at the 1977 national conference on testing in New York stressed the need to recognize the profound problem that exists when using intelligence tests with culturally different populations. The information sampled by IQ tests stems from general cultural knowledge—that is, the culture of the white, urban, middle class—and the skills sampled by the tests are those taught by middle-class parents regardless of their color or ethnicity.

At the risk of repeating the same caveat, it must be remembered that minority children who do well on IQ tests as a whole come from homes that convey the same values, the same aspirations, the same environmental circumstances, and the same attitudes as the majority white middle class in America. The issue of color and ethnicity is irrelevant and misleading. The children of people such as retired General Colin Powell and the Reverend Jesse Jackson, for example, will do as well on the standard traditional tests of mental aptitude as any white middle-class child, because they experienced similar influences and models in the home and in the environment. They will, in a sense, be conditioned by very similar circumstances. They will have similar cognitive styles and analogous exposure to the middle-class pedagogy and school environment. The point is that psychological tests are necessarily biased in favor of those who come from that milieu and against those who are culturally or socio-economically different. The basic problem in the use of intelligence tests with culturally different populations concerns the skills and knowledge that are presumably based on the assumption of common experience.

As Anastasi (1988) states, intelligence tests are merely samples of behavior, whether that behavior consists of tracing a maze, arranging a sequence of pictures, knowing the capital of France, or defining the term *justice*. Moreover, almost all tests of mental aptitude comprise items that call for the use of analogous thinking in solving problems. Tests take for granted that the individual being assessed understands the underlying concept of the analogy and has developed a cognitive strategy to solve it. It does not really matter that the analogy is framed in nonverbal symbols; the result, for those who do not understand how to solve analogous problems, will be the same. The rationale underlying sampling procedures presumes that if individuals know the capital of France, they are also likely to have other kinds of similar information; people who can abstract the similarities between farming and manufacture will also know how to think abstractly when it comes to solving other problems; and, similarly, people who can remember and repeat eight digits backward will also be able to manipulate and control other data in their head. Thus, it takes no particular stretch of the imagination to realize that aptitude tests, whether they might be the Stanford-Binet, the Wechsler Intelligence Scale for Children, or one of the group variety, such as the Lorge-Thorndike or the Scholastic Aptitude Test, are in essence tests of developed abilities; as such, they are, in a sense, essentially tests of achievement.

What Is Intelligence?

Another fundamental problem exists in defining the word *intelligence*. One thing is certain: There is little agreement on what it is. Many definitions have been proposed, including the most cynical of all, which states that intelligence is whatever IQ tests measure. Some have searched for an adequate meaning by linking the definition of intelligence to real-life situations associated with adaptability in neighborhood and family settings. But are we not still plagued with defining and recognizing what constitutes intelligence in family and neighborhood settings? What should an individual from a ghetto project environment do if he or she happens to find a closed envelope, stamped and addressed, lying on the ground? Is it more adaptable to post the letter at the nearest mailbox or open it to see if there is any money inside? Is finding employment in the ghetto or knowing how to herd a flock of sheep or finding one's way in a city or in the woods of Kentucky an appropriate way of testing adaptability? Each one undoubtedly requires intelligent behavior, but society does not reward that kind of intelligence, whatever it is. Intelligence, as measured by tests of mental aptitude, is fundamentally "school-learn-ing" ability and not general or common adaptation to life situations.

In view of the issues and pitfalls alluded to above, serious objections have been raised since the 1970s concerning the reasons for testing. Many have called for a moratorium on all tests that would seek to measure capacity to reason or predict successful performance either in school or on the job. One distinguished black professor went so far as to label test-ing a means of engendering the intellectual genocide of blacks, particu-larly when the results are interpreted to ascribe genetic inferiority to Af-rican Americans. Indeed, it is precisely because of those concerns, especially with regard to the interpretation of test results, that some edu-cators and psychologists have turned toward culturally relative assess-ment. However, neither the abandonment of testing per se nor the adop-tion of culturally relative assessment will do much to solve the problem.

If testing does have a purpose in the educational preparation of mi-norities, it should be geared in such a way that it will inform instruction. The procedures should help in initiating and fostering pedagogically sound programs and settings that will optimize the learning potential of individuals to help them reach what Lev Vygotsky (1978) has called *the zone of proximal development*, that is, the optimum level of functioning that one can achieve under ideal developmental conditions.

The fundamental question concerns the alternatives: Will testing continue to buttress institutional and structural racism in the schools in general and society at large or can assessment become the means of open-ing up opportunity for all individuals, regardless of their ethnic and socioeconomic backgrounds? Assessment, if it is to be educationally and ethically viable, must adhere to the principle that it serves the good of individuals by augmenting the effectiveness of the teaching-learning process. On the other hand, when it necessarily abrogates the principle of social justice, testing contributes to the violation of civil rights of in-dividual citizens.

The Goals and Purposes of This Book

This publication includes work that represents the culmination of the major trends in the field of cross-cultural assessment throughout the last quarter of this century. In some respects, it is designed to respond to the increasing spate of criticisms of psychometrics that began in the early seventies. It pinpoints the weaknesses of traditional tests and follows in the wake of Binet to provide a means by which assessment can be useful in the educational enterprise.

This book is essentially concerned with advances in the theory and practice of appraising cognitive potential. Such a term, however, represents another way of saying intelligence, or mental aptitude, or capacity to learn. All of those concepts are implied in the notion of IQ. But how can we study the theory and practice of assessing intelligence if we have not even agreed on the meaning of the term? How can we place each movement or innovation in context unless we first examine the pitfalls associated with the notion? As William Turnbull (1975), late president of the Educational Testing Service at Princeton, wrote, "As long as the *definition* of intelligence remains a matter of choice, with that choice not made explicit, the likelihood of finding agreement on any propositions about the *measurement* of intelligence is slim indeed" (p. vii).

Although intelligence, as a concept, has never been adequately defined, it is still regarded by the public at large and, indeed, by many practicing teachers, counselors, and professionals in the area of social work, as an important entity. Confusion is widespread concerning its definition, and many still confuse IQ with the concept of intelligence. Even in the field of social science, there are those who still maintain that intelligence tests measure something innate that is fixed at the moment of conception and genetically linked.

This is not the place to reiterate the various attempts at settling the arguments concerning the meaning of intelligence. Suffice it to say that there has been a plethora of definitions, each one suffering from a number of evident weaknesses. In their efforts to be all-encompassing, most definitions are vague, use undefinable terms, place overemphasis on the ability to reason abstractly, or consider intelligence as an entity. What is the reason for such widespread bedlam in the use of the term?

Intelligence in Historical Context

The first initiative to define intelligence was the work of Sir Francis Galton, who based his concept on the belief that mental tests measure, to some extent, one basic intellectual ability, which Spearman called *g*.

As an aftermath of that kind of reasoning, the concept of fixed mental aptitude, compressed in the concept of an intelligence quotient or IQ, became a dominant axiom until far into the 20th century. Besides this general capacity, believed to be pure intelligence, the notion included specific factors, or *s*, for an array of minor types of abilities. Such theories evolved into the hierarchical pyramid advanced in the models of Burt and Vernon with Spearman's *g* at the top.

On the other hand, there were those researchers, such as Thurstone and Guildford, who proposed a second approach. Rather than linking all mental abilities to a single factor, they held that intelligence is multifaceted. In fact, intelligence should be perceived (to use Tyler's words) as essentially a plural word. Guildford elaborated on Thurstone's multifactorial approach by proposing his famous structure of intellect (SI) in the shape of a cube encompassing 120 possible cells, each representing a hypothetical mental ability. From such beginnings, the multifactorial theory of intelligence has spawned the movement toward the differentiation of aptitudes, particularly in the application to such well-known instruments as the Differential Aptitude Battery commonly used in schools and employment situations and the General Aptitude Test Battery extensively used in counseling by the U.S. Department of Labor.

The standard tests of mental aptitude are the Stanford-Binet and the Wechsler group, including the Wechsler Scale of Adult Intelligence (WAIS and WAIS-R), the Wechsler Intelligence Scale for Children (WISC and WISC-R), and the Wechsler Preschool and Primary Scale of Intelligence (WPPSI). These individually administered tests, originally standardized on norming populations that tended to focus on white Anglo-Saxon middle-class individuals, have been subjected to heated debate and criticism precisely because of the initial homogeneous nature of the standardization samples, which excluded minorities. Those two traditional tests have since been restandardized to include minorities, in the form of the Stanford-Binet and the Wechsler scales, WAIS-R and WISC-R. However, the restandardized models are still subjected to critical scrutiny because of the paucity of sociodemographic variables in sampling procedures. Thus, as Dana (1993) demonstrated, "these tests apparently measure the construct of intelligence somewhat differently across groups" (p. 186). In other words, they lack cross-cultural construct validity. However, despite their limitations, standardized tests can be useful when used with the care and protocol that Jerome Sattler has recommended, and such uses are discussed by Professor John E. Lewis in Chapter 7.

Cattell's Model of Fluid and Crystallized Intelligence

Changes in the conceptualization of intelligence have inspired new approaches to cognitive assessment. Cattell (1963) proposed a departure from the notion of a fixed and unitary g factor and advanced the theory of fluid and crystallized intelligence. Cattell's theory regards fluid intelligence as a basic capacity to adapt to new situations. It is also an inherent capacity for learning and problem solving that is independent of both education and cultural influences. To adapt to novel situations, fluid intelligence must encompass flexible inductive skills. Crystallized intelligence emerges from a person's use of fluid intelligence to interact with society. It is therefore a product of formal education. Thus, the means by which crystallized intelligence organizes knowledge and concepts reflects how the members of a given society process information and solve problems. These are "developed abilities," which can be quantified and assembled to make up tests for general mental ability. The outcome of such measures is necessarily static.

In Cattell's formulation, intelligence is the product of an active mind that is malleable and responsive to instruction. Intelligent behavior is seen in the processing of information, the anticipation of new situations, and the planning for effective solutions based on past experience. Given such a perspective, it follows that any adequate assessment of intelligence must address both these fluid and crystallized characteristics.

Traditional standardized tests of intelligence have focused principally on assessing global intellectual abilities. The original Binet tests were aimed at predicting how well Parisian children learn within the "normal" school classroom. The Stanford-Binet test developed by Lewis Terman and Maud Merrill was based on Binet's model and similarly related to correlations between performance on samples of behavior and achievement within the school system. The Wechsler Intelligence Scales were constructed around David Wechsler's (1958) notion that intelligence is a "global capacity of the individual to act purposefully, to think rationally, and to deal effectively with the environment" (p. 7).

Organization and Structure of the Book

This book is intended to provide an overview of the major innovations in the field of intellectual assessment. Each chapter covers one aspect of the innovations and theoretical formulations that have been occurring over the past quarter of a century. But although the focus is on what is new in the field of cross-cultural assessment, the intention is to show the ways and means that the traditional standardized tests have been modified to make them appropriate for use with culturally different individuals, providing the limitations are kept well in mind. One chapter is devoted to cross-cultural issues in the assessment of personality.

The Kaufman Assessment Battery for Children

The Kaufman Assessment Battery for Children (K-ABC; Kaufman & Kaufman, 1983b) represents one of the three central methodologies with which this book is concerned. It is of prime importance in the advance of innovations in cross-cultural assessment. Like Sternberg, the Kaufmans were interested in the assessment of fluid intelligence and achievement. Originally developed for psychological and clinical assessment—and particularly for the educational evaluation of exceptional children, including the learning-disabled—the K-ABC is a landmark system of testing for educational planning and placement and, as the chapter on cross-cultural research signifies, it is especially important for minority group assessment, for preschool assessment, and for limited neuropsychological assessment (Kaufman & Kaufman, 1983b).

The K-ABC is not limited to the measurement of intellectual potential, for it combines an achievement element that involves mental processing or problem solving in novel situations from one that involves factual, school-related knowledge. The 16 subtests include mental processing assessment, yielding aggregated global scores for Sequential Processing, Simultaneous Processing, and a Mental Processing Composite. These tests of mental processes tap fluid intelligence in the form of adaptable and flexible behavior in response to unfamiliar situations and problems. There is also a Nonverbal Scale that is a shortened form of the Mental Processing Scale where pantomime is employed with motoric responses.

Cross-Cultural Research Results With the K-ABC

The system developed by Alan and Nadeen Kaufman represents a pivotal leap in cross-cultural assessment. As demonstrated in Chapter 2, the testing program has been thoroughly researched with regard to relevance in cross-cultural situations. The reliability data compared favorably with the Wechsler tests, and in 43 studies, emphasis was placed on construct and criterion-related validity. In general, the K-ABC is especially important in testing children who have limited English language proficiency or who speak a nonstandard English dialect. Research with children who speak different languages, such as Spanish and French, indicates that the K-ABC is equally useful as a diagnostic and placement tool and that it can provide important clues for remedial procedures in the school systems.

The fact that the K-ABC separates mental processing scores from achievement scores may explain why it is more useful in assessing minority children, compared to conventional tests, such as the WISC-R or even the System of Multicultural Multipluralistic Assessment (SOMPA), which depend on traditional test results as a base. In fact, the research done on Hispanic children would indicate that the K-ABC is more appropriate and more useful than the WISC in establishing the intellectual potential and functioning level of minority children. Moreover, the flexibility in interpretation of the K-ABC tends to provide richer information with which to design effective posttest intervention strategies, as the case studies in Chapter 2 reveal. In fact, the results of the K-ABC can clearly determine the characteristics of the testee's cognitive performance and verbal achievement.

Feuerstein's Learning Potential Assessment Device

The second system of assessment with which this book is concerned is the Feuerstein methodology and particularly the Learning Potential Assessment Device (LPAD) with its programmatic follow-up in Instrumental Enrichment. Feuerstein's methodology epitomizes a departure from the conventional views of intelligence. In sharp contrast to Spearman's theory, which tended to imply an immutable IQ fixed by genetic endowment at the moment of birth, Feuerstein derives his definition of intelligence from Vygotsky, who perceives it as a dynamic process that changes with development and learning. Although genetics has some relevance, the significant factors in the development of intelligence emanate from the cultural environment, from influences in the home, and from conditioning within the school and social environment. As learners interact with other people, their learning stimulates cognitive development. As cognitive development proceeds, a zone of proximal development can be depicted to reflect the gap between the learner's actual development and the learner's developmental potential. It is this potential that enables the counselor, psychologist, or teacher to help in the remedial and reconditioning process to raise the learner's ability to function. Testing is intentionally dynamic and geared to a remedial program whereby cognitive gaps are apprehended and instructional procedures are designed to enhance cognitive functioning.

Feuerstein's major concern has been to assess the untapped cognitive potential of individuals, particularly the culturally deprived, and to remedy any deficiencies through an active intervention process that helps the individual build a new and effective cognitive structure. The process of assessment rests on a fundamental tenet of modifiability of the cognitive structure. Linked with this is the conviction that the mediated learning experience can enhance and condition intellectual functioning.

Two chapters are devoted to Feuerstein's methodology because each one deals with a related but separate phase of the procedure. Chapter 4 is concerned with the LPAD. This dynamic method begins with a clear delineation of psychometric goals as follows:

1. To assess students' cognitive modifiability by observing how they function in situations designed to produce a change.
2. To assess the extent of modifiability in terms of cognitive functioning and the significance of a student's attained functioning in the hierarchy of universal cognitive operations, ranging from perception to abstract thinking.
3. To determine the transfer value of what is learned in one area to other areas of operations.

4. To identify the student's preferred modalities for learning and the problem-solving strategies that work best.

Feuerstein's method engages both the student and assessor or counselor in an active modification procedure. When the client performs the task, the counselor's role is to intervene wherever necessary and to present alternative ways of perceiving, interpreting, and problem solving. Change in the client's approach to the task is noted, as well as the amount of intervention necessary to produce that change. The assessment process is therefore transformed from one of the neutral examiner to that of the active and involved appraiser. Assessment takes on a new meaning and becomes part of the educational process. Furthermore, the test items must be clear and well-sequenced to permit a starting point at the individual's level of cognitive functioning. The assessment strategies focus on the *process* of intellectual reasoning rather than on its *product*, and the emphasis is placed on change in cognitive skill.

The LPAD, thus, provides the means to tap an individual's acquisition components and performance components of intelligence. It enables the appraiser to identify where cognitive deficits lie, and it is designed to help fashion a program of remediation and cognitive conditioning so that the very structure of cognitive functioning can be permanently modified.

Instrumental Enrichment

The chapter on Instrumental Enrichment describes Feuerstein's program for remediation of impairments that occur frequently in people who have been culturally deprived. Narrol, Silverman, and Waksman (1982) have demonstrated that individuals who exhibit certain cognitive deficits are amenable to remedial help. Some writers maintain that Feuerstein's basic assumption that everyone is modifiable may be an overgeneralization. Nevertheless, researchers such as Sundberg and Gonzales (1981) have shown that this dynamic approach contributes significantly toward the clarifying of the special needs of minority individuals and groups.

The Feuerstein methodology is now in operation in various countries throughout the world. It has shifted the focus away from quantitative product scores to qualitative observations and interpretations of the process of mental ability functioning, based on the assumption that intelligence is a multifaceted, multidimensional, and fluid construct that continually undergoes change. This approach attempts to determine not only the characteristics of the various components of intelligence but also how they function. What is significant in the three central systems of assessment is that the procedures have been radically changed from an emphasis on calibrating and labeling a static measure of developed ability to a focus on fostering remedial change and reeducation. Taken together, the LPAD and the concept of mediated learning experience encompass what Reuven Feuerstein refers to as *structural cognitive modifiability.*

Sternberg's Triarchic Theory

Robert Sternberg would probably agree that traditional standardized tests do assess some aspects of intelligence, but he would also contend that the results of such tests do not describe the individual's real capacity because they do not take into account the entire spectrum of intelligent behavior. Thus, Sternberg has incorporated in his triarchic theory the view that any comprehensive consideration of the nature of intelligence must take into account three essential facets:

1. The internal world of the individual or the mental mechanisms that underlie intelligent behavior
2. The individual's experience
3. The relationship of the individual to the external world

These aspects of intelligence Sternberg has labeled the componential, the experiential, and the contextual subtheories.

Sternberg's triarchic theory of intelligence has had a profound impact on the psychometric enterprise. In his provocative Chapter 6 of this book, he speculates on the performance of inhabitants of a mythical planet, Velda, and demonstrates why it is so important for us to see the function of intelligence as situational and why it is significant for us to define intelligent behavior within its cultural context.

Using Traditional Assessment Across Cultures

Traditional standardized objective tests are still frequently employed in evaluating the intellectual potential of minorities and culturally different individuals. In Chapter 7, John Lewis addresses the issues of misuse when diverse clients are tested and delineates alternatives for using the traditional instruments in culturally appropriate ways. The chapter comprises an introduction on preassessment issues, a recapitulation and summary of the culture free/culture fair movement, a brief critical review of Jane Mercer's SOMPA, and a discussion of comprehensive assessment and test-of-limits procedures.

The issues and methods are presented in a succinct and precise summary form. As the author points out, even the so-called culture-fair tests are really only culture-reduced because they assume that examinees have been socialized and educated in the culture in which the test originated. However, such procedures can help in the evaluation of the atypical individual when used with discretion and in combination with traditional measures of intelligence, such as the Stanford Binet Fourth Edition or the revised version of the Wechsler Adult Intelligence Scale. The problems inherent in translated tests are also addressed, along with suggestions for ameliorating the difficulty of using language-based tests with linguistically different clients. Although dynamic assessment and the measuring of cognitive modifiability are dealt with in greater detail in other chapters, Lewis touches briefly on the overall concepts so as to place the Feuerstein methodology in the context of the total assessment enterprise. The chapter ends with a set of recommended assessment practices and procedures. Lewis reminds assessors of the culturally diverse that they have an ethical and professional obligation to become aware of the pitfalls and to make every effort to take into account the caveats he has summarized.

Multicultural Assessment and the Buros Institute of Mental Measurements

The chapter by Gargi Roysircar Sodowsky, Jorge E. Gonzalez, and Phoebe Y. Kuo-Jackson is geared to three basic goals. It deals with the 1993 Buros Nebraska Symposium on Testing and Measurement, which represents an important milestone in stimulating awareness of the problems and issues inherent in the use of tests in counseling and clinical practice. It provides a critical evaluation of commercial ability, achievement, and language tests that purport to have multicultural relevance. And it presents a critical analysis of commercially available personality measures commonly used with minority populations.

This chapter represents a unique contribution to the book as a whole, in that it points up the ways in which misdiagnosis can occur, resulting from racial and cultural client-clinician mismatch, particularly in the use of personality measures. The authors introduce some of the most recent and innovative concepts and practices in the field of multicultural and cross-cultural assessment. The properties and significance of the TEMAS (Multicultural Thematic Apperception Test) are discussed, as are such innovative concepts as *sociorace* by Janet Helms and the Oklahoma Racial Attitudes Scale-Preliminary Form (ORAS-P) by Sandra Choney and John Behrens, the Multicultural Counseling Awareness Scale by Joseph Ponterotto, and the Multicultural Inventory by the chapter's senior author, Gargi Sodowsky herself.

The second section is devoted to a critical analysis of Jane Mercer's SOMPA as well as the psychometric properties and factor structure of the WISC-III and the WIAT (the Wechsler Individual Achievement Tests), followed by a delineation of some of the most advanced tests that purport to have multicultural relevance. The third section, dealing with an evaluation of select personality tests, provides readers with an estimate of relevance of two major personality tests, namely, the Strong Interest Inventory, Fourth Edition, and the Minnesota Multiphasic Personality Inventory (MMPI).

As Sodowsky points out in her conclusion, we need to take into account both the etic and emic descriptions of minority people in interracial, interethnic, and intercultural milieus when using any assessment instrument in cross-cultural or multicultural situations.

Conclusions

No one volume can cover all the variables and issues associated with the business of psychological and educational assessment. The central mission of this book has been to pull together the most recent advances in assessing human subjects across cultures. We have attempted to demonstrate and to describe the significant issues and alternatives that are relevant in the final years of this century and that will continue to affect the lives of the great majority of people in various parts of the world. The problems of assessing those who veer from the social, cultural, and linguistic norms of society are not unique to the United States.

The world is increasingly becoming one global village. More and more, the industrial nations of the world will face the need to absorb immigrants into the economic, social, and industrial fabric. If we are to optimize the potential of all individuals, we must find the ways and means of identifying and cultivating the capabilities of all individuals, regardless of their origin or background. Equally important, from a moral and ethical standpoint, we must be conscious of the enormous power of assessment to be disastrous in the lives of those individuals who derive from different cultural and/or socioeconomic environmental circumstances. Educators and social scientists of all persuasions have a moral and ethical duty to ensure that the tests they use are relevant and useful. In particular, we need to be certain that the results, and especially the interpretations associated with those results, will do no harm.

Let us recall the caveat of Ernest Hemingway, when he reminded his fellow writers that their fundamental purpose and moral duty was to discover what is true and to use that truth in ways that are useful. In a very similar way, those of us who deal in the area of psychometrics and the application of test results must devote our psychometric enterprise to discovering what is true, using that truth for the betterment and uplift of those who are subjected to our assessment devices.

The contents of this book are not exhaustive. We have been highly selective in pinpointing the central thrust of the issues and the alternatives in cross-cultural assessment that have occurred in the past two decades. As we approach a new century, we hope this book will be an important contribution within the context of education and the social sciences in all countries where the issues of cross-cultural assessment are significant.

2 Kaufman Assessment Battery for Children

Theory and Application

ELIZABETH O. LICHTENBERGER
ALAN S. KAUFMAN
NADEEN L. KAUFMAN

The Kaufman Assessment Battery for Children (K-ABC) is a battery of tests measuring intelligence and achievement of normal and exceptional children ages 2½ through 12½ years. It yields four scales: Sequential Processing, Simultaneous Processing, Mental Processing Composite (Sequential and Simultaneous), and Achievement.

The K-ABC is becoming a frequently used test in intelligence and achievement assessment by both clinical and school psychologists (Kamphaus, Beres, Kaufman, & Kaufman, 1995). In a nationwide survey of school psychologists conducted in 1987 by Obringer (1988), respondents were asked to rank the following instruments in order of their usage: Wechsler's scales, the K-ABC, and both the old and new Stanford-Binets. The Wechsler scales earned a mean rank of 2.69, followed closely by the K-ABC, with a mean of 2.55, the L-M version of the Binet (1.98), and the Stanford Binet Fourth Edition (1.26). Bracken (1985) also found similar evidence of the K-ABC's popularity. Bracken surveyed school psychologists and found that for ages 5 through 11 years, the Wechsler (1974) Intelligence Scale for Children-Revised (WISC-R) was endorsed by 82%, the K-ABC by 57%, and the Binet IV by 39% of the practitioners. These results suggest that clinicians working with children should have some familiarity with the K-ABC (Kamphaus et al., 1995).

The K-ABC has been the subject of great controversy from the outset, as evidenced by the strongly pro and con articles written for a special issue of the *Journal of Special Education* devoted to the K-ABC (Miller & Reynolds, 1984). Many of the controversies, especially those regarding the validity of the K-ABC theory, will likely endure as unresolved for some time (Kamphaus et al., 1995). Fortunately, the apparent controversy linked to the K-ABC has resulted in numerous research studies and papers that provide more insight into the K-ABC and its strengths and weaknesses.

The K-ABC was developed with the intention of creating a test battery that would improve upon existing individually administered intelligence tests. To delineate the areas that were in the greatest need of improvement within the assessment arena, perspectives from clinical experience with existing measures of intelligence, knowledge of empirical research and test construction, and criticisms of existing measures were combined. In the K-ABC interpretive manual (Kaufman & Kaufman, 1983a), the following are listed as goals kept in mind in the development of the K-ABC:

1. To measure intelligence from a strong theoretical and research basis
2. To separate acquired factual knowledge from the ability to solve unfamiliar problems
3. To yield scores that translate to educational intervention
4. To include novel tasks
5. To be easy to administer and objective to score
6. To be sensitive to the diverse needs of preschool, minority group, and exceptional children

This chapter will discuss primarily the first and last goals. The tasks on the K-ABC were developed to conform to a specific model derived from neuropsychological and cognitive theories, which are discussed in the following section. The final goal of meeting the needs of minority group children is multifaceted and complex. The many efforts that were made to be sensitive to the needs of such groups will also be discussed in detail in the following pages.

K-ABC Theory

The K-ABC intelligence scales are based on a theoretical framework of Sequential and Simultaneous information processing, which relates to *how* children solve problems rather than *what* type of problems they must solve (e.g., verbal or nonverbal). In stark contrast is Wechsler's theoretical framework of the assessment of *g*, a conception of intelligence as an overall global entity. As a result, Wechsler used the Verbal and Performance Scales as a means to an end; that end is the assessment of general intelligence. In comparison, in the K-ABC, the individual importance of the Sequential and Simultaneous Scales in interpretation is emphasized, rather than the overall Mental Processing Composite score (Kamphaus et al., 1995).

The Sequential and Simultaneous framework for the K-ABC stems from an updated version of a variety of theories (Kamphaus et al., 1995). The foundation lies in a wealth of research in clinical and experimental neuropsychology and cognitive psychology. The Sequential and Simultaneous theory was primarily developed from two lines of theory: the information processing approach of Luria (1966) and the cerebral specialization work of Sperry (1968, 1974), Bogen (1969), Kinsbourne (1978), and Wada, Clarke, and Hamm (1975).

The neuropsychological processing model developed from the neurophysiological observations of Alexander Luria (1966, 1973, 1980) and Roger Sperry (1968), the psychoeducational research of J. P. Das (1973; Das, Kirby, & Jarman, 1975, 1979; Naglieri & Das, 1988, 1990), and the psychometric research with the K-ABC (Kaufman & Kaufman, 1983a). The neuropsychological processing model possesses several strengths relative to previous models in that it (a) provides a unified framework for interpreting a wide range of important individual difference variables; (b) rests on a well-researched theoretical base in clinical neuropsychology and psychobiology; (c) presents a processing, rather than a product-oriented, explanation for behavior; and (d) lends itself readily to remedial strategies based on relatively uncomplicated assessment procedures (Kaufman & Kaufman, 1983a; McCallum & Merritt, 1983; Perlman, 1986).

This neuropsychological processing model describes two very distinct types of processes that individuals use to organize and process information received to solve problems successfully: successive or sequential, analytic-linear processing versus holistic/simultaneous processing (Levy & Trevarthen, 1976; Luria, 1966). These processes have been identified by numerous researchers in diverse areas of neuropsychology and cognitive psychology (Perlman, 1986). From Sperry's (1974) cerebral specialization perspective, these processes represent the problem-solving strategies of the left hemisphere (analytic/sequential) and the right hemisphere (Gestalt/holistic). From Luria's theoretical approach, successive and simultaneous processes reflect the coding processes that characterize *Block 2* functions.

Regardless of the theoretical model, successive processing refers to the processing of information in a sequential, serial order. The essential nature of this mode of processing is that the system is not totally surveyable at any point in time. Simultaneous processing refers to the synthesis of separate elements into groups. The essential nature of this mode of processing is that any portion of the result is, at once, surveyable without dependence on its position in the whole. The model assumes that the two modes of processing information are available to the individual. The selection of either or both modes of processing depends on two conditions: (a) the individual's habitual mode of processing information as determined by social-cultural and genetic factors, and (b) the demands of the task (Das, Kirby, & Jarman, 1979).

In reference to the K-ABC, Simultaneous processing refers to the mental ability to integrate information all at once to solve a problem correctly. Simultaneous processing frequently involves spatial, analogic, or organizational abilities (Kaufman & Kaufman, 1983a; Kamphaus & Reynolds, 1987). There is often a visual aspect to the problem, and visual imagery is used to solve it. A prototypical example of a Simultaneous subtest is the Triangles subtest on the K-ABC, which is similar to Wechsler's Block Design. To solve both of these subtests, children must be able to see the whole picture in their mind and then integrate the individual pieces to create the whole.

In comparison, Sequential processing emphasizes the ability to place or arrange stimuli in sequential or serial order. The stimuli are all linearly or temporally related to one another, creating a form of serial interdependence within the stimulus (Kaufman & Kaufman, 1983a). The K-ABC subtests assess the child's Sequential processing *abilities* in a variety of modes. For example, Hand Movements involves visual input and a motor response, Number Recall involves auditory input with a vocal response, and Word Order involves auditory input and a visual response. These different modes of input and output allow the examiner to assess the child's sequential abilities in a variety of ways. The Sequential subtests also provide information on the child's short-term memory and attentional abilities.

According to Kamphaus et al. (1995), one of the controversial aspects of the K-ABC was the fact that it took the equivalent of Wechsler's Verbal Scale and redefined it as *achievement*. The Kaufmans' analogs of tests such as Information (Faces & Places), Vocabulary (Riddles and Expressive Vocabulary), and Arithmetic (Arithmetic) are included on the K-ABC as achievement tests and viewed as tasks that are united by the demands they place on children to extract and assimilate information from their cultural and school environment. The K-ABC is predicated on the distinction between problem solving and knowledge of facts. The former *set of skills* is interpreted as intelligence; the latter is defined as achievement. This definition presents a break from other intelligence tests, where a person's acquired factual information and applied skills greatly influence the obtained IQ (Kaufman & Kaufman, 1983a).

Minority Group Assessment

One of the most frequent topics of discussion and empirical study has been how tests are biased and discriminatory against various racial, ethnic, or socioeconomic groups (Flaugher, 1978; Jensen, 1980; Reynolds, 1982). To meet the needs of minority group children, sensitive and thoughtful methods of assessment are necessary. During the K-ABC's development, many efforts were made to use sensitivity in the choice of materials, item format, and the selection of children for the standardization sample. The success of the K-ABC's attempts at being more fair in assessing minority group children is discussed in detail in the following chapter on research findings.

Many existing intelligence tests include subtests that have school-related content. This tends to promote bias in assessment of cognitive aptitude. Thus, the K-ABC excludes school-related subtests from the K-ABC Mental Processing Composite and places such tasks on a separate scale titled Achievement. In addition, the K-ABC Mental Processing Scales include teaching items. Teaching items are important because some children who are culturally disadvantaged may fail to understand the nature of the task presented to them. At the beginning of each Mental Processing subtest, the examiner administers one sample and two teaching items. If a child does not understand (he or she fails the item), then the examiner is instructed to demonstrate the correct answer and use any verbal or nonverbal means to communicate the nature of the task. Thus, the allowed flexibility in the teaching items ensures that the child understands what is expected of him or her.

Not only can foreign language and nonverbal communication be used to teach the tasks on the Mental Processing Scales, but also in the scoring of the K-ABC, correct answers are accepted if they are given in subcultural slang or a foreign language. These rules enhance the use of the K-ABC for Hispanic and other bilingual children. Directions for administering the Sequential and Simultaneous Processing Scales in Spanish are provided in the appendices (Kaufman & Kaufman, 1983a, 1983b), which also include lists of correct Spanish responses for all Mental Processing and Achievement subtests requiring verbalization.

The overall role of language was deliberately diminished in the K-ABC Mental Processing Scales in an effort to reduce the contamination of problem-solving ability with level of language development or fluency in verbal expression. Both formal and informal educational experiences can affect language development and verbal fluency. In addition, subcultural background and personality are noted to be related to verbal fluency (Labov, 1970). In reducing the language component of the Mental Processing subtests, nonverbal concrete stimuli were used. Only 3 of the 10 processing tests require vocalization for response: Number Recall, Magic Window, and Gestalt Closure. Furthermore, all three tests require only brief verbalization. Therefore, despite potential difficulties with language, bilingual children and culturally disadvantaged children are not greatly penalized in their K-ABC Processing Scale scores.

Careful thought and sensitivity were used in the selection of specific K-ABC items. The *K-ABC Interpretive Manual* describes three areas that were considered in item selection. The empirical results of item bias statistics were carefully examined, using methods developed by Angoff (1956) and Rasch (1966). The subjective perceptions and attitudes of two black and two Hispanic educators who were hired to review the preliminary version of the K-ABC were also taken into account. Finally, the current literature was examined to look for findings on tasks that have been repeatedly shown to be fair cross-culturally or to produce minimal black-white differences (Bogen, DeZure, Tenhouten, & Marsh, 1972; Gerken, 1978; Jensen & Figueroa, 1975).

Assessment of minority groups was also aided by efforts made in obtaining the K-ABC standardization sample. In the development of the test, additional black children, above the proportional numbers of blacks needed for national norming, were assessed. The data obtained from this extra sample were used to create supplementary norms by race and socioeconomic status for whites and blacks. This allows an examiner to match a child's socioeconomic and ethnic background to an appropriate reference group to find percentile ranks for the Global Scales in the supplementary tables.

Standardization and Properties of the Scale

Stratification of the K-ABC standardization sample closely matched the 1980 U.S. Census data on the variables of age, gender, geographic region, community size, socioeconomic status, race or ethnic group, and parental occupation and education. In addition, unlike most other intelligence measures for children, stratification variables included educational placement of the child (see Table 2.1).

Reliability and validity data provide considerable support for the psychometric aspects of the test. A test-retest reliability study was conducted with 246 children after a 2- to 4-week interval (mean interval = 17 days). The coefficients for the Mental Processing Composite were .83 for age 2 years, 6 months, through 4 years, 11 months; .88 for ages 5 years through 8 years, 11 months; and .93 for ages 9 years to 12 years, 5 months. Test-retest reliabilities for the Achievement Scale composite for the same age groups were .95, .95, and .97, respectively (Kamphaus et al., 1995). The test-retest reliability research reveals that there is a clear developmental trend, with coefficients for the preschool ages being smaller than those for the school-age range. This trend is consistent with the known variability over time that characterizes preschool children's standardization test performance in general (Kamphaus & Reynolds, 1987). Split-half reliability coefficients for the K-ABC Global Scales range from .86 to 0.93 (mean =.90) for preschool children, and from .89 to .97 (mean = .93) for children ages 5 to 12 years, 6 months (Kamphaus et al., 1995).

There has been a considerable amount of research done on the validity of the K-ABC. The *K-ABC Interpretive Manual* (Kaufman & Kaufman, 1983a) includes the results of 43 such investigations, and several

TABLE 2.1 Representation of Kaufman Assessment Battery for Children (K-ABC) Standardization Sample by Educational Placement ($N = 2,000$)

Educational Placement	N	Percentage in K-ABC Standardization Sample	Percentage in U.S. School-Age Population[a]
Regular classroom	1,862	93.1	91.1
Speech impaired	28	1.4	2.0
Learning disabled	23	1.2	2.3
Mentally retarded	37	1.8	1.7
Emotionally disturbed	5	0.2	0.3
Other[b]	15	0.8	0.7
Gifted and Talented	30	1.5	1.9[c]
Total K-ABC Sample	2,000	100.0	100.0

a. Data from U.S. Department of Education (1980a).

b. Includes other health-impaired, orthopedically handicapped, and hard of hearing.

c. Data from U.S. Office for Civil Rights (1980), p. 5.

additional validity studies have appeared in the professional literature (Kamphaus et al., 1995; Kamphaus & Reynolds, 1987). Construct validity was established by looking at five separate topics: developmental changes, internal consistency, factor analysis (principal factor, principal components, and confirmatory), convergent and discriminant analysis, and correlations with other tests. Factor analysis of the Mental Processing Scales offered clear empirical support for the existence of two, and only two, factors at each age level and for the placement of each preschool and school-age subtest on its respective scale. Analyses of the combined processing and achievement subtests also offered good construct validation of the K-ABC's three-scale structure (Kaufman & Kamphaus, 1984).

Although the K-ABC and the WISC-R differ from one another in a number of ways, there is strong evidence that the two measures correlate substantially (Kamphaus & Reynolds, 1987). In a study of 182 children enrolled in regular classrooms, the Mental Processing Composite correlated 0.70 with WISC-R Full Scale IQ, thus, sharing a 49% overlap in variance (Kamphaus et al., 1995; Kaufman & Kaufman, 1983a). There have also been numerous correlational studies conducted with handicapped and exceptional populations that may be found in the interpretative manual. The overall correlation between the K-ABC and the WISC-R range from .57 to .74, indicating that the two tests overlap a good deal, yet also show some independence (Kamphaus et al., 1995).

Overview

Although the K-ABC has been the subject of past controversy, it appears that it has held its own and is used often by professionals. The K-ABC is well designed with easy to use easels and manuals. The information in the manuals is presented in a straightforward, clear fashion, making use and interpretation of the K-ABC relatively easy (Merz, 1985). There has been a considerable amount of research done on the validity of the K-ABC, and much of that information is thoroughly presented in the manual. The reporting of the reliability and validity data in the manual is complete and understandable. However, there is not enough information presented on the content validity of the test. The various tasks on the subtests on the K-ABC are based on clinical, neuropsychological, and/or other research-based validity; however, a much clearer explication of the rationale behind some of the novel subtests would have been quite helpful (Merz, 1985).

The K-ABC measures intelligence from a strong theoretical and research basis, evident in the quality of investigation and the amount of research data presented in the manual (Merz, 1985). The K-ABC was designed to measure the intelligence and achievement of children 2 $\frac{1}{2}$ to 12 $\frac{1}{2}$ years old, and the research done to date suggests that, in fact, the test does just that. The Nonverbal Scale significantly contributes to the effort to address the diverse needs of minority groups and language handicapped children. Overall, it appears that the goals listed in the interpretative manual have been met and that this battery is a valuable assessment tool (Merz, 1985).

Keith and Dunbar (1984) present an alternate means of interpreting the K-ABC, based on exploratory and confirmatory factor analytic data. The two K-ABC Reading subtests are eliminated in their alternate analysis, and factors labeled Verbal Memory, Nonverbal Reasoning, and Verbal Reasoning are presented. For school-age children whose Achievement Scale splits in half, this model may help interpret their profile. A problem with the Keith and Dunbar interpretation is that they do not offer evidence to support their Verbal Memory and Nonverbal Reasoning labels. Keith and Dunbar (1984) conclude that considerable caution should be used when interpreting K-ABC results. In the K-ABC *Interpretive Manual* (Kaufman & Kaufman, 1983a), it is also stressed that a child's profile may need to be approached from an alternative model, if the author's model does not create a good interpretation of the profile.

Practical Application of the K-ABC

The following pages will present case studies of several children who were referred for evaluation to the psychoeducational clinic directed by Drs. Nadeen Kaufman and Elizabeth Lichtenberger. These cases were selected to demonstrate the applicability of the K-ABC for use with children who have diverse cultural and ethnic backgrounds. These children were each referred for a learning problem of some sort, although some children also demonstrated concurrent emotional and/or attentional problems.

In each of the cases presented, the K-ABC was administered as the primary instrument to measure cognitive ability, but several supplemental subtests, as well as tests of achievement were administered to provide a comprehensive understanding of the children. For all reports in this book, names are changed and pertinent background information has been modified to protect the confidentiality of the children.

Case Study: John V.

Referral and Background Information

John is an almost 4-year-old male with Vietnamese parents who was referred for an evaluation by his preschool teacher. The reason for referral is to assess John's lack of communication skills and his delay in speech and to offer possible recommendations to remediate current deficits. At present, John uses one-word utterances, with a limited vocabulary, to communicate. His parents are concerned about what can or should be done to improve his language skills.

John lives at home with his mother, father, and his 6-year-old brother. His brother is described as having no language or academic difficulties. Mrs. V. has lived in the United States for 16 years and Mr. V. has lived in the United States since age 4. Only English is spoken in the home on a regular basis, although both Mr. and Mrs. V. can speak both Vietnamese and English. Mr. and Mrs. V. stated that John may understand a few words of Vietnamese. Mrs. V. described her pregnancy and delivery of John as normal. John reached his developmental milestones, except for language acquisition, within the normally expected time frame. According to Mrs. V., John began speaking at an earlier age than his brother with words such as *I, Mommy, Daddy,* and *doggy.* However, after age 1½ , John stopped speaking. At age 1, a head injury was reported by John's parents. However, no negative consequences were observed. No other major illnesses or injuries were reported.

John attended nursery school from ages 30 months to 42 months, 2 days a week for 3 hours per day. Mrs. V. indicated that John appeared quiet and sad at that time and did not want to play with other children. Currently, John is attending preschool 7 hours a day, 5 days a week. At preschool, his demeanor is described as autonomous. According to his teacher, he does not like to be told what to do, yet he is an "emotional and sensitive" child.

At age 2 years, 11 months, John was taken for an evaluation of his speech and language development. As part of the evaluation, John's hearing was checked and found to be normal. At that time, John used two true words, *hello* and *ba,* which means "day" in Vietnamese. According to the speech and language evaluation, John primarily relied on aggressive gestures, such as pushing, grabbing, and pointing, to communicate his needs. He performed well with manipulative toys. He appeared to have a good memory and recognized familiar objects in the environment, yet he responded inconsistently to his name and the word/command, *no.* John was able to attend to activities that were self-chosen but had very limited attention span for more structured tasks. A parent questionnaire revealed receptive language development equivalent to that of about 18 months. His expressive language development was assessed to be at 12 months. John primarily communicated with gestures. As a result, John was diagnosed with a severe speech and receptive/expressive language disorder. Recommendations were made for John to attend individual and group therapy for an initial period of one year. According to his parents, John did not complete the treatment and attended only a couple of sessions. Shortly thereafter, John began to attend his current preschool.

Appearance and Behavioral Characteristics

John is a very cute, Vietnamese American, almost 4-year-old boy, who appears to be his stated age. He has large dark eyes, dark skin, and a thin frame, and he is of average height. When John was first introduced to the examiners, he clung to his mother and was rather quiet and timid. John would not let his mother leave the room. Therefore, she stayed at his side throughout all of the testing. About 15 or 20 minutes into the first testing session, John was able to relax a little and interact more by playing with toys on the floor with his mother and the examiners. Throughout all of the testing, John sat either on his mother's lap or in a chair beside her.

John had great difficulty communicating with the examiners. While playing with a toy house, John knew what to do with the people and the furniture; however, he was unable to communicate verbally with the examiners. It was very clear within the first few minutes of interacting with John that his ability to communicate verbally was extremely limited and significantly impaired. He was able to say a few words, but it was difficult to understand what he was saying most of the time. As a result, John's mother would often have to interpret for the examiners. When John did not know or was unable to verbally identify an object, he would often become frustrated and repeatedly say the words *in* or *look mommy, there.*

Throughout most of the testing, John had great difficulty paying attention, and it appeared that he had difficulty understanding and following directions on many occasions. For example, the examiner showed John a set of pictures and asked him to find the cow and point to it. John then pointed to, and verbally identified (when able to), some and/or every object on the page, appearing unable to understand what the exact task was. On most of the tasks where an easel was used, John would impulsively attempt to grab the easel and turn the pages himself. Eventually, the examiner had to hold his hands to keep him from touching the easel or test pages. When John became bored or did not know how to perform a task, he often disengaged from the examiner by looking away or down. When he disengaged, he sometimes appeared to be sad or frustrated. John was clearly unable to verbally communicate his lack of desire or inability to continue a task.

During the testing, John appeared to be a relatively happy child. He was playful, and he smiled and laughed a lot. He had difficulty in several areas: separation from mother, verbal comprehension and expression following directions, perseveration, paying attention, impulsivity, mental stamina, and cooperative and interactive play. On a task in which John was to imitate the examiner and tap each key of a xylophone once, he perseverated on the first key, then tapped the last two keys. Then, on a second trial where he was to tap twice, he again perseverated on the first key.

Tests Administered

Peabody Picture Vocabulary Test—Revised (PPVT-R)
K-ABC
Kaufman Survey of Early Academic and Language Skills (K-SEALS)
McCarthy Scales of Children's Abilities: Selected Subtests
Vineland Adaptive Behavior Scales: Expanded Form

Test Results and Interpretation

Because of the pervasive receptive and expressive language problems displayed by John, it is not possible to measure his cognitive functioning independent of his ability to understand spoken instruction and to give vocal responses to test items. All scores, therefore, must be interpreted in the context of his extreme language difficulties. On the K-ABC, John earned a Mental Processing Composite (IQ equivalent) of 92 ± 10, an Average level of performance compared to other children almost 4 years of age. That score is meaningless, however, because of the huge discrepancy between the two scales that compose the composite score. On the Simultaneous Processing Scale, he earned a standard score of 114 ± 12, indicating that he has Above Average ability (82nd percentile) in solving problems that require an integrated, holistic approach. In contrast, he scored at the Lower Extreme level (1st percentile) on the Sequential Processing Scale (standard score = 67 ± 10), reflecting his poor ability when solving problems in a linear step-by-step fashion. However, his level of ability at solving step-by-step problems must remain indeterminate because of the extreme perseveration that he evidenced on a test requiring him to copy the examiner's hand movements and the likelihood that he failed to understand a task involving the repetition of a series of numbers spoken by the examiner.

The K-ABC Simultaneous Processing Scale comprises three tasks that are easily communicated with a minimum of words. John understood what he was supposed to do and performed better than other children his age on this scale, even though two of the subtests demand verbal labeling. He performed exceptionally well (91st percentile) on two subtests that measure spatial visualization ability: a visual memory task that required him to look at a photo of a person and then point to that person in a group photograph, and a visual closure task that required him to name an incomplete "inkblot" drawing. He performed as well as the average 5-year-old on the three subtests included on the Simultaneous Processing Scale.

Because the Simultaneous Processing Scale does not include reasoning or conceptual tasks for children younger than age 4, John was given the Perceptual-Performance Scale of the McCarthy Scales of Children's Abilities. He earned a standard score of 32 ± 7 (mean for normal children = 50), reflecting performance at the 4th percentile, comparable to the average skills of a 36-month-old child. He performed most poorly on the conceptual and reasoning subtests, scoring below the level of the average 30-month-old on a test of logical classification skills and at a 24- to 42-month-old level on tests of solving picture puzzles and drawing a child. He did not understand what he was supposed to do on the logical skills task or on a sequential test requiring him to tap a xylophone (30-month-old level). He scored at the 5-year level on a test requiring him to copy structures out of blocks. Like the K-ABC subtests on which he excelled, the block building task demands spatial visualization, and the directions are easily understood; on another task of this sort (copying designs with a pencil), he performed at a 36-month-old level. He was able to pass three out of four items on imitative subtests of the McCarthy Motor Scale (42-months-old level), again indicating his ability to perform at his approximate age level when he understands what he is supposed to do.

John was administered the K-SEALS to try to quantify his language development, both receptively and expressively. He earned standard scores of 71 on the Vocabulary subtests and 70 on the overall battery composite. He failed every item on the Numbers, Letters, and Words subtest, demonstrating no apparent learning of pre-reading and pre-math concepts. He performed at equal levels on Expressive Skills (3rd

CASE 2.1 John V., Vietnamese child, age 3 years, 11 months, possible development delays

Kaufman Assessment Battery for Children (K-ABC) Profile

Global Score	Standard Score	Percentile Rank
Simultaneous Processing	114 ± 12	82
Sequential Processing	67 ± 10	1
Mental Processing Composite	92 ± 10	30

Sequential Processing Subtest	Scaled Score	Percentile Rank
Hand Movements	6	9
Number Recall[a]	3	1
Magic Window	8	25
Face Recognition	14	91
Gestalt Closure	14	91

Achievement Subtest	Standard Score	Percentile Score
Expressive Vocabulary	74 ± 13	4
Faces & Places	84 ± 16	14
Arithmetic	73[a] ± 11	4

Kaufman Survey of Early Academic and Language Skills (K-SEALS)

Language Skill	Standard Score	Percentile Rank
Expressive Skills	71 ± 8	3
Receptive Skills	69 ± 9	2
Early Academic & Language Skills Composite	70 ± 6	2

Subtest	Scaled Score	Percentile Rank
Vocabulary	71 ± 7	3
Numbers, Letters & Words	77[a] ± 8	6

Peabody Picture Vocabulary Test—Revised (PPVT-R)

Standard Score = 41
Percentile = < 1
Age Equivalent = 1-11

percentile) and Receptive Skills (2nd percentile). All of these scores classify John at the juncture of the Well Below Average and Lower Extreme categories, compared to children his age. He made many articulation errors on the Articulation Survey and performed below the level of the average 2-year-old on all K-SEALS scales and subtests.

CASE 2.1 Continued

McCarthy Scales of Children's Abilities

	Subtest Age Score	Standard Score	Percentile
Perceptual-Performance		32 ± 7^b	4
Block Building	5-0		
Puzzle Solving	3-0		
Tapping Sequence	2-6		
Draw-A-Design	3-0		
Draw-A-Child	3-0		
Conceptual Grouping	< 2-6		
Pictorial Memory	No response		
Word Knowledge, I	< 2-6		
Verbal Fluency	No response		
Opposite Analogies	No response		
Number Questions	No response		
Numerical Memory, I & II	No response		
Counting & Sorting	No response		
Imitative Action	3-6		

Vineland Adaptive Behavior Scales: Interview Edition (Expanded Form)

	Subtest Age Score	Standard Score	Percentile
Communication Domain	1-9	64 ± 5	1
	2-5		
	1-7		
	4-0		
Daily Living Skills Domain	3-9	98 ± 5	45
	3-10		
	4-4		
	3-3		
Socialization Domain	1-11	64 ± 6	1
	1-6		
	1-6		
	1-11		
Motor Skills Domain	2-11	78 ± 4	7
	3-1		
	2-10		

a. Caution: Standard Score corresponds to a raw score of 0.
b. Mean = 50; SD = 10.

John also scored at a deficient level on a test of receptive vocabulary (PPVT-R), earning an age equivalent of 23 months and a standard score of "Below 41." The test required John to point to the one picture (out of four) that corresponds to an object or action named by the examiner. John may not have understood what type of response was expected on the PPVT-R, perhaps lowering his score. That notion is supported by his higher scores on two K-ABC achievement tests, both measures of expressive language. He earned a standard score of 74 (4th percentile) on a vocabulary test requiring him to name pictures of objects and a standard score of 84 (14th percentile) on a test of general information (naming famous people and places). He understood what he was supposed to do on both tasks. He performed below a 30-month-old level on a McCarthy Scales vocabulary test that assesses both receptive and expressive vocabulary. His overall performance on language and cognitive tests indicate a mild to moderate language deficiency at the present time that is likely to become moderate to severe in the future without immediate, intensive speech and language therapy.

John's intelligence level is at an Average to Above Average level on tests that are readily communicated without verbiage and that do not emphasize concepts. He has very well-developed spatial visualization skills and simultaneous processing abilities. He seems best able to communicate verbally when solving visual perceptual and visual memory problems that he understands and finds interesting. Because verbal concepts and language skills are so important for academic growth and intellectual growth during the early school years, the success of the language intervention will affect his performance on future intelligence tests.

The Vineland Adaptive Behavior Scales, Interview Edition, Expanded Form was administered to John's mother. On the Vineland, John obtained an Adaptive Behavior Composite standard score of 70 ± 4. This score places him at the 2nd percentile compared to other children his age and classifies his general adaptive functioning as moderately low.

John's standard scores in the adaptive behavior domains are as follows: Communication, which measures what he understands, says, and reads, 64 ± 5; Daily Living Skills, which measures practical skills that are needed to take care of oneself, 98 ± 5; Socialization, which measures the skills that people need to get along with others as well as their play activities and use of leisure time, 64 ± 6; and Motor Skills, which has to do with important physical skills, 78 ± 8. His performance in the Daily Living Skills domain, which corresponds to the percentile rank of 45, is at the Adequate adaptive level. His performance in the Motor Skills domain, which corresponds to the percentile rank of 7, is at the Moderately

Low adaptive level. His performance in the Communication and Socialization domains, which both correspond to the percentile rank of 1, is classified as Low when compared with other children his same age. His performance on the Vineland Adaptive Behavior Scales underscores the need for a thorough reevaluation in the future to validate the diagnostic impressions based on John's present level of functioning.

Summary and Diagnostic Impressions

John is an almost 4-year-old Vietnamese American boy. He was referred for a psychoeducational evaluation by his preschool. The purpose of the referral was to assess John's overall language skills. John's parents are concerned about his limited communication skills and would like to know the severity of his language impairment. John's hearing has been thoroughly evaluated and was found to be normal; therefore, auditory impairment may be ruled out at this time.

John appears to be his stated age, yet his communication skills are far below age appropriate. In fact, his communication and verbal ability is limited to one word utterances. This is clearly indicative of a child with a severe language disorder. John is a friendly child and appears to be happy; however, he becomes rather frustrated and upset when he cannot verbalize his needs. John's impaired language abilities and difficulty with paying attention, following directions, and staying on task make it very difficult for him, as well as for those who interact with him. John is unable to verbalize his frustration; therefore, he often disengages from a task by looking away or down. After John disengages, he sometimes looks sad and withdrawn, suggesting that he is somewhat aware of his problem.

At the present time, John's pervasive language difficulties make it very difficult to properly assess his cognitive functioning. This is further complicated by John's inability to pay attention and to respond to verbal instruction. It is difficult to sort out John's cognitive and verbal functioning; therefore, these test results should be interpreted with caution. Test results suggest that John is of Average to Above Average Intelligence on tasks that do not emphasize verbal ability. He does much better on visual-spatial tasks; however, he has difficulty with all basic concepts such as size, shape, and quantity.

At this time, the following diagnoses are viewed as appropriate:

Phonological Disorder (*DSM-IV* code: 315.39)
Mixed Receptive-Expressive Language Disorder (*DSM-IV* code: 315.31)

Recommendations:

1. John should receive long-term intensive language therapy. The therapy should focus on speech articulation, as well as receptive and expressive communication skills. John would benefit from both individual and group language therapy. Working on his language skills in a group setting with other children will help improve John's communication with others.

2. Whenever possible, encourage John to use the correct words for things. To improve John's ability to express himself and to increase his vocabulary, identify or label objects out loud on a consistent basis. If John wants something and is unable to properly identify it verbally, tell him what the word is and then encourage him to repeat it back. When he correctly responds, reward him with verbal praise. Attempts that are recognizable should be considered correct at this stage of development, until his articulation is gradually shaped and improved. John's language difficulties may be complicated by the fact that two languages are spoken at home. At this time in his development, John would benefit from having only one language spoken to him. Because English is the language that is spoken in school, it is recommended that English be the primary language at home as well.

3. John should continue to attend school in order to further expose him to age-appropriate peers who will model language and behavior. A school that will provide individual attention and instruction by specialists in the area of delayed or impaired language preschoolers will be ideal for John. John is not ready to attend a pre-kindergarten academic setting at this time. The most urgent priority for his well-being now is for him to receive as much speech and language training as possible.

4. John is naturally curious and likes to explore his physical environment. New learning, such as those prerequisite basic concepts that must be acquired before higher levels of learning can begin, can be introduced with the aid of concrete, colorful materials. Keeping John interested is

the key to maintaining his attention and effort. The use of music, song, easy preschool instruments, such as a drum, triangle, or tambourine, can also attract his attention and provide reinforcement.

5. Considering John's significant receptive and expressive language disorder, a full psychoeducational reevaluation is also recommended to reassess his progress and abilities after extensive remediation.

Examiners: Kristee Beres, Ph.D., and Jose Gonzalez, M.A.
Supervisor: Nadeen Kaufman, Ed.D.

Case Study: Roberto G.

Referral and Background Information

Roberto G., age 10 years, 10 months, was referred for an evaluation by his pediatrician. His pediatrician is currently evaluating Roberto for Attention Deficit Hyperactivity Disorder (ADHD) and requested a psychoeducational testing to rule out any potential learning disability. In addition, Mr. and Mrs. G. hope to obtain information regarding how best to meet Roberto's educational and emotional needs. Roberto lives at home with his biological parents and 4-year-old sister. The family is originally from Mexico City, Mexico, and has lived in the United States for the past few months, due to Mr. G.'s job. They intend to return to Mexico within the next 6 months. Roberto is bilingual; however, the primary language spoken in his home is Spanish.

According to Mrs. G., she had a normal pregnancy, and Roberto was born weighing 3 kg. Childhood developmental milestones are reported by Mrs. G. to be within normal limits. He had his tonsils removed at the age of 7. Roberto's parents stated that he has some sleep difficulties, taking a long time to fall asleep and waking up during the night and very early in the morning. Roberto's parents and teacher reported that he occasionally complains of dizziness, particularly after exercise or when at church. They had not yet sought medical evaluation for complaints of Roberto's dizziness.

Roberto was diagnosed with ADHD in Mexico. Before moving to the United States, Roberto had received various treatments for his ADHD, such as multisensory teaching and computerized treatments. His parents indicated that they questioned the effectiveness of these treatments. Roberto was also treated with Ritalin for 9 months; however, due to Roberto's complaints of dizziness and depression, his parents stopped his medication about 6 months ago. Roberto's pediatrician completed a thorough medical evaluation of Roberto and found that there were no hearing, vision, or other medical problems. His doctor noted that his overall diagnostic impression of Roberto is ADD without hyperactivity. He stated that the side-effects Roberto reportedly experienced when on Ritalin could be a "wear-off effect," which can occur when the doses are too far apart. The doctor commented that Ritalin or another stimulant medication could be tried again. According to the pediatrician, Roberto may have a tic disorder, possibly a variant of Tourette's syndrome. The symptoms that Mr. and Mrs. G. reported to the pediatrician include both vocal tics, such as animal noises, as well as motor tics, such as eye blinking and grimacing. Roberto has never received treatment for his mild tic disorder.

Roberto's educational history began at age 2 years, 6 months, when he entered preschool in Mexico City, Mexico. From kindergarten through third grade, Roberto attended a bilingual, private school in Mexico City. His parents reported that, through third grade, he was performing academically at an average level. The structure of his school environment in Mexico City was very predictable. According to Mr. and Mrs. G., Roberto was given the same type of assignments each week. The curriculum placed an emphasis on grammar and vocabulary; very little reading was required in either English or Spanish. After the family's move to the United States a few months ago, Roberto began attending fourth grade. Both Roberto and his parents reported that the demands of his current school are very different from those in Mexico. For example, more reading is emphasized and less predictability is available in the pattern of assignments. Mr. and Mrs. G. reported that since his transition to the new school, Roberto has been having difficulty both academically and socially. They stated that his primary difficulties are in classes which are verbally demanding. Many of these difficulties appear to result from the discrepancy between the structure of Roberto's education in Mexico and in the United States. According to Mr. and Mrs. G., Roberto has difficulty keeping up with the changing requirements in the classroom and struggles with reading and problem solving in mathematics. Mr. and Mrs. G.

reported further difficulties with Roberto's writing and spelling skills. They noted that he tends to spell phonetically, confusing rules he has learned in Spanish with those applicable to English. They also indicated that Roberto struggles to attend to details. For example, when focusing on his spelling, Roberto will neglect his punctuation and capitalization. Mr. and Mrs. G. noted that Roberto's fourth-grade teacher emphasizes the importance of details, and Roberto is often graded down in this area.

According to Mr. and Mrs. G., an additional area of academic difficulty is Roberto's difficulty completing his homework. Mr. and Mrs. G. reported that, without supervision, Roberto tends to become stuck on a section of the homework and is unable to continue. Consequently, his homework takes him a substantial amount of time, and he becomes frustrated. His parents described Roberto as unmotivated. They are concerned that, should he fail fourth grade, he will be in the same grade as his younger brother, whom they describe as a high achiever in all areas.

Roberto's parents stated that they are also concerned about his social abilities because he has struggled to make friends since his move to the United States. His parents indicated that Roberto is very sensitive to the teasing that goes on in the classroom, and he acts in an immature manner around his peers. They commented that some of these behaviors were also noted in Mexico: Roberto would not be able to forget a fight and would become very upset after being teased. Mr. and Mrs. G. commented that Roberto had low self-esteem before, but that it has become worse since the move. They noted that Roberto cries easily and that he often "acts silly." Roberto was described by his parents as very fidgety and nervous, and they commented that he is very badly affected by failure. They indicated that Roberto "gives up easily" and becomes frustrated and irritable.

In an interview with Roberto's fourth-grade teacher, she indicated that, although Roberto has made progress since the holiday break, he would not have done so without the individualized assistance she is providing. His teacher noted that she needs to call on Roberto "at least a hundred times a day" in order to get his attention. She commented that he is easily distracted, particularly in class discussions, during which he loses concentration "as soon as the other children begin talking." His teacher further indicated that Roberto prefers working on worksheets to participating in class discussions but noted that Roberto's work is very often incomplete. According to his teacher, Roberto states that he does not always understand the vocabulary she uses. She noted that, since Roberto revealed his difficulty understanding her at times, he appears to be more comfortable asking her to clarify instructions when necessary. The primary concerns reported by his teacher are Roberto's poor study skills and his inability to work independently.

Appearance and Behavioral Characteristics

Roberto is an attractive, almost 11-year-old Hispanic boy with sandy-blond hair and freckles on his nose. At both testing sessions, he was casually dressed in a school uniform of blue sweatpants, shirt, and sneakers. Roberto was friendly and responsive to the examiners, and rapport was easily established. He spoke comfortably and described his difficulty adjusting to his new school, commenting that "the beginning of the year was hard," and he shared several jokes with the examiners at various times during the testing. Roberto spoke with a slight Spanish accent, and at times, his language appeared slightly stilted. Although he appeared comfortable overall in the testing situation, he made some spoken errors, such as confusing *mother* and *father* and *brother* and *sister*, which appeared to be related to anxiety when first meeting the examiners. Despite these difficulties when speaking initially, Roberto did not appear to have trouble understanding the examiner's instructions or casual conversation.

Throughout the testing, Roberto tended to verbally mediate as he worked. When drawing pictures, he spontaneously narrated the scene for the examiners to hear, and when presented with passages to read, he chose to read out loud. Roberto's ability to pay attention to the task presented was inconsistent. He had to be encouraged to refocus his attention on several occasions, and he tended to fidget constantly and swing in his chair, particularly when faced with higher-level items. At those times, Roberto would stare at the clock or at a picture on the wall, and he had to be prompted to attend to the task. However, despite Roberto's moderate level of fidgeting and looking away at various times throughout the testing, he was able to answer the question or complete the task he was working on accurately. Thus, although Roberto appeared to be inattentive because of his motor activity, his appearance was misleading because he was able to respond appropriately. At other times, Roberto became completely focused and engrossed in a task and was able to attend throughout the presentation of a subtest without fidgeting, even as the items became challenging.

In addition to excess motor activity, mild facial tics, such as a stretching of his mouth and a widening of his eyes, were apparent during various points in the evaluation. These tics appeared to be more evident during moments of high anxiety. During one subtest, after Roberto had to concentrate intensely for some time, he complained of feeling dizzy; however, no other somatic complaints were noted.

Roberto appeared to be confident about what he did and did not know. He persevered throughout the testing; however, when he was unable to answer a question, he stated calmly, "this is too hard for me, I won't do this one." On the K-TEA Mathematics Computation subtest, when faced with long division problems and two-digit multiplication problems, although Roberto commented that he could do these problems, he also noted that " I certainly won't do those. Those will take me too long." It appears that Roberto would rather not attempt a difficult task than try and fail. This is supported by his parents' comment that Roberto gives up easily and is badly affected by failure. Similar behaviors were also evident on the K-TEA Reading Comprehension subtest. When faced with difficult items, Roberto stated that he did not know the answer and went on to the next item. Despite this reluctance to attempt some higher level tasks, given Roberto's level of motivation and his ability to complete all tasks presented to him, this assessment is judged to be a valid measure of Roberto's cognitive and academic abilities.

Tests Administered

K-ABC

Kaufman Test of Educational Achievement—Comprehensive Form (K-TEA)

Wechsler Intelligence Scale for Children—Third Edition (WISC-III): Similarities

Woodcock-Johnson—Revised Tests of Cognitive Ability (WJ-R): Selected Subtests

Peabody Individual Achievement Test Revised (PIAT-R): Written Expression

Developmental Test of Visual Motor Integration (VMI)

Intermediate Visual and Auditory Continuous Performance Test (IVA)

Kinetic Family Drawing (KFD)

Draw-a-Person Test

Peabody Picture Vocabulary Test—Revised (PPVT-R)

Test Results and Interpretation

Cognitive and Achievement Abilities

To assess his cognitive abilities, Roberto was administered the K-ABC, as well as subtests from the WJ-R. The K-ABC is an individually administered test of a child's intellectual functioning and cognitive strengths and weaknesses. This battery measures global areas of functioning, including Sequential Processing, Simultaneous Processing, and Nonverbal Processing. Sequential Processing emphasizes the temporal order of stimuli, whereas Simultaneous Processing involves solving problems using an integrated holistic style. On the K-ABC, Roberto earned a Sequential Processing Standard Score of 100 æ 8 (50th percentile), a Simultaneous Processing Standard Score of 117 ± 6 (87th percentile), and a Nonverbal Processing Standard Score of 116 ± 6 (86th percentile). Roberto's global scores suggest a child who is functioning in the Average to High Average range of cognitive ability. The 17-point difference between his Sequential Processing and Simultaneous Processing Standard Scores is statistically significant, indicating that Roberto performs at a higher level when he solves problems by integrating many stimuli at once, rather than when solving problems in a linear, step-by-step manner. Because two of the three subtests of the Sequential Processing Scale are partly influenced by language ability, Roberto's performance on this Global Scale may be affected by language factors. As such, Roberto's High Average ability in Simultaneous Processing is likely the most valid measure of his cognitive ability. In addition, this High Average cognitive ability is further confirmed by Roberto's High Average performance on the Nonverbal Processing Scale. The discrepancy between Roberto's Sequential and Simultaneous Processing renders his Mental Processing Composite Score of 111 ± 6 meaningless as an estimate of his overall cognitive ability, as it is reflecting nothing more than a midpoint of several diverse skill areas. Thus, the interpretation of the two separate global scales and his unique strengths and weaknesses provide the most meaningful understanding of Roberto's abilities.

Within the Simultaneous Processing Scale, Roberto exhibited a relative strength in his reasoning and analytic abilities. This was evident from his strong performance (98th percentile) on a subtest requiring him to assemble several identical colored triangles to match an abstract design. His strong reasoning and analytical skills were further supported by his Above Average performance on a task that required Roberto to select the meaningful picture of an abstract design that best completes a visual analogy, as well as on another task on which he was required to place photographs of an event in chronological order.

In comparison to these scores, a significant relative weakness (37th percentile) was noted on a Simultaneous Processing subtest that measured Roberto's ability to recall the locations of pictures arranged randomly on a page. It should be noted that this score is still within the Average range when compared to other children of his age; however, it reflects a weakness relative to his overall High Average level of holistic processing. This difficulty indicates a possible weakness in Roberto's visual short-term memory, or more specifically, his spatial memory. To further investigate this hypothesis, Roberto was administered a subtest from the WJ-R that required him to recognize a subset of previously presented pictures within a field of distracting pictures. On this subtest, Roberto scored within the High Average range, at the 88th percentile. This indicates that Roberto's visual-perceptual skills are intact, and his ability to recall visually presented stimuli (not the location) is Above Average to Average.

To assess Roberto's visual-motor abilities, the VMI was administered, and his handwriting and drawings were evaluated. On the VMI, Roberto was asked to copy a series of geometric forms. Roberto did exceptionally well on this subtest, scoring at the 94th percentile. This indicates that Roberto's visual-motor ability is currently above an age-expected level. On the unstructured drawing tasks, Roberto appeared to grip the pencil appropriately and drew people who were of age-appropriate quality. Similar to the structured and unstructured drawing tasks, Roberto's handwriting appeared to be of age-appropriate quality. He wrote neatly and legibly in cursive.

Within the Sequential Scale of the K-ABC, Roberto obtained a relative weakness (37th percentile) on a subtest requiring him to point to silhouettes of common objects in the same order as these objects were named by the examiner. This subtest includes a 5-second interference task that requires the child to name a series of colors before pointing to the silhouettes. It appears that this color naming was very disruptive for

CASE 2.2 Roberto G., Hispanic child, age 10 years, 10 months, possible
learning disability and Attention Deficit Hyperactivity Disorder

Kaufman Assessment Battery for Children (K-ABC) Profile

Global Score	Standard Score	Percentile Rank
Simultaneous Processing	117 ± 6	87
Sequential Processing	100 ± 8	50
Mental Processing Composite	111 ± 6	77
Nonverbal Scale	116 ± 6	86

Sequential Processing Subtest	Scaled Score	Percentile Rank
Hand Movements	11	63
Number Recall	10	50
Word Order	9	37
Gestalt Closure	11	63
Triangles	16	98
Matrix Analogies	13	84
Spatial Memory	9	37
Photo Series	13	84

Achievement Subtest	Standard Score	Percentile Rank
Riddles	99 ± 9	47

Wechsler Intelligence Scale for Children—Third Edition (WISC-III)

Language Skill	Scaled Score	Percentile
Similarities	13	84

Woodcock-Johnson—Revised Tests of Cognitive Ability (WJ-R) Profile

Subtest	Standard Score	Percentile Rank
Long-Term Retrieval		
Visual-Auditory Learning	102 ± 5	55
Memory for Names	115 ± 4	84
Visual Processing		
Picture Recognition	117 ± 6	88
Short-Term Memory		
Memory for Words	96 ± 7	39
Comprehension-Knowledge		
Oral Vocabulary	93 ± 6	31

CASE 2.2 Continued

Kaufman Test of Educational Achievement (K-TEA): Comprehensive Form

	Standard Score ± 90 Confidence Interval	Percentile Rank
Composite		
Reading Composite	100 ± 5	50
Mathematics Composite	96 ± 5	39
Battery Composite	97 ± 3	42
Subtest		
Mathematics Application	99 ± 7	47
Reading Decoding	119 ± 6	90
Spelling	94 ± 5	34
Reading Comprehension	86 ± 6	18
Mathematics Computation	93 ± 7	32

Peabody Individual Achievement Test (PIAT-R)

Subtest	Scaled Score	Percentile
Written Expression	9	37

Peabody Picture Vocabulary Test—Revised (PPVT-R)

Standard Score	79
Percentile	8

Roberto. He appeared to have difficulty retrieving the names of several of the colors, such as gray. It is also likely that the verbal comprehension required on this subtest created a difficulty for Roberto. When originally presented with the silhouettes, he called the cup a *teapot*. Clearly, Roberto's language background may have affected his performance on this subtest, as well as on another Sequential task that required him to repeat a series of digits in the same order as the examiner said them.

In addition to the cognitive testing discussed above, tests of language ability were administered to determine the impact of language factors on his performance. Tests included were: the Riddles subtest of the K-ABC, the Oral Vocabulary, Visual-Auditory Learning, Memory for Names, and Memory for Words subtests of the WJ-R, the Similarities subtest of the WISC-III, and the PPVT-R. On an expressive language subtest of the K-ABC, measuring his ability to infer the name of a concrete or abstract verbal concept when given several of its characteristics, Roberto scored at the 47th percentile. On a WJ-R task designed to measure his knowledge of word meanings, Roberto scored at the 31st percentile. This test consisted of two parts: recalling antonyms and synonyms. Roberto appeared to have greater difficulty recalling synonyms than antonyms. When providing the antonym of a word, Roberto tended to use the prefix *dis*. For example, he said that the antonym of *accumulate* was *disaccumulate*. In comparison to these results, Roberto scored at the 84th percentile on a WISC-III expressive language subtest in which he was required to explain the similarity between two paired items. These results indicate that, although Roberto may have some difficulties with word retrieval, his strong abstract reasoning and analytic abilities assist him in the formation of verbal concepts, and he has the verbal abilities to express these concepts.

To assess Roberto's receptive language ability, he was administered the PPVT-R, which is a test of receptive language. Roberto struggled on this task, which required him to identify the picture named by the examiner (8th percentile), and he often asked for words to be repeated on this task. Similarly, on a WJ-R short-term memory task in which he was required to repeat lists of unrelated words presented by means of an audiotape, Roberto scored at the 39th percentile. This is both a receptive and an expressive task, and Roberto indicated his difficulty on this task, commenting that it was difficult to understand the audiotape. The words on these two tasks were presented out of context. This may have been difficult for Roberto because he appears to make use of the context to understand content, as evidenced by his performance on a subtest of the WJ-R, measuring his ability to associate new visual symbols with familiar words in oral language and to translate a series of symbols into verbal sentences (55th percentile). In this subtest, it appeared that Roberto made use of the context of the symbols to recall their meaning, and this strengthened his performance.

In contrast to his weak performance on the test of receptive language, Roberto had very little language difficulty on a WJ-R test of long-term retrieval in which he was required to recall names of space creatures shown on a page (84th percentile). This test involves both an auditory and visual stimulus, and the names used are unfamiliar words, such as *Zarp* or *Plik*. Roberto's strong visual processing, together with the fact that he was recalling meaningless names that are not related to any culture or language, may have strengthened his performance on this test. On the basis of these results, it is clear that Roberto may have some difficulty understanding English words used in his everyday environment. This is supported by the report of his teacher that Roberto indicated that he does not always understand the words she is using.

A brief informal assessment was conducted in Spanish to obtain a sense of Roberto's performance in his native language. Roberto was required to read a passage of a book in Spanish and to answer some comprehension questions, and a spelling test was also administered. When reading in Spanish, Roberto had very little difficulty decoding higher level words; however, his pace and tempo were slow, and this was similar to the way he read in English. On the spelling test administered, Roberto missed 5 out of 15 words. An analysis of his errors indicated a confusion between the representation of sounds in Spanish and English. For example, he wrote a *y* for *ll* when spelling *llanta*.

In addition to his cognitive abilities, Roberto's academic achievement was also assessed. To assess his performance in mathematics applications, reading decoding, spelling, reading comprehension, and mathematics computation, Roberto was administered the Kaufman Test of Educational Achievement—Comprehensive Form (K-TEA), which is an individually administered test of academic achievement. Roberto scored within the Average range on all subtests, with the exception of the Reading Decoding subtest, on which he scored at the Above Average range (90th percentile) and the Reading Comprehension subtest, on which he scored at the Below Average range (18th percentile). The discrepancy between Roberto's performance on the Reading Decoding subtest and his performance on the Reading Comprehension subtest is significant, indicating that Roberto is more proficient at recognizing and correctly pronouncing a list of words in isolation than understanding and correctly answering questions about passages. This result further confirms Roberto's difficulty in linguistic comprehension, as noted earlier in this report.

In listening to Roberto's reading and pronunciation of unfamiliar words during the K-TEA Reading Decoding, his skill in phonics was apparent. Although he scored in the Average range (34th percentile) on Spelling, which was not as strong as his performance in Reading Decoding, Roberto's performance on the Spelling subtest provided further confirmation of his use of phonics. For example, he spelled *celebrate* as *cele-brait*, and *accident* as *axident*. Roberto made excellent use of his phonetic skills to sound out the words presented on the Reading Decoding task; however, his results on Reading Comprehension indicate that he was not always able to extract the meaning of the words. His performance on the Reading Comprehension subtest was inconsistent; he was able to answer some difficult, higher level questions, and struggled on some easier ones. It is likely that his difficulty in interpreting the question, as indicated by several statements such as "I don't understand," affected his perfor-mance. It is important to recognize the impact that Roberto's academic background may have had on his performance in comprehension and written passages. According to his parents, in Mexico, Roberto was taught English with very little emphasis on reading; instead, the focus was purely on grammar and spelling. It is only since he began attending school in the United States that he has had more exposure to reading comprehension, and this appears to be an area of difficulty for him. On the basis of Roberto's academic and language background, his relative difficulties in Spelling and Reading Comprehension, as compared to his higher score on Reading Decoding, are not unexpected.

An additional area of academic achievement assessed was Roberto's written expression and writing fluency. On the Written Expression sub-test of PIAT-R, Roberto scored at the 37th percentile. A specific difficulty was evident with the use of run-on sentences. Roberto did not make use of paragraphs, his sentences were not related to each other in content, and he did not make reference to events that happened prior to the scene depicted in the picture prompt. This result indicates that Roberto has not obtained age-appropriate written expression skills in English, particu-larly with regards to organization, structure, and planning of his writing. For example, Roberto used only three periods throughout the one page of his story.

As indicated earlier in this report, Roberto's High Average abilities in Simultaneous Processing and Nonverbal Processing are the most valid measures of his cognitive ability. These measures are discrepant with his overall Average academic achievement, as measured by the K-TEA. However, as discussed above, it appeared that language factors may have affected Roberto's performance on the achievement subtests. In ad-dition, Roberto's educational and cultural background, combined with the fact that he has not experienced the same educational opportunities as the children living in the United States to whom he is being compared on these tests, make the diagnosis of a learning disability inappropriate.

Assessment of Attention and Concentration Abilities

Roberto was administered the IVA, which is a test developed to help in the identification and diagnosis of ADHD. It is a computerized task that involves a similar situation to that which children are exposed to in the classroom and requires sustained attention to a mildly boring repetitive task. During the administration, Roberto attended and appeared motivated to perform to the best of his ability. The results indicate that the administration was valid and can be interpreted. Roberto's performance reflected a directed and steady focus of attention; however, his auditory reaction speed and mental processing speed were slow. This test supports Roberto's relative strength and greater ability for mental processing in the visual modality. As English is Roberto's second language, it is expected that the auditory presentation, which was in English, may have affected the speed at which he processed the stimuli. The results further indicate that Roberto's visual strength is at its peak when task demands are high, and he is stimulated by activity. He performs less well when test demands are low and his attention is free to wander. On the basis of the IVA results, it appears that Roberto's attentional difficulties do not completely meet ADHD diagnostic criteria. However, it is important to note, that whereas Continuous Performance Tests rarely identify a false positive, they are known to, at times, identify a false negative. In other words, this test alone cannot definitively rule out a diagnosis of ADHD. Multiple factors including reports of his behavior in multiple settings need to be considered. Although these results are not consistently supportive of ADHD, there is confirmation that Roberto's attention is variable. Therefore, it appears that our results are similar with his pediatrician's finding of ADD without hyperactivity.

Summary and Diagnostic Impressions

Roberto G., age 10 years, 10 months, was born in Mexico City, Mexico, and relocated to the United States recently. The G. family plans to return to Mexico City within the next 6 months. Roberto was referred for an evaluation by his pediatrician, who is currently assessing Roberto for ADHD. The aim of this psychoeducational evaluation is to rule out a learning disability and to provide Mr. and Mrs. G. with recommendations to help their son. Roberto has had previous educational and medical treatments for ADHD; however, none of these proved to be very successful, according to Mr. and Mrs. G.

Roberto is bilingual; however, the primary language spoken in his home is Spanish. He spoke with a slight accent, and at times his language appeared slightly stilted. Although he made some spoken errors, he did not appear to have difficulty understanding the examiners. Roberto's attention appeared to be inconsistent, and he frequently had to be encouraged to attend to the task. There was some evidence of fidgeting and excessive motor activity.

According to the results from the K-ABC, Roberto's intellectual functioning is currently in the Average to High Average range. He earned a Sequential Processing Standard Score of 100 ± 8 (50th percentile), a Simultaneous Processing Standard Score of 117 ± 6 (87th percentile), and a Nonverbal Processing Standard Score of 116 ± 6 (86th percentile). Due to the possible impact of language factors on the Sequential Scale, Roberto's High Average abilities in Simultaneous Processing and Nonverbal Processing are the most valid measures of his cognitive ability. Roberto showed a strength in his ability to solve problems in an integrated, holistic manner. This testing provided evidence of difficulty in word retrieval and receptive language processing in the English language. Roberto's language background likely affected his performance throughout the testing.

Roberto's academic achievement, as evidenced on the K-TEA, was in the Average range, with the exception of his reading scores. There was a discrepancy between his Reading Decoding, which was in the Above Average range, and his Reading Comprehension, which was Below Average. This discrepancy indicates that whereas Roberto is able to make use of his strong phonetic skills to decode words, he has more difficulty extracting the meaning from a passage and interpreting questions. Clearly, Roberto's language and academic background played an important role in this difficulty. His slow reading pace was noticed when reading both Spanish and English. On both Roberto's reading and spelling, a confusion was noted between the representation of sounds in Spanish and English. On the PIAT-R Written Expression subtest, specific difficulties were noted in the area of run-on sentences, in the use of paragraphs, and in relating his sentences together in content.

Roberto's performance on the IVA, a test requiring sustained attention to a repetitive task, indicates that he was able to maintain his focus of attention throughout the test. This test provides further support for Roberto's relative strength in visual processing and indicates some difficulty in auditory response speed. This difficulty is not unexpected considering that the auditory presentation was in English, which is Roberto's second language. Although this test does not completely support the diagnosis of ADHD, it should be noted that this test alone cannot definitively rule out a diagnosis of ADHD. Multiple factors including reports of his behavior in multiple settings need to be considered.

Overall, it appears that Roberto's academic achievement is fairly consistent with his Average to High Average cognitive abilities, although there are significant discrepancies between his cognitive abilities and reading comprehension. His difficulties with reading comprehension are likely affected by his bilingualism and style of instruction in Mexico. Roberto's educational and cultural background, combined with the fact that the tests administered were normed on children living in the United States, make the diagnosis of a learning disability inappropriate. Considering these background factors discussed above, Roberto is performing at a very high level and should be commended for his achievements.

Recommendations

1. It is strongly recommended that Roberto be referred to a pediatric psychiatrist to evaluate whether his facial grimaces, vocalizations, and other tic-like behaviors are symptoms of Tourette's syndrome.

2. Roberto clearly benefits from individualized instruction. This has been supported by his teacher. He should continue to sit toward the front of the class and would benefit from being placed in as small a class as possible, with few distractions and a highly structured, consistent routine.

3. Roberto would benefit from being encouraged to ask for help when he does not understand directions or has missed part of the instructions.

Before giving him oral instructions, it is essential to make sure that Roberto is paying attention. It is also important to state oral instructions in a clear and concise manner.

4. Roberto would benefit from teaching methods that incorporate nonverbal input and visual reinforcement whenever possible, such as using gestures, drawing on the board, or modeling the steps of a process.

5. It is recommended that Roberto be taught strategies for monitoring his comprehension of text, such as paraphrasing the main idea of a paragraph after reading it. He could be taught to form a visual picture of the elements of the paragraph and could be encouraged to actually draw a semantic map of the material, using the main idea and supporting details to structure the map. It is recommended that Roberto be taught to relate new information to those ideas that he already understands by using analogies from his own experience. Before assigning independent reading, it would be useful to check that Roberto has the necessary vocabulary and background knowledge to understand the story. Roberto appears to make use of context clues when possible, and this should be further encouraged.

6. To increase Roberto's interest in reading, he should be allowed to select materials that are high-interest and low vocabulary level. A system of using reinforcers to increase the amount of time Roberto spends in daily reading should be established. In order for Roberto to see that reading can be fun, the family could play language games together, such as *Scrabble, Up Words,* or *Boggle.* Roberto could also be encouraged to play computer games that require reading to get from one level to the next, as well as to listen to taped books as he reads along.

7. To help Roberto increase his understanding of the English language, he would benefit from hearing English being spoken at home. The family members are encouraged to engage in discussions in English together at dinner time and to watch English television programs.

8. Positive reinforcements could be used to help sustain Roberto's attention during difficult tasks. He should be allowed to participate in an enjoyable activity after he has demonstrated a period of sustained

effort on more difficult tasks. Roberto's frustration level could be monitored by understanding that sudden behavioral outbursts may be a signal that a task is too difficult or that a short break is needed. As indicated by Roberto's parents, Roberto has some difficulty accepting failure. When Roberto fails at a task, he would benefit from being provided with opportunities to succeed at another task. This will prevent him from developing a sense of helplessness and a lack of motivation toward learning.

9. Roberto's acting out behavior, as indicated by his parents, may be his attempt at coping in social situations that he finds confusing and difficult to understand. It may also reflect Roberto's discomfort with his mild tics, which may be a source of social embarrassment for Roberto. Roberto displayed a good sense of humor during the assessment, and he could be taught to use humor productively in social situations instead of acting "silly." He could also be encouraged to participate in drama activities, which would provide an acceptable outlet for his acting out behavior.

10. As described above, Roberto exhibited variable attention during the evaluation, which was evidence of only a very mild problem with attention, as his pediatrician suggested. Many children and parents effectively deal with mild difficulties such as these. To provide assistance for Mr. and Mrs. G. to better understand the difficulties Roberto is having and to obtain specific ideas about what they may do to help him, a book is recommended. It is titled *Taking Charge of ADHD*, written by Russell A. Barkley in 1995, and published by Guilford Press. Mr. and Mrs. G. will find helpful suggestions for parenting in general in this book.

Examiner: Shelley Suntup, M.A.
Supervisors: Liz Lichtenberger, Ph.D., and Carren Stika, Ph.D.

3 Kaufman Assessment Battery for Children (K-ABC)

Recent Research

ELIZABETH O. LICHTENBERGER
ALAN S. KAUFMAN

The Kaufman Assessment Battery for Children (K-ABC; Kaufman & Kaufman, 1983b) was developed with a main goal of being sensitive to the needs of minority groups, different ethnic groups, and different cultural groups. Many attempts were made in the creation and selection of items, in the structure of the processing scales with a separate achievement scale, and in the selection of the standardization sample to make the test more fair and less biased than previous measures of intelligence. Chapter 2 details the theory behind the K-ABC and the specific ways in which the test was developed with multicultural sensitivity. This chapter will discuss the research findings that support how well the K-ABC serves as an assessment tool for various cultural and minority groups.

Introduction

The children who are referred to school psychologists or clinicians in other settings for an assessment often come from diverse backgrounds with unique circumstances. In a thorough evaluation of a child, a major component is usually measuring the child's cognitive aptitude or intelligence. This is a critical part of an evaluation, as it often plays a significant role in determining whether a child qualifies for special services, and it is also necessary for an extensive understanding of each unique child. If a child is administered a test that is known to be discriminatory against a group to which the child belongs, then the scores obtained may be an inaccurate reflection of the child's true abilities. This misuse of tests can be problematic in that assumptions will be made based on data that are distorted by the bias of the test, which may lead to inappropriate conclusions being drawn (Cordary, 1996).

Biases regarding ethnicity, culture, and gender in assessment have been discussed in the literature for some time. In 1968, during the annual meeting of the American Psychological Association, the Association of Black Psychologists called for a moratorium on the use of psychological testing on disadvantaged children. The Association of Black Psychologists also mandated that the government implement some type of intervention and legal sanctions regarding current testing practices.

Additional professional groups have addressed the issues regarding assessment of minority group children in publications. A report published by the American Psychological Association in the *American Psychologist* comprehensively discusses the topics involved in test bias (Cleary, Humphreys, Kendrick, & Westman, 1975). The American Psychological Association's (1972) *Ethical Standards of Psychologists* and *Standards for Educational and Psychological Tests* (Davis, 1974) also both discuss the topic of assessment of minority group children, including issues ranging from development of tests to the appropriate use of such tests. An important set of federal guidelines entitled *Elimination of Discrimination in the Assignment of Children to Special Educational Classes for the Mentally Retarded* (U.S. Department of Health, Education, and Welfare, Office of Civil Rights, 1972) was proposed to outline principles in educational assessment practices.

In the empirical realm, it is important to define *test bias* objectively. One operational definition was put forth by Jensen (1980). In an effort to distinguish *fairness* and *unfairness* from the concept of *bias*, Jensen's definition used statistical constructs to define bias (Cordary, 1996). He stated, "In mathematical statistics, bias refers to a systematic over or underestimation of a population parameter by a statistic based on samples drawn from the population" (p. 375).

Another operational definition of test bias was put forth by Cleary (1968). This definition states that a test is categorized as

> biased for members of a subgroup of the population if in the prediction of a criterion for which the test was designed, consistent non-zero errors

of prediction are made for members of the subgroup. In other words, the test is biased if the criterion score predicted from the common regression line is consistently too high or too low for members of the subgroup. With this definition of "bias," there may be a connotation of "unfair," particularly if the use of the test produces a prediction that is too low. If the test is used for selection, members of a subgroup may be rejected when they were capable of adequate performance. (p. 115)

In examining bias, empirical investigation may demonstrate via statistics whether a test is indeed biased. Typically, investigation into bias examines three facets of validity: content, criterion-related, and construct (Jensen, 1980). Using these criteria, one can objectively judge a test and whether it may be biased. Reynolds (1982) stated, "The proper investigation of psychometric bias requires a multifaceted approach that can evaluate for bias at all levels including total score, individual scales, and items" (p. 176). In view of the definitions of bias presented above, the following pages will present research on the individual differences between various cultural groups' performance on the K-ABC and will provide evidence in support of the K-ABC's fairness with regard to content, construct, and criterion-related validity.

African American–White Group Differences on the K-ABC

The literature has shown that tests of intelligence typically produce differences in scores between cultural groups, such as African American and white children. Most often white children score approximately one standard deviation higher than African American children on tests that are measures of intelligence. For example, the mean difference on the Wechsler Intelligence Scale for Children-Revised (WISC-R; Wechsler, 1974) Full Scale IQ between African Americans and whites is 15.9 points (Kaufman & Doppelt, 1976) and on the Stanford-Binet Fourth Edition the average mean difference is about 12 points (Thorndike, Hagen, & Sattler, 1986). Various explanations have been generated to explain why these differences occur, including environmental differences such as education and cultural variables, child rearing practices, genetic differences between the groups, and, of course, the hypothesis that IQ tests are culturally biased.

In contrast to findings with other measures of intelligence, the data from studies of the K-ABC have not found the same large group difference between African Americans and whites. In fact, the findings reported in the *K-ABC Interpretive Manual* (Kaufman & Kaufman, 1983a) indicate that the mean difference between African American and white children is about half what is traditionally reported. Table 3.1 indicates that, on average, white children score only 7 points higher than African American children on the K-ABC Mental Processing Composite, which is in contrast to the 15.9 point difference in favor of whites on the WISC-R Full Scale IQ.

Vincent (1991) examined African American–white IQ differences from the norms of the K-ABC, the recent renorming of the Wechsler Adult Intelligence Scale-Revised, the Stanford Binet-IV and Raven's Progressive Matrices. In this study, African American–white IQ differences were examined in adults before and after 1980, in addition to examining African American–white IQ differences in children before and after 1980. Vincent's (1991) findings are reported in Table 3.2.

The data presented by Vincent (1991) indicate a consistent difference in IQ between African American and white adults, with African American adults scoring approximately one standard deviation lower than white adults in studies reported both pre- and post-1980. However, with children there is a change noted that seems to point to an "overall trend of a lessening of racial IQ differences in children" (Vincent, 1991, p. 268). In examining the African American IQ differences from the U.S. mean, findings that showed 14-18 point differences in studies prior to 1980 are in contrast to more recent findings, which show differences in the single digits (5-9 points).

Vincent (1991) reported five post-1980 studies that were not part of a standardization or re-standardization of a test, including studies by Naglieri and Hill (1986b) and Krohn and Lamp (1989) that reported data on the K-ABC as well as other tests. When socioeconomic status (SES) was controlled in these studies, one study showed no significant difference between African American and white IQ scores (Krohn & Lamp, 1989), whereas Naglieri and Hill (1986b) showed a significant decrease in African American–white score differences. Vincent (1991) noted that, although the results of these SES-controlled studies do

TABLE 3.1 African American–White Differences on the K-ABC and WISC-R

Intelligence Scale Score	African Americans		Whites		Difference
	N	Mean	N	Mean	
K-ABC Standard Score	807		1,569		
Sequential Processing		98.2		101.2	–3.0
Simultaneous Processing		93.8		102.3	–8.5
Mental Processing Composite		95.0		102.0	–7.0
WISC-R IQ	305		1,870		
Verbal		87.8		102.0	–14.2
Performance		87.2		102.2	–15.0
Full Scale		86.4		102.3	–15.9

SOURCE: Adapted from Kaufman and Kaufman, 1983a. K-ABC data are for children ages 2.5 through 12.5 tested in the sociocultural norming and standardization programs. WISC-R data (Kaufman & Doppelt, 1976) are for children ages 6 through 16 tested in the WISC-R standardization program.

NOTE: K-ABC = Kaufman Assessment Battery for Children (Kaufman & Kaufman, 1983b).
WISC-R = Wechsler Intelligence Scale for Children-Revised (Wechsler, 1974).

> not explain racial differences because one's socioeconomic status may be due not only to one's ability, but also to one's access to economic and educational opportunities, it calls into question the idea that one test is less biased than another. (p. 268)

Vincent (1991) interprets his findings, which emphasize the decreased racial difference, as evidenced in the K-ABC, as indicating that U.S. attempts at providing more equal opportunity are beginning to show results. However, alternative interpretations are feasible. In the Naglieri and Hill (1986b) study, the K-ABC African American–white difference of 6 points is one third smaller than the 9-point WISC-R discrepancy. Furthermore, differences of about 9 to 10 points for SES-matched groups of African Americans and Whites are not a new finding; such differences have been found for decades (see Shuey, 1966). In addition, the small IQ differences found on several tests by Krohn and Lamp (1989) are for preschool children, ages 4 to 6 years old. Much smaller African American–white differences for preschool versus school-age children are not a new finding; such results have also been demonstrated on SES-matched samples on the McCarthy (1972) Scales of Children's Abilities and on the Wechsler (1967) Preschool and Primary Scale of Intelligence (WPPSI) (Kaufman, 1973; Kaufman & Kaufman, 1973).

TABLE 3.2 U.S. African American–White IQ Differences

Study	Test	Age	African American/White IQ Scores	African American/White IQ Difference	African American/White IQ Difference From U.S. Mean
Adult pre- and post-1980					
Jensen (1969)	Various tests	Adult	85/100	15	15
Vincent & Cox (1974)	Raven's Standard Progressive Matrices (SPM)	Adult	83/99	16	17
Sattler (1988)	Wechsler Adult Intelligence Scale-Revised	Adult	87/101	14	13
Children pre-1980					
Kaufman & Doppelt (1976)	Wechsler Intelligence Scale for Children-Revised (WISC-R)	6-16	86/102	16	14
Baughman & Dahlstrom (1968)	Stanford-Binet Intelligence Scale (SB, L-M)	5-13	86/101	15	14
Jensen (1973)	Raven's Coloured Progressive Matrices (CPM)	11	82/96	14	18
		6	82/100	18	18
Children post-1980 (normative studies)					
Raven et al. (1986)	Raven's SPM	12	94/101	7	5
Kaufman & Kaufman (1983b)	Kaufman-Assessment Battery for Children (K-ABC)	2-12	95/102	7	6
Thorndike et al. (1986)	Stanford-Binet, 4th ed. (SBIV)	7-11	93/103	10	7
		2-6	92/105	12	9
Children post-1980 (SES-controlled studies)					
Naglieri & Hill (1986a)	K-ABC	9-12	92/98	6	8
	WISC	9-12	92/102	9	8
Krohn & Lamp (1989)	SBIV	4-6	93/94	1	7
	K-ABC	4-6	94/97	3	6
	SB, L-M	4-6	93/97	4	7

SOURCE: Adapted from Vincent (1991).
NOTE: IQs are reported as an M of 100 and SD of 15. Stanford-Binet data are adjusted accordingly. Raven's CPM and SPM scores are presented in the context of 1986 U.S. norms.

Jensen (1984) provided several possible explanations as to why the diminished African American–white differences on the K-ABC are in contrast to what has been previously demonstrated with other intelligence tests. Jensen generated several hypotheses for further exploration; however, he did not provide empirical conclusions regarding actual ethnic group performance. One of Jensen's explanations for the diminished African American–white difference was that K-ABC subtests were given preference because of their past record for showing smaller African American–white differences than other tests. Jensen explains that subtests that were given preference because of their known small African American–white differences include those such as Gestalt Closure and Face Recognition. Jensen states that theoretical or psychometric justification for selecting items or tests on the basis of their degree of discrimination between different populations cannot be found. Although Jensen's statement has some truth, there are numerous humanistic reasons for giving preference to less discriminatory items (Kaufman, 1984). Jensen (1984) states that "certain other K-ABC tests were expressly selected because previous studies had shown especially small black-white differences" (p. 398). However, this was simply not the case. "Primary considerations were always theoretical relevance, factor-analytic data, interest to children, ease of administration and scoring, neuropsychological value and novelty" (Kaufman, 1984, p. 441). It was primarily these qualities that it was critical for tasks to have, and if such tasks were found to have small racial differences, then that was even better for the K-ABC. Selecting subtests expressly or specifically for the potential to produce small race differences was not done in the development of the K-ABC. *The K-ABC Interpretive Manual* (Kaufman & Kaufman, 1983a) does not imply in any way that this procedure was used.

An example of the primary importance of theoretical relevance, neuropsychological value, and empirical evidence being used in task development can be seen in the K-ABC's Number Recall task. African American–white differences are known to be larger on Digits Backward than Digits Forward, but this information is not what led to the exclusion of Digits Backward from the Sequential Processing Scale. Rather, empirical evidence from the neuropsychological research, suggesting that Digits Backward may be a Simultaneous task (Kaufman, 1979), was the convincing factor that led to the exclusion of the task. Alone, Digits Forward has been used in many cases as a marker test of successive processing (Das et al., 1979).

Furthermore, Sternberg (1984) and Jensen (1984) both proposed that subtests on the Sequential Processing Scale that "overemphasize" short-term rote memory, such as Number Recall and Word Order, may lead to smaller African American–white differences. Rote memory tasks have been found to produce smaller African American–white differences (Sternberg, 1984); however, the abilities needed to succeed on the Sequential Processing tasks are diverse and include more than simply rote memory. Both strategy generation and mediation are needed to recall stimuli despite color interference or to copy a sequence of hand movements (Kaufman, 1984). Kamphaus and Reynolds (1987) refute the contention of overgeneralization across multiple dimensions made by Sternberg (1984).

Another possible explanation put forth by Jensen (1984) for the diminished African American–white difference was that the K-ABC standardization sample was more heterogeneous with regard to mental ability. The Kaufmans' sample included children who were affected by mental retardation, learning disabilities, speech and language impairments, and other handicaps, in addition to including greater representation of minorities. Jensen suggests that this heterogeneity is a possible explanation for discrepancy with other intelligence tests. It was hypothesized that the sampling composition led to an artificial shrinkage of group differences expressed in standard score terms (Jensen, 1984).

Bracken (1985) and Jensen (1984) both mention that the K-ABC standardization sample included a disproportionate number of minorities in urban settings and of higher SES. In comparison to the 1980 U.S. Census statistics, the standardization sample did include a disproportionate number of African American children from the highest SES group. The level of parental education was taken as an indicator of SES in the K-ABC standardization sample. For African Americans, the two highest levels of education seemed to be overrepresented, with the percentages in the K-ABC standardization sample being 23.2% and 14.5%, whereas the U.S. Census statistics reported only 16.9% and 8.8% of African Americans falling in the two highest levels of parent education or SES. However, Kamphaus and Reynolds (1987) note that the impact of this is minimal; "based on a reweighing of cases taken from the actual standardization data and use of the sociocultural norm group, the difference can account for no more than about 2 IQ points of reduction at best" (p. 166).

Kaufman, O'Neal, Avant, and Long (1987) also suggest that more evidence supportive of the smaller group differences is apparent in the *K-ABC Interpretive Manual* (Kaufman & Kaufman, 1983a), which provided data on the same sample of children administered both the Peabody Picture Vocabulary Test-Revised (PPVT-R) and the K-ABC. The PPVT-R produced African American–white differences of 15 points on the standardization sample that produced much smaller racial or ethnic differences on the K-ABC. Thus, the hypothesis that the diminished differences between ethnic groups is due to sampling problems does not appear to be supported, because the African American–white reduced differences were not also found on the PPVT-R. This finding also is contrary to Vincent's (1991) contention that the K-ABC yields African American–white differences of the same magnitude as other cognitive batteries.

Jensen (1984) also suggests that scaling artifacts may be related to the diminished African American–white differences. Kaufman and Kaufman (1983a) note that as many as 10% to 20% of the children in any age group may fail to pass a single item in the subtest, which leaves an unusually large number of raw scores of zero on some subtests. This may indicate that the "bottom" of some K-ABC subtests is insufficient, and the range of item difficulty will not discriminate true ability differences between white and African American children when raw scores of zero are so frequently obtained. Jensen (1984) admits that the "biasing effects of the scale artifacts would not be very large" (p. 400). However, he notes that the effects may nonetheless affect the reported diminished group difference, albeit by a minuscule amount.

Jensen (1984) and Naglieri and Jensen (1987) propose that because the K-ABC's subtests are less heavily laden with g, and because African American–white differences on tests of intelligence are positively correlated with g-loadings, this may also provide an explanation for the diminution of African American–white differences on the K-ABC. When matched pairs of African American and white children were administered both the K-ABC and the WISC-R, Naglieri and Jensen (1987) found that

The lesser white-black discriminability of the K-ABC relative to the WISC-R is attributable to (1) the smaller g-loadings of the K-ABC subtests and (2) the presence of other factors, particularly sequential short-term memory which, to some degree, offsets the white-black difference in g. (p. 21)

Some of Jensen's (1984) own data show that the K-ABC Mental Processing Composite does, in fact, have g-loadings as strong as the WISC-R. The mean g-loading reported by Jensen for the composite is in the low 60s, which is similar to that shown in studies with the WISC-R, with ranges from the low .50s to the low .60s. The g-loadings of K-ABC subtests, WISC-R, and Stanford-Binet are further shown by Jensen to be congruent, suggesting that all three tests measure almost the same g (Kaufman, 1984). Thus, although Jensen states that the K-ABC has smaller g-loadings, which lead to diminished racial differences, he provides evidence that does not support his own point (Kaufman, 1984).

Native American–White Group Differences on the K-ABC

A small number of studies are available examining the performance of Native Americans on the K-ABC. Two studies are presented in the *K-ABC Interpretive Manual* (Kaufman & Kaufman, 1983a), one involving 33 Navajo children ages 5 years, 5 months, through 12 years, 4 months, and the second involving 40 Sioux children ages 8 years, 2 months, to 12 years. Table 3.3 presents the data from these two studies.

As explained in the *K-ABC Interpretive Manual* (Kaufman & Kaufman, 1983a), the Sioux and Navajo Native American groups are culturally different groups. The sample of Sioux children was noted to be more integrated into American society than the sample of Navajo children. In contrast to the sample of Navajo children, in which the majority spoke primarily Navajo and lived on a reservation, the Sioux sample spoke English well and attended regular public schools.

The findings of these studies (Kaufman & Kaufman, 1983a) indicated that both the Sioux and Navajo groups earned scores on the Simultaneous Processing Scale that were approximately at the normative mean of 100. A discrepancy between the two Native American groups was found in processing style preference. The Navajo group scored 12 points higher on Simultaneous than Sequential Processing, but the Sioux chil-

TABLE 3.3 WISC-R and K-ABC Global Scale Means and Standard Deviations for Native Americans

Scale	Navajos (n = 33) Ages 5 years, 5 months to 12 years, 4 months		Sioux (n = 40) Ages 8 years, 2 months to 12 years		Crow (n = 57) Ages 7 years to 12 years, 6 months		White (n=60) Ages 7 years to 12 years, 6 months	
	Mean	SD	Mean	SD	Mean	SD	Mean	SD
Kaufman-Assessment Battery for Children (K-ABC)								
Sequential Processing	87.7	11.3	99.6	12.4	106.1	10.2	111.7	9.9
Simultaneous Processing	99.8	10.2	101.3	10.7	116.8	8.6	112.9	9.6
Mental Processing Composite	94.2	10.3	100.6	10.7	114.3	8.6	114.2	9.4
Achievement	81.7	11.2	93.3	12.8				
Wechsler Intelligence Scale for Children-Revised								
Verbal IQ	74.9	13.5	91.4	14.6				
Performance IQ	102.8	11.8	103.6	11.8				
Full Scale IQ	86.9	11.1	96.8	12.6				

SOURCE: Adapted from Kaufman and Kaufman (1983a). The data on Crow and white children are adapted from Davidson (1992). The Crow and white subjects were only administered three of the K-ABC global scales.

dren displayed no discrepancy in their style of processing information. Kaufman and Kaufman (1983a) noted that, on closer examination of the Navajo profile, three subtest scores were observed to be extremely depressed: Number Recall, Word Order, and Riddles.

> All three involve auditory stimuli and demand good verbal comprehension skills; the low scores may reflect their limited proficiency in English . . . and render the Sequential Processing, Mental Processing Composite, and Achievement standard scores as underestimates of their true ability. (Kaufman & Kaufman, 1983a, p. 153)

The Sioux and Navajo groups' performances on the WISC-R and K-ABC were compared (Kaufman & Kaufman, 1983a). The Sioux sample earned a mean WISC-R Full Scale IQ 4 points below its K-ABC Mental Processing Composite (96.8 versus 100.6). The Navajo sample exhibited a 7-point difference between its mean WISC-R Full Scale IQ (86.9) and K-ABC Mental Processing Composite (94.2). It appears that the combination of language factors and cultural variables had a greater impact on the WISC-R Full Scale mean than the K-ABC Mental Processing Composite, which was only slightly lower than the normative mean.

A more recent study of Native American students' performance on the K-ABC was performed by Davidson (1992). Fifty-seven American Indian children and 60 white children, all ages 7 to 12.5, served as subjects for this study. The majority (67%) of the Native American group were from the Crow tribe. A unique feature of the subject pool was that all of the children had been referred for testing from various sources for possible inclusion in an enrichment program for students of high ability. An inclusion criterion for subjects in this study was a K-ABC Mental Processing Composite above the 50th percentile.

Davidson's (1992) findings indicated that, in a group of children with average to superior intellectual ability, there were no significant differences between whites and Native Americans on the K-ABC Mental Processing Composite (Table 3.3 presents the means and standard deviations for the white and Native American children). However, differences were noted in the processing styles of whites versus Native Americans. As a group, the Native American children scored significantly higher than the white children on Simultaneous Processing. Closer analysis revealed that 47% of the total group of Native American subjects significantly favored Simultaneous Processing over Sequential Processing, whereas only 16% of the total group of white students showed the same discrepancy.

Davidson (1992) suggests that it may be "overly simplistic to state that most or all [Native American] students process information in a simultaneous/holistic manner or that most or all white students process information in a sequential manner" (p. 114). A greater number of Native American (53%) and white (73%) children showed no significant discrepancy between Sequential and Simultaneous Processing.

In a more detailed analysis of relative strengths, Native Americans scored significantly higher than white children on Gestalt Closure, Triangles, and Spatial Memory (Davidson, 1992). These subtests require a combination of simultaneous processing abilities and spatial abilities. However, the author cautions the reader not to assign cognitive traits to children based on cultural research. Instead, each child should be considered as an individual.

Hispanic–White Group Differences on the K-ABC

Data in the *K-ABC Interpretive Manual* (Kaufman & Kaufman, 1983a) on Hispanics included 157 cases in the standardization sample, plus three cases tested just after the completion of the standardization program. The sample of Hispanic children is broken down into 32 preschool age children (2 years, 6 months, through 4 years, 11 months) and 128 school age children (5 years through 12 years, 6 months). In both age groups, Hispanic children

> scored about equally well on the Sequential and Simultaneous Processing Scales, but performed about 5 points better on the Mental Processing Composite than on the Achievement Scale. Despite this similarity in relative performance on the Global Scales, the means for preschool children were 5 to 7 points higher than the means for school age children. (Kaufman & Kaufman, 1983a, p. 150)

The Kaufmans' (1983a) standardization sample showed that the Hispanic group means were very close, only 2 points away from the normative mean of 100. However, the average mean on the Achievement Scale was approximately half a standard deviation below the normative mean.

In comparing Hispanic children's performance on the K-ABC and the WISC-R (Mercer, 1979), differences are apparent. On the WISC-R, Hispanic children scored 11 points below white children on the Full Scale IQ, with a Verbal IQ mean 14 points below white children and a Performance IQ mean only 6 points below white children. Table 3.4 shows the differences in Hispanic and white children's performance on the K-ABC and the WISC-R.

It is likely that the linguistic demands and cultural content of the WISC-R Verbal Scale affected the performance of the Hispanic children. On the K-ABC Mental Processing Scales, mental functioning can be demonstrated by Hispanic children with little penalty for linguistic and cultural differences. However, the K-ABC Achievement Scale is still clearly affected by the linguistic and cultural factors, which lead to a larger difference between white and Hispanic children's performance.

Similar to what was reported in the K-ABC standardization data with preschool children (Kaufman & Kaufman, 1983a), Whiteworth and Chrisman (1987) reported that they also found no significant differences between Hispanic and white preschoolers (ages 4-5) on any of the K-ABC global scales. They examined the performance of 30 Mexican American and 30 white children on both the K-ABC and the WPPSI. Subjects were not matched "exactly" for socioeconomic status (SES), but the majority of both the Hispanic and white parents had completed at least some college, placing them in the upper SES division.

The means for the K-ABC standard scores and the WPPSI IQs from Whiteworth and Chrisman's (1987) results are presented in Table 3.4. Results of univariate analyses of variance showed that none of the five K-ABC global scores were significantly different in the two ethnic groups ($p > .05$). Differences between Hispanic and white children on the K-ABC Sequential, Simultaneous, and Mental Processing Composite ranged from only 1.4 to 1.9 standard score points. The only significant difference found between the two cultural groups was on their performance on the Verbal Scale of the WPPSI; Mexican American preschoolers scored significantly lower, $F(1, 58) = 5.06$, $p < .05$, with a 7.6-point difference between the groups. The authors conclude by saying that "the K-ABC is somewhat less biased for this group of Mexican-American preschoolers than the WPPSI, quite possibly because the K-ABC intelligence scales are less verbally loaded than the WPPSI as suggested by the test's developers" (Whiteworth & Chrisman, 1987, p. 700).

TABLE 3.4 Hispanic–White Differences on the K-ABC and WISC-R

Intelligence Scale Score	Hispanics		Whites		
	N	Mean	N	Mean	Difference
Study 1					
K-ABC Standard Score	106		1,569		
Sequential Processing		98.7		101.2	–2.5
Simultaneous Processing		99.5		102.3	–2.8
Mental Processing Composite		95.8		102.0	–3.1
WISC-R IQ	520		640		
Verbal		87.7		102.0	–14.3
Performance		97.9		103.8	–5.9
Full Scale		91.9		103.1	–11.2
Study 2					
K-ABC Standard Score	30		30		
Sequential Processing		101.1		102.5	–1.4
Simultaneous Processing		99.4		101.1	–1.7
Mental Processing Composite		100.0		101.9	–1.9
WPPSI IQ	30		30		
Verbal		95.1		102.7	–7.6
Performance		109.3		109.7	–.4
Full Scale		102.1		107.5	–5.4

SOURCE: In Study 1, K-ABC data were adapted from Kaufman and Kaufman (1983a), p. 151. WISC-R data are from Mercer (1979). In Study 2, data were adapted from Whiteworth and Chrisman (1987).

NOTE: K-ABC = Kaufman Assessment Battery for Children (Kaufman & Kaufman, 1983b). K-ABC data are for children ages 2.5 through 12.5 tested in the sociocultural norming and standardization programs. WISC-R = Wechsler Intelligence Scale for Children-Revised (Wechsler, 1974).

Content Validity

The literature on African American, Native American, Mexican American, and white group differences in performance on the K-ABC global scales and other measures of intelligence have been presented to give background for further discussion of the culture-fairness of the K-ABC. The following pages present research on the validity and reliability of the K-ABC in the context of multicultural fairness.

When constructing a test, items should be examined during the development phases to identify potential bias, whether due to gender or ethnic factors. The content validity studies for the K-ABC involved evaluation via both statistical methods and more subjective judgments (Kaufman & Kaufman, 1983a). Independent outside reviewers were asked to review the initial edition of the K-ABC and identify items that were biased on the basis of gender or culture. Two African American and two Hispanic educators reviewed the items and identified ones that were problematic in their opinion. The items that the reviewers viewed as unfair were eliminated before the standardization process. Additional statistical techniques were also used to assess potential item bias. As explained in the *K-ABC Interpretive Manual* (Kaufman & Kaufman, 1983a, p. 60), the Rasch-Wright one-parameter latent trait methodology and an adaptation of the method presented by Angoff and Ford (1973) were used to assess gender and race bias. In view of the many content validity evaluations performed on the initial K-ABC items, Kamphaus and Reynolds (1987) stated, "It appears that the K-ABC item pool was tested more rigorously than many other clinical tests prior to publication" and "the K-ABC can suffer little criticism for failing to address the issue of item bias" (p. 22).

A study performed by Willson, Nolan, Reynolds, and Kamphaus (1989) examined gender and race differences on individual K-ABC items. The authors noted that it is particularly important to examine the K-ABC at the item level because of the subtest profile analysis and discrepancy analysis advocated by the Kaufmans (1983a). Willson et al. (1989) also recognized that biased items are more likely to affect a subtest score than a Mental Processing Composite.

On the 10 K-ABC mental processing subtests, 2,932 item comparisons were made (Willson et al., 1989). A total of 23 items were deemed to be biased against African American children, and 13 were found to be biased against white children. Table 3.5 displays the results of the race bias item analysis. When gender bias was examined, 12 items were found to be biased against males, and 16 items were biased against females. The results of the Willson et al. (1989) gender-bias item analysis can be found in Table 3.6. Neither the ratio of racially biased nor the gender-biased items exceeded chance expectations.

The subtest that presented the most biased items for both gender and race was Gestalt Closure. The number of Gestalt Closure items showing gender bias was 12, with 5 biased against males and 7 biased against females. When considering race, the number showing race bias was 8, with all identified items reportedly biased against African American children. However, the authors note that there was no identifiable reason for a greater number of items in Gestalt Closure being biased (Willson et al., 1989).

TABLE 3.5 Number of Items Showing Race Bias on Subtests of the Kaufman-Assessment Battery for Children (K-ABC)

	Bias Against	
Subtest Name	African American	White
Gestalt Closure	8	0
Number Recall	2	4
Triangles	1	1
Word Order	2	1
Matrix Analogies	1	3
Photo Series	4	2
Spatial Memory	2	1
Hand Movements	1	1
Face Recognition	0	0
Magic Window	2	0
Total	23	13

SOURCE: Adapted from Willson et al. (1989).
NOTE: Includes ages 2.5 through 4.5 only.

In light of the large number of comparisons examined (2,932), a relatively small number of items (64) in the total item pool were found to be functioning differently by race or gender. Willson and colleagues (1989) note that by chance alone (at the .001 level), it is expected that up to six items may be considered biased just due to Type I errors. It is also important to consider that of the 2% of the total item pool identified as possibly biased, most of those items were essentially counterbalanced. The authors concluded that "eliminating such items would have a minuscule effects on race or gender differences in mean scores" (Willson et al., 1989, p. 296). Thus, the effect of the small number of biased items is likely to be of no real practical consequence.

Item bias on the K-ABC was also examined in a sample of gifted and nongifted children from the standardization sample (Nolan, Watlington, & Willson, 1989). The items found to be gender- or race-biased in the sample of gifted and nongifted children are listed in Table 3.7.

In the analysis of the differential item functioning for gifted children, no items were found to be biased against the gifted African American children. However, eight items were found to be biased against the gifted white children. Thus, regarding racial bias in the gifted sample, significantly more items were biased against the gifted white children (Nolan et al., 1989).

TABLE 3.6 Number of Items Showing Gender Bias on Subtests of the
Kaufman-Assessment Battery for Children (K-ABC)

	Bias Against	
Subtest Name	Male	Female
Gestalt Closure	5	7
Number Recall	0	2
Triangles	1	2
Word Order	1	2
Matrix Analogies	1	0
Photo Series	1	2
Spatial Memory	2	0
Hand Movements	1	0
Face Recognition	1	0
Magic Window	0	0
Total	13	15

SOURCE: Adapted from Willson et al. (1989).
NOTE: Includes ages 2.5 through 4.5 only.

The differential item functioning on the K-ABC in the nongifted sample revealed different results. Three items were found to be biased against nongifted African American children, and four items were biased against nongifted white children. Chi square statistic results indicated that there were not significantly more items biased against either race in the sample of nongifted children.

Nolan et al. (1989) also examined gender bias in the samples of gifted and nongifted children. Results of the gifted sample showed that one item in Photo Series and one item in Spatial Memory were biased against gifted males. Items found to be biased against gifted females included one item in Hand Movements and one in Number Recall. There was no significant difference in the number of biased items in the male versus female group of gifted children.

Concerning gender bias in the nongifted sample, Nolan et al. (1989) reported that a total of 10 items were biased against males and 6 items were biased against females. Three items in Gestalt Closure, three items in Triangles, two items in Hand Movements, and two items in Number Recall were found to be biased against nongifted male children. Items identified as biased for nongifted female children included two in Gestalt Closure, two in Triangles, one in Number Recall, and one in Photo Series. Within the group of nongifted children, no statistically significant differ-

TABLE 3.7 Number of Items Showing Race Bias on Subtests of the Kaufman-Assessment Battery for Gifted and Nongifted Children

		Biased Against			
		Gifted		Nongifted	
Subtest Name	Number	African American	White	African American	White
Gestalt Closure	25	0	1	1	3
Number Recall	21	0	0	0	0
Triangles	18	0	1	1	1
Word Order	19	0	0	0	0
Matrix Analogies	17	0	2	0	0
Photo Series	21	0	2	0	0
Spatial Memory	20	0	2	0	0
Hand Movements	20	0	0	0	0
Face Recognition	15	0	0	0	0
Magic Window	15	0	0	1	0
Total	191	0	0	3	4

SOURCE: Adapted from Nolan et al. (1980).
NOTE: Includes ages 2.5 through 4.5.

ences were found between genders. However, between the gifted and nongifted samples, the number of biased items was found to be significantly different.

Nolan et al. (1989) found that there was no systematic pattern underlying the biased items. On the basis of gender, a total of 4.2% of the items were found to be biased for nongifted children, whereas 1.0% of the items were biased for gifted children. On the basis of race, 2.0% of the items were biased against gifted white children. In the sample of nongifted children, 1.8% of the items were found to be racially biased. Overall, findings revealed that out of the 2,932 items, only 35 (1.2%) were found to be biased. Thus, these results indicate that the K-ABC is a relatively nonbiased test at the item level. Most of the significant findings are probably a result of chance factors based on the huge number of comparisons and nothing more. For example, of the 16 biased items in the gender analysis for the nongifted sample, 10 occurred on subtests with culturally neutral stimuli (Triangles, Hand Movements, Number Recall). There is no rational (i.e., content-based) explanation for any particular design, sequence of hand movements, or series of numbers to be unfair to males or females.

In conclusion, the present review of the studies on content validity and item bias demonstrate that Kaufman and Kaufman's (1983a) attempt to develop a test of intelligence for children that is relatively free of bias at the item level has been successful. The literature available on the K-ABC has not tapped all possible groups in which bias may be present, but the findings thus far do seem to suggest that the items on the Mental Processing Scale of the K-ABC are relatively free of bias on the basis of age, gender, and race (African American-white). Given these findings, Willson et al. (1989) and Nolan et al. (1989) believe that there is substantial empirical evidence to support that the K-ABC is a viable tool for the assessment of children who are gifted or nongifted, from diverse racial backgrounds, and of either gender.

Construct Validity

Another facet of validity to be addressed in the context of examining the cultural fairness of the K-ABC is construct validity. How well a particular instrument measures a theoretically defined construct is described as construct validity (Kazdin, 1992). Some believe that construct validity is the most important type of validity (Messick, 1980). Extensive work was done to provide substantial evidence of the K-ABC's construct validity (Kaufman & Kaufman, 1983a). The *K-ABC Interpretive Manual* (Kaufman & Kaufman, 1983a) organizes the discussion of construct validity around five main areas: developmental changes, internal consistency, factor analysis, convergent and discriminant validation, and correlations with other tests. These five areas of construct validity correspond to those described by Anastasi (1988). Of these areas, the ones that are most relevant to the differential validity of the K-ABC will be discussed in detail in the following pages.

Factor Analysis. One way to explore for evidence of differential construct validity is factor analysis. With the K-ABC's foundation being solidly situated on the distinction between sequential and simultaneous processing, it was very important to demonstrate that there are, in fact, two factors underlying the K-ABC Mental Processing Composite, and these factors are consistent across race and gender. Factor analytic evidence to support the K-ABC Achievement Scale is also important to present (Kaufman & Kaufman, 1983a).

The organization of the K-ABC Mental Processing Scales into Sequential and Simultaneous components was supported by a factor analytic study of the national standardization sample conducted by Kaufman and Kamphaus (1984). Using a two-factor solution, the highest mean loadings across all ages on the Simultaneous factor were found in the Simultaneous subtests (.40 to .69), and on the Sequential factor, the highest loadings were found on the Sequential subtests (.43 to .75). Only one of the sequential tasks, Hand Movements, had an additional moderate loading of .36 on the Simultaneous factor. However, no substantial loadings on the Sequential factor were found on any of the Simultaneous processing subtests.

When Kaufman and Kamphaus (1984) examined a three-factor solution, including an achievement factor, the six K-ABC Achievement subtests were found to have loadings ranging from .49 to .77 on the achievement factor. The Mental Processing subtests of the K-ABC were found to have loadings on the sequential and simultaneous factors that were similar to those found in the two-factor solution. One Achievement subtest, Arithmetic, was found to load highly (ranging from .38 to .66) on the sequential and simultaneous factors.

Recognizing the need for further research on gender differences in simultaneous and sequential processing, Kamphaus and Kaufman (1986) assessed the factorial validity of the K-ABC for boys and girls separately. Across every age group for boys, the two-factor solutions were found to be most meaningful. The results for girls were similar, with the two-factor solution selected for every age, except for age 5, in which a three-factor solution was found most meaningful. The three-factor solution for 5-year-old girls "revealed that Factor 1 was Simultaneous Processing, Factor 2 was Sequential Processing, and Factor 3 was Visual Memory" (Kamphaus & Kaufman, 1986, p. 211). Table 3.8 displays the results of the factor analysis for boys and girls ages 5 to 12.5.

To address the issue of the generalizability of the factorial validity of the K-ABC for diverse cultural and ethnic groups, Reynolds and Willson (1984) conducted a factor analytic study using groups of African American and white children from the standardization sample. Bias on

TABLE 3.8 Mean Varimax-Rotated Loadings on Sequential and Simultaneous Factors for Separate Groups of Girls and Boys at Ages 5 to 12.5 Years, Kaufman-Assessment Battery for Children

| | School Age (Ages 5 to 12.5) | | | |
| | Girls | | Boys | |
Subtest	Sequential	Simultaneous	Sequential	Simultaneous
Sequential Processing Scale				
3. Hand Movements	34	**40**	38	39
5. Number Recall	**81**	14	**80**	12
7. Word Order	**66**	31	**77**	25
Simultaneous Processing Scale				
4. Gestalt Closure	14	**53**	04	**53**
6. Closure	17	**76**	20	**70**
8. Matrix Analogies	29	**58**	28	**55**
9. Spatial Memory	29	**55**	21	**59**
10. Photo Series	26	**68**	22	**72**

SOURCE: Adapted from Kamphaus & Kaufman (1986).
NOTE: Decimal points are omitted from factor loadings. Loadings of .35 and above are highlighted in boldface.

a test may be indicated if a difference is present in the factor structure for different groups, such as African Americans and whites.

The two-factor solution for the Mental Processing subtests was examined for African Americans and whites (Reynolds & Willson, 1984). The findings for each group were compared using the coefficient of congruence (Reynolds, 1982). The overall results of the analysis demonstrate that the two-factor processing model is supported across race for both African Americans and whites. All of the coefficients of congruence were found to exceed .80, and the majority (12 out of 15) of the coefficients were larger than .91 (see Table 3.9).

Although the two factors underlying the Mental Processing Scales of the K-ABC were found to be congruent for African Americans and whites, some important differences emerged when the Achievement Scales were added into the analysis to form a three-factor solution (Reynolds & Willson, 1984). In fact, Kamphaus and Reynolds (1987) noted, "Such disparity in factor structures is highly unusual in the testing literature" (p. 45). The findings of the study indicated that for the group of African American children, the K-ABC Achievement subtests and the

TABLE 3.9 Coefficients of Congruence Between African Americans and
Whites at Five Age Levels for the Sequential and Simultaneous
Factor Loadings of the Kaufman-Assessment Battery for Children

Age	Sequential Processing Factor	Simultaneous Processing Factor
3 years to 3 years, 11 months	.91	.84
4 years to 4 years, 11 months	.91	.80
5 years to 5 years, 11 months	.92	.97
6 years to 6 years, 11 months	.83	.93
7 years to 12 years, 5 months	.95	.98

SOURCE: Adapted from Reynolds & Willson (1984).

Mental Processing subtests are less differentiated. Reynolds and Willson (1984) indicated that many of the Mental Processing subtests seem to load at higher values on the achievement factor for the African American group, with the most overlap being found on the Sequential and Achievement Scales. Thus, although the results from the group of white children are similar to the overall results in the normative sample, when the results of the group of African American children are considered separately, it appears that it may be necessary to conceptualize the performance of these children in a new way.

To explain the diminished differentiation between Achievement and Mental Processing factors with the group of African American children, the authors hypothesized that knowing the name of objects may be more difficult than the mental processing necessary to combine the stimuli for African American children, relative to the white children (Reynolds & Willson, 1984). This hypothesis grew from the group differences of factor loadings for Magic Window with 3-year-olds and for Gestalt Closure across many ages. Similarly, for an Achievement test such as Riddles, the mental process of reasoning may be more demanding for an African American child, who may be lacking in experience with the verbal concepts.

To examine the validity of the K-ABC factor structure with minority groups other than African Americans, Valencia and Rankin (1986) conducted a comparative factor analysis for Hispanic and white fifth graders. The groups were matched on SES (mainly low to low-middle) and language status (English dominant). The white sample comprised 45 boys and 55 girls, and the Mexican American group comprised 50 children of each gender.

Valencia and Rankin's (1986) findings indicated that the factors that emerged for both the white and Mexican American groups corresponded to the Sequential, Simultaneous, and Achievement Scales composing the K-ABC. Coefficients of congruence were computed between each group and the normative sample, as well as between the study's white and Mexican American samples. The coefficients of congruence between the normative sample and both the white and Mexican American groups were .97 for the Simultaneous factor. Between the Mexican American and white groups, the coefficient for the Simultaneous factor was .96. For the Sequential factor, the coefficients were .93 between the standardization group and the white group and .94 between the Mexican American group and the standardization group. Finally, a coefficient of congruence of .99 was found for the Sequential factor between the white and Mexican American group. Table 3.10 shows the two-factor solution for the white and Mexican American groups.

Like Reynolds and Willson (1984), who examined a sample of African American and white children, Valencia and Rankin (1986) found that the Achievement tests tended to load on the Mental Processing factors for Mexican American children. Thus, when a three-factor solution was computed in the analysis, the coefficients of congruency for the first factor (achievement) and second factor (Simultaneous) were .95 and .91, respectively, but a much lower coefficient of .18 was found for the third factor (with Simultaneous/achievement loadings for the Mexican American group and Sequential processing loadings for the white group).

Comparable to the factor analytic findings with African American children, when the Mexican American children's Achievement scores are included in the analysis, the factors become incongruent with those of the White group. In Valencia and Rankin's (1986) study, the Mexican American group had two Achievement subtests with significant loadings on a Mental Processing factor (Faces and Places and Riddles). The behavior of the Sequential Processing subtests was also similar to that exhibited in the earlier study with African American children, with the Mexican American group showing loadings on the Achievement Scale of .34 and .44 for two of the three Sequential subtests. It appears, from the factor analytic studies of the ethnic minorities examined, that the K-ABC Achievement Scales are highly affected by verbal intelligence and may therefore be a less "pure" measure of achievement for those groups than they are for white children.

TABLE 3.10 Factor Structure of the Mental Processing Subtests for the
Standardization, White and Mexican American Fifth Grade
Samples, Kaufman-Assessment Battery for Children

Subtest	Standardization[a] (N = 200)		White (n = 100)		Mexican American (n = 100)	
	Simultaneous	Sequential	Simultaneous	Sequential	Simultaneous	Sequential
Sequential Processing Scale						
3. Hand Movements	43	37	52	22	45	27
5. Number Recall	13	92	11	59	23	57
7. Word Order	24	69	14	86	08	71
Simultaneous Processing Scale						
4. Gestalt Closure	52	04	48	02	24	08
6. Closure	69	18	59	–05	66	–01
8. Matrix Analogies	62	23	58	23	64	24
9. Spatial Memory	54	27	59	19	50	13
10. Photo Series	75	22	44	21	65	17

SOURCE: Adapted from Valencia & Rankin (1986).

a. Factor Loadings are based on Varimax rotated principal factor analysis using a 10-year-old cohort from the K-ABC standardized sample (see Kaufman & Kaufman, 1983, p. 105).

NOTE: Decimals are omitted.

In summary, the factor analytic results of samples of white, African American, and Mexican American children with the K-ABC contribute to the construct validity of this instrument across ethnic groups. Although the K-ABC's Achievement subtests appear not to be a pure measure of achievement for the minority groups, the Mental Processing subtests consistently produced a two-factor solution consistent with the Sequential and Simultaneous breakdown of the scales for all groups. Thus, there is strong evidence for the validity of these constructs in this test of intelligence.

Correlations With Other Tests. During its standardization, the K-ABC was administered with other tests that are widely accepted as criteria of intelligence, and the correlations between the K-ABC and these other measures of intelligence provide further evidence of differential construct validity. Kaufman and Kaufman (1983a) indicate that the K-ABC met the goal of construct validity described by Anastasi (1988) as having correlations that are moderate, but not too high with available tests, and thus, it contributes uniquely to the assessment of intelligence. The *K-ABC Interpretive Manual* (Kaufman & Kaufman, 1983a) provides correlational data on different samples, including children of combined ethnic groups, African American children, Hispanic children, Native American children, and white children.

The interpretive manual presents data from a combination of five studies that correlated the WISC-R with the K-ABC using samples of normal children with a variety of ethnic backgrounds. Overall, results indicated that the K-ABC Mental Processing Composite correlated with the WISC-R Full Scale IQ at .70, and the correlation between the K-ABC Achievement Scale and the WISC-R Full Scale IQ was just as high, with a coefficient of .76. The WISC-R Verbal IQ correlation with the K-ABC Achievement Scale was stronger than the correlation between Achievement and Performance IQ, .78 and .51 respectively, which is likely related to the underlying school-based, culture-related verbal knowledge that is necessary to succeed on both the Verbal and Achievement Scales.

The relationship between the K-ABC and other measures of intelligence has also been empirically examined in separate ethnic minority groups. The present chapter will review three studies of African American children comparing K-ABC scores with those on the WISC-R (Naglieri & Jensen, 1987), WPPSI (Kaufman & Kaufman, 1983a), and SB-LM (Krohn, Lamp, & Phelps, 1988).

Naglieri and Jensen (1987) administered the K-ABC and the WISC-R to 87 African American fourth and fifth graders and to a cohort of white children matched on gender, schooling, and SES. The results demonstrated strong correlations between the K-ABC Mental Processing Composite and the WISC-R Full Scale IQ for both African American and white children (correlations of .73 and .72, respectively). Table 3.11 displays partial results of this study. The Simultaneous Processing Scale revealed the strongest relationship to the Performance IQ, with correlations of .79 and .76 for African American and white children respectfully. The strength of these correlations is reflective of the nonverbal and spatial nature of the tasks on each of these scales. The Sequential Processing Scale did not show correlations as high on either of the WISC-R Scales

TABLE 3.11 Correlations Between K-ABC Global Scales and WISC-R IQs From Samples of African American, Native American, Mexican American, and Mixed Ethnic Background Children

| | | | WISC-R Scale | | |
| | | | Verbal IQ | Performance IQ | Full Scale IQ |
K-ABC Scale	Sample	n			
Sequential Processing	Mixed	182	.49	.30	.47
	White	86	.33	.33	.40
	African American	86	.33	.33	.37
	Native American	35	.36	.46	.46
	Mexican American	42	.26	.25	.29
Simultaneous Processing	Mixed	182	.51	.68	.68
	White	86	.55	.76	.75
	African American	86	.50	.79	.73
	Native American	35	.40	.55	.53
	Mexican American	42	.48	.74	.70
Mental Processing Composite	Mixed	182	.59	.61	.70
	White	86	.56	.69	.72
	African American	86	.52	.75	.73
	Native American	35	.43	.60	.57
	Mexican American	42	.46	.63	.63
Achievement	Mixed	182	.78	.51	.76
	White	86	.85	.47	.77
	African American	86	.83	.50	.77
	Native American	35	.83	.45	.78
	Mexican American	42	.48	.44	.54

SOURCE: Mixed—Adapted from Kaufman & Kaufman (1983a). White/African American—Adapted from Naglieri & Jensen (1987). Native American—Adapted from Naglieri (1984). Mexican American—Adapted from Fourqurean (1987).

NOTE: K-ABC = Kaufman Assessment Battery for Children (Kaufman & Kaufman, 1983b). WISC-R = Wechsler Intelligence Scale for Children-Revised (Wechsler, 1974).

(.33 on both the Verbal I and Performance IQ for the African American sample).

Similar to findings discussed in the *K-ABC Interpretive Manual* (Kaufman & Kaufman, 1983a), Naglieri and Jensen (1987) found a very strong relationship between the K-ABC Achievement and WISC-R Verbal IQ. Correlations between these two scales were found to be .83 for the African American sample and .85 for the white sample. The authors discuss that this finding is parallel with results of previous research and seems likely due to the requirements of these scales, which both involve verbal knowledge obtained through formal education and acculturation.

The second correlational study involving a sample of African American children is discussed by Kaufman and Kaufman (1983a) in the construct validity section of their *K-ABC Interpretive Manual*. A sample of 40 African American preschool children ages 4 to 5 were administered both the WPPSI and the K-ABC. The results indicated that the correlations between the K-ABC and the WPPSI were lower than those typically reported with the WISC-R. The "restriction in range of the black children's IQs and K-ABC standard scores" seemed to be responsible for the lower magnitude of the correlations (Kaufman & Kaufman, 1983a, p. 115). When the restriction of range was corrected, an increase was noted in the correlation between the WPPSI Full Scale IQ and the K-ABC Mental Processing Composite; the coefficients jumped from .55 to .84. Thus, when the correction for range restriction was made at the preschool level with a sample of African American children, the K-ABC again was able to demonstrate its construct validity.

The third study examining the relationship of the K-ABC to other measures of cognitive ability using a sample of African American children was performed by Krohn et al. (1988). This investigation used the Stanford-Binet Intelligence Scale (SB-LM) rather than a Wechsler scale as a comparative test, with a sample of 38 African American preschool children from a Head Start program. Pearson product-moment correlations were reported with a correction for range restriction. Convergent validity was strongly supported in this low-SES African American preschool sample with correlation coefficients of .82 between the SB-LM and the K-ABC Mental Processing Composite and of .87 between the SB-LM and the K-ABC Achievement Scale. The strong relationship, especially between the Achievement Scale and the SB-LM, is not surprising, as the SB-LM has been described as "being largely a measure of scholastic aptitude, heavily loaded with verbal abilities" (Krohn et al., 1988, p. 19).

Further examination of the construct validity of the K-ABC with minorities has occurred with samples of Mexican American children. Two studies to be discussed here examined the relationship of the WPPSI and the K-ABC in samples of Mexican American preschool children (Valencia, 1984; Whiteworth & Chrisman, 1987), and one investigation analyzed a school-age sample of Mexican American children to determine the relationship between the WISC-R and the K-ABC (Fourqurean, 1987).

With 42 English-speaking Mexican American Head Start children as subjects, Valencia (1984) provided evidence of the construct validity of the K-ABC. This sample's performance was similar to the Hispanic preschool age children represented in the standardization sample on the Mental Processing Composite (difference in standard scores was one third of a point), but the current sample's mean score of 90.6 on the Achievement Scale was nearly two thirds of a standard deviation lower than that of the normative Hispanic group. The author indicated that this difference was significant.

In examining the correlations between the WPPSI and the K-ABC global scales, it was desirable to correct the scores for restriction of range (Valencia, 1984). The correlation coefficients increased substantially in magnitude after the correction. About 80% of the corrected correlation coefficients were reported to be in the range from .64 to .76. The largest correlations were reported between the WPPSI Full Scale IQ and the K-ABC Mental Processing Composite (.76), the Full Scale IQ and Simultaneous Processing Scale (.76), and the K-ABC Achievement Scale and WPPSI Verbal IQ (.76). Overall, "approximately 50% of the variance in K-ABC performance was shared with WPPSI performance scores" (Valencia, 1984, p. 370).

The results of this correlational study of Hispanic preschool children using the WPPSI and K-ABC provides evidence that is helpful in reinforcing the findings of other validity studies. Although there is substantial overlap in the two measures of intelligence, the K-ABC seems to provide unique information about a child's manner of processing information. Furthermore, the K-ABC provides a way to assess a child with less emphasis on the verbal requirements.

Whiteworth and Chrisman (1987) provided further support for the construct validity of the K-ABC in their examination of a preschool sample of Mexican American children administered the WPPSI and K-ABC. Their specific sample included 60 children ages 4 to 5, with half of the group Mexican American and half of the group white. English was the primary language spoken by all subjects. As reported earlier in this chapter, the authors found no significant differences between the white and Mexican American preschoolers on any of the K-ABC global scales, although the difference on the Achievement Scale did approach significance ($p = 0.063$). The verbal and culturally loaded requirements of the

Achievement Scale were viewed as the reason for the discrepancy between ethnic groups' performance.

The results of Whiteworth and Chrisman's (1987) correlational analysis were similar to those reported by Valencia (1984) and those from the standardization data (Kaufman & Kaufman, 1983a). The pattern of correlations for the White sample were found to be analogous to the Mexican American sample (Whiteworth & Chrisman, 1987). The highest correlations for both groups were found between the K-ABC Achievement and the WPPSI Full Scale IQ and Verbal IQ. For the white group, the correlations with the Achievement Scale were .83 and .79 for the Full Scale IQ and Verbal IQ, respectfully. The group of Mexican American children had correlations with the Achievement Scale of .75 and .73 between the Full Scale IQ and Verbal IQ, respectively.

Whiteworth and Chrisman (1987) concluded that they believe the Kaufmans have succeeded in developing a test that is "certainly fairer for Mexican American preschoolers than the WPPSI" (p. 700). The overall results showed moderate correlations between the Kaufman and Wechsler global scales; therefore, they do support the concurrent validity with the WPPSI. However, the tests are clearly not so overlapping that they are not each unique. The K-ABC Mental Processing subtests strive to be less verbally and culturally loaded, and this makes the K-ABC different from other measures of cognitive ability.

A final study that considers validity of the K-ABC through the performance of a Mexican American sample was conducted by Fourqurean (1987). A group of 42 Latino learning disabled children ages 6 to 12.5 were subjects for this study. The WISC-R was used as the criterion measure and was administered 1 week apart from the K-ABC. The author reported that the results of the correlation analysis showed results similar to those in the *K-ABC Interpretive Manual* (Kaufman & Kaufman, 1983a). Yet, some interesting exceptions were noted with the Sequential Processing Scale. Neither the WISC-R Verbal, Performance, nor Full Scale IQ was found to correlate significantly with the Sequential Processing Scale in this sample of learning disabled Latino children. However, the author noted that there was a severely restricted range of scores on both variables, but no attempt was made to correct for the restriction. Thus, artificially low correlations may be expected, warranting caution in interpretation.

The correlations reported between the Simultaneous Processing Scale and WISC-R IQs ranged from .48 to .70, correlations between the K-ABC Achievement Scale and WISC-R IQs ranged from .44 to .54, and correlations between the Mental Processing Composite and WISC-R IQs ranged from .46 to .63. Correlations are detailed in Table 3.11. As noted previously, the restricted range noted on all variables was not corrected and may have deflated the existing relationships. Despite this difficulty, the results are supportive of the literature demonstrating the construct validity of the K-ABC in minority samples.

A final minority group to discuss in the context of the construct validity of the K-ABC is Native Americans. With this particular group, only a small number of studies are available to examine. *The K-ABC Interpretive Manual* (Kaufman & Kaufman, 1983a) discusses two studies, each from very different Native American groups. One of the Native American samples consisted of 40 Sioux children and the other of 33 Navajo children. With both samples, restriction of range was reported on all variables, which resulted in correlation coefficients considerably smaller in size than for other minority groups. Table 3.11 presents data from the Navajo sample (Naglieri, 1984). With both the Sioux and Navajo samples, the K-ABC Mental Processing Composite was found to correlate more highly with the WISC-R Performance IQ than the Verbal IQ. In the Sioux sample, the correlation with Verbal IQ was .44, compared to a correlation with Performance IQ of .65. In the Navajo sample, the correlations were .43 and .60, respectively. As reported in all other groups, the Achievement Scale was found to correlate the highest with the WISC-R Verbal IQ for both the Native American samples. The overall moderate correlations found in these studies of Native American children also seem to lend supportive evidence to the construct validity of the K-ABC.

Criterion-Related Validity: Predictive Validity

Measures of intellectual functioning are often used to predict success in school. Beyond that prediction, measures of intellectual functioning are used as a criterion on which to base specific educational interventions. The importance of demonstrating predictive validity in an instrument such as the K-ABC is clear. In the K-ABC, the Achievement Scale is intended as the best and most meaningful predictor of a child's future scholastic accomplishments; however, the Mental Processing Scales also need to prove themselves as significant predictors of future achievement in school.

The *K-ABC Interpretive Manual* (Kaufman & Kaufman, 1983a) presents six predictive validity studies, four with samples of mainly white children with average intelligence, one with a sample of educable mentally retarded children, and one with a sample of culturally different Navajo children. The overall results of the studies employing primarily samples of white children with average intelligence, which used tests such as the Peabody Individual Achievement Test (PIAT; Dunn & Markwardt, 1970), the California Achievement Test, the Iowa Tests of Basic Skills, and the Woodcock Johnson Psychoeducational Battery (Woodcock & Johnson, 1977) as criterion measures, indicate that the K-ABC has ample predictive validity with this population (see Kaufman & Kaufman, 1983a, for more detailed discussion). The issue of the K-ABC's predictive validity with culturally different groups has also been addressed by researchers. Predictive validity was examined by Valencia and Rankin (1988) in a group of Mexican American children, by Naglieri and Hill (1986a) in a group of African American children, by Naglieri (1984) in a group of Navajo children, and by Glutting (1986), in a group of African American and Puerto Rican children.

Valencia and Rankin (1988) investigated the possible bias in the predictive validity of the K-ABC with a sample of 76 white and 90 Mexican American fifth- and sixth-grade boys and girls. Subjects were matched for SES and English proficiency. The criterion variable was the Comprehensive Tests of Basic Skills (CTBS; 1974), Level 2, form S. Subjects were administered three areas of the CTBS, Reading, Language, and Mathematics, and these were combined into a Total Battery Score.

No significant differences emerged in the mean K-ABC Mental Processing Composite scores between cultural groups, but there were significant differences found between the mean scores on Achievement (Valencia & Rankin, 1988). On both the K-ABC Achievement Scale and all areas of the CTBS, the white children performed significantly higher ($p < .0001$). Table 3.12 presents the means, standard deviations, and t values for the two samples.

Valencia and Rankin (1988) also analyzed the data by Pearson product-moment correlational analysis, and the results are presented in

TABLE 3.12 Comparison of Mean Scores on K-ABC and CTBS for White and Mexican American Samples

Scale/Test	White (n = 76)		Mexican American (n = 90)		t	P
	Mean	SD	Mean	SD		
Kaufman-Assessment Battery for Children (K-ABC)						
Mental Processing Composite	100.21	10.77	98.13	10.83	1.23	> .05
Achievement	102.63	11.29	91.19	8.56	7.42	.0001
Comprehensive Tests of Basic Skills (CTBS)						
Reading	503.22	72.36	431.32	50.03	7.53	.0001
Language	509.12	67.71	455.13	57.62	5.55	.0001
Math	459.57	59.68	431.20	41.71	3.59	.0001
Total	478.30	72.31	418.73	45.21	6.46	.0001

SOURCE: Adapted from Valencia and Rankin (1988).

Table 3.13. In all instances, the correlations between the K-ABC Mental Processing Composite and the CTBS scores were considerably lower for the Mexican American sample. The K-ABC composite was found to be a weak predictor for the Mexican American group, but it was a moderate predictor for the white group.

High predictive validity was indicated in the white sample, with correlations ranging from .66 to .79 between the K-ABC Achievement Scale and CTBS. A moderate level of predictive validity was indicated in the Mexican American sample, with correlations ranging from .49 to .67 between the K-ABC Achievement Scale and CTBS.

Valencia and Rankin (1988) also examined their data to predict CTBS scores from ethnic membership, K-ABC Mental Processing Composite scores, and the interaction of ethnicity and the composite. The regressions of the CTBS on the interaction between ethnic group and Mental Processing Composite indicated that the regression lines for the white and Mexican American groups were not parallel. For all CTBS areas, the interaction term was significant (Table 3.14).

The conclusions drawn from the results of this study (Valencia & Rankin, 1988) were that there was "strong evidence of bias in regard to differential predictive validity" (p. 262). The authors concluded that the

TABLE 3.13 Comparison of Validity Coefficients Between K-ABC Scores and CTBS Scores for White and Mexican American Samples

	Comprehensive Tests of Basic Skills (CTBS)							
	Reading		Language		Math		Total	
Kaufman-Assessment Battery for Children Scale	*r*	*z*	*r*	*z*	*r*	*z*	*r*	*z*
Mental Processing Composite								
White (*n* = 76)	.57		.55		.58		.59	
		2.67**		2.81**		2.07*		2.43*
Mexican American (*n* = 90)	.23		.17		.32		.28	
Achievement								
White (*n* = 76)	.79		.69		.66		.76	
		1.63		1.71		1.62		1.28
Mexican American (*n* = 90)	.67		.52		.49		.67	

SOURCE: Adapted from Valencia and Rankin (1988).
*$p < .05$. **$p < .01$.
NOTE: z = computed using Fisher's z-test for the difference between correlation coefficients.

K-ABC had more power to predict the CTBS scores of white children than Mexican American children. Because the reliability of the K-ABC Mental Processing Composite was approximately equal for each group, differential reliability was not deemed a reason for the difference in predictive power. The authors hypothesized that the criterion test itself may be biased, which could explain the difference in predictive validity between the groups. Thus, true variance in a criterion test cannot be predicted from an unbiased test when the criterion may be biased itself. The authors conclude by saying "caution is urged in using the K-ABC [Mental Processing Composite] to predict CTBS scores for upper-primary grade Mexican American children" (Valencia & Rankin, 1988, p. 263).

Investigation of the differential predictive validity of the K-ABC for white and African American children was completed by Naglieri and Hill (1986a). Eighty-six African American children and 86 white children, matched on SES, grade, school, and gender served as subjects for this study. Regression lines were used for predicting the CTBS and K-ABC Achievement Scale by the K-ABC and the WISC-R, using the Potthoff (1966) technique. Naglieri and Hill (1986a) explain that "this technique provides an F ratio that tests the equivalence of regression coefficients and intercepts simultaneously. If this test is significant, subsequent F

TABLE 3.14   Interaction Tests of Differential Test Validity for the
Kaufman-Assessment Battery for Children (K-ABC) and the
Comprehensive Tests of Basic Skills (CTBS) for White and
Mexican American Samples

	Dependent Variable					
Independent Variable	R^2	F	P	Increment	F	P
CTBS Reading						
Ethnic group	.257	56.740	.0001	.257	31.826	.0001
K-ABC Mental Processing	.379	49.847	.0001	.123	32.180	.0001
Composite						
Interaction	.426	40.165	.0001	.047	13.285	.0001
CTBS Language						
Ethnic group	.58	30.867	.0001	.158	30.867	.0001
K-ABC Mental Processing	.264	22.267	.0001	.106	23.476	.0001
Composite						
Interaction	.308	24.068	.0001	.044	10.301	.0001
CTBS Mathematics						
Ethnic group	.073	12.900	.0001	.073	12.900	.0001
K-ABC Mental Processing	.262	28.964	.0001	.189	41.743	.0001
Composite						
Interaction	.303	23.455	.0001	.041	9.529	.0001
CTBS Total						
Ethnic group	.203	41.875	.0001	.203	41.874	.0001
K-ABC Mental Processing	.364	46.613	.0001	.161	9.529	.0001
Composite						
Interaction	.418	38.732	.0001	.054	15.031	.0001

SOURCE: Adapted from Valencia and Rankin (1988).

tests are performed to evaluate, separately, the regression coefficients and the intercepts" (p. 353).

The results of the study (Naglieri & Hill, 1986a) indicate that there was no difference in the correlation between African American and white students' CTBS total achievement and WISC-R Full Scale IQ scores (both were .63). There was also no difference between group correlations of the WISC-R Verbal IQ and CTBS scores (both were .67), and no meaningful differences were noted between African American children (.39) and white children (.41) on the Performance IQ-CTBS correlations. Using the WISC-R scores as a predictor for African American and white students' achievement regressions lines was found not to be significant $F(2, 168) = 0.07$, $p > .05$. K-ABC Mental Processing Composite scores and CTBS total achievement scores were found to correlate .43 for African American children and .51 for white children. Using K-ABC scores as a predictor for achievement, regression lines were also not found to be significant $F(2, 168) = 1.51, p > .05$.

Naglieri and Hill (1986a) did further analyses using the K-ABC Achievement scores as a criterion. No significant differences were found between the regression lines for African American and White children when the WISC-R Full Scale IQ was used to predict K-ABC Achievement scores, $F(2, 168) = 0.80, p < .05$. However, when the K-ABC Achievement score was predicted from the K-ABC Mental Processing Composite, significant differences emerged overall, $F(2, 168) = 3.87, p < .05$, and in the Y-intercept, $F(1, 169) = 7.07, p < .01$. The authors further examined the K-ABC Mental Processing Scales individually. When the Simultaneous Scale was used as a predictor, they found significant differences overall, $F(2, 168) = 4.01, p < .05$, and in the Y-intercept, $F(1, 169) = 6.93, p < .01$. Similarly, when the Sequential Scale was used as a predictor, there were significant differences overall, $F(2, 168) = 7.92, p < .01$, and in the Y-intercept, $F(1, 169) = 15.72, p < .01$.

The authors indicated that their results regarding the WISC-R were similar to previous research and suggested that no bias was present in the prediction of African American student achievement using WISC-R scores. African Americans earned WISC-R IQs that were 9.1 to 8.1 points lower than whites' IQs, whereas African Americans' scores on the K-ABC Mental Processing Scales were only 3 to 6.9 points lower than those of whites, on average. On the CTBS and the K-ABC Achievement Scale, African Americans earned scores 4.9 to 6.9 points lower than those of whites. Using the K-ABC Mental Processing Composite scores to predict African American students' K-ABC Achievement needs to be done with caution, according to Naglieri and Hill (1986a). The authors state, "Significant differences in the regression line intercepts suggest that using the Mental Processing Composite resulted in errors in prediction of African American student performance on the K-ABC Achievement Scale" (Naglieri & Hill, 1986a, p. 354). However, the authors also note that differential prediction in achievement was not found when the K-ABC composite was used to predict CTBS achievement scores, and they further suggest that replication of their study is necessary to confirm their results.

To examine the predictive validity of another cultural group, Naglieri (1984) studied the performance of 35 Navajo children ages 6 to 12.5 on several tests: the K-ABC Mental Processing Composite and Achievement Scale, the WISC-R, and the PIAT (Dunn & Markwardt, 1970). The PIAT was administered 10.5 months after the IQ measures. No control group was used for this study. The results of the correlational analyses are presented in Table 3.15.

Naglieri's (1984) results showed strong correlations between the WISC-R Verbal Scale and both the PIAT and the K-ABC Achievement Scale. The author suggests that this indicates that a verbal/acquired knowledge component is present in the Verbal IQ and that for this Navajo sample, the Verbal IQ is likely reflecting language skills, rather than verbal intelligence. The correlational analysis of the K-ABC Processing Scales and the achievement tests revealed that the Sequential and Simultaneous Scales were about equally related to achievement (correlations of .45 and .43, respectively). According to the author, the strong correlation (.82) between K-ABC Achievement and the PIAT Total Score supports the fact that achievement tests have more in common with each other than with simultaneous and sequential tasks. Overall, the results are supportive of the predictive validity of the K-ABC with a Navajo population.

The final study to be discussed in terms of the K-ABC's predictive validity was one involving a sample of 65 white, 24 African American, 27 English-dominant Puerto Rican, and 30 Spanish-dominant Puerto Rican kindergarten children (Glutting, 1986). In this study, four criterion measures were used: the K-ABC Achievement Scale, the Needs Assessment Survey Reading and Mathematics subscales (NASR & NASM), and Teacher-Assigned Grades. The criterion tests were administered to the subjects between 3 to 8 months after the predictors (the K-ABC Mental Processing Composite and Nonverbal Scale). The K-ABC Mental Processing Composite and Achievement Scale were not administered to the Spanish-dominant Puerto Rican group because of their limited English proficiency. The K-ABC Nonverbal IQ scores were 104.09 (white), 89.83 (African American), 98.00 (English-dominant Puerto Rican), and 85.70 (Spanish-dominant Puerto Rican). The mean scores on the criteria measures for each group are listed in Table 3.16.

The results of the correlational analyses showed significant predictions using the K-ABC Mental Processing Composite for all groups ($p <$ .05) with each of the criterion measures (ranging from .39 to .76, mean = .61). Correlations using the K-ABC Nonverbal Scale as a predictor

TABLE 3.15 Pearson Correlation Coefficients Among WISC-R, K-ABC, and PIAT Standard Scores in a Navajo Sample

	Kaufman-Assessment Battery for Children (K-ABC)					
	Simultaneous Processing	Sequential Processing	Mental Processing Composite	Achievement Scale	Nonverbal Scale	Peabody Individual Achievement Test (PIAT), Total
Weschler Intelligence Scale for Children (WISC-R)						
Verbal	.40	.36	.43	.83	.27	.64
Performance	.55	.46	.60	.45	.42	.23
Full Scale	.53	.46	.57	.78	.38	.55
K-ABC						
Simultaneous Processing						.43
Sequential Processing	.39					.45
Mental Processing Composite	.91	.74				.52
Achievement Scale	.54	.51	.61			.82
Nonverbal Scale	.92	.55	.92	.47		.42

SOURCE: Adapted from Naglieri (1984).
NOTE: $n = 35$.

showed significant predictions for the white, African American, and Spanish-dominant Puerto Rican groups for all nine criteria (ranging from .45 to .70, mean = .60). In contrast was the English-dominant Puerto Rican group, for which only one of the three validity coefficients was significant. For the English-dominant Puerto Rican group, only the NASM scale correlated significantly with the Nonverbal Scale IQ, $r = .38$, $p < .05$.

Glutting (1986) explains that although there was only one significant correlation in the English-dominant Puerto Rican group, this is "not indicative of predictive bias" (p. 230). However, the author does state that for the English-dominant Puerto Rican group, the K-ABC Nonverbal Scale may be a questionable predictor because of the nonsignificance of the correlations.

The Potthoff procedure was used by Glutting (1986) to examine bias of the K-ABC scales in predicting achievement. With the K-ABC Mental

TABLE 3.16   Mean Scores by Ethnic Group on the NASR, NASM, Grade, and the K-ABC Achievement Scale

	Ethnic Group			
	White n = 65	African American n = 24	English- Dominant Puerto Rican n = 27	Spanish- Dominant Puerto Rican n = 30
Criterion				
Needs Assessment Survey, Reading (NASR) Scale	52.29	44.46	46.78	38.73
Needs Assessment Survey, Mathematics (NASM) Scale	55.32	48.25	50.44	42.27
Grade	24.75	21.50	23.82	22.77
K-ABC Achievement Scale	96.71	84.88	84.07	

SOURCE: Adapted from Glutting (1986).

NOTE: K-ABC = Kaufman Assessment Battery for Children (Kaufman & Kaufman, 1983b). The K-ABC Achievement Scale was administered in English and was not given to the Spanish-dominant Puerto Rican group.

Processing Composite as the predictor, the NASR, NASM, and K-ABC were free of bias. However, when comparing whites and African Americans, significant results were found with the grade criterion. "Black kindergartners with low [composite] scores were underpredicted on the Grade criterion, whereas high-scoring blacks were overpredicted" (Glutting, 1986, p. 231). When examining the K-ABC Nonverbal standard score as the predictor with Potthoff analyses, the author found that the Nonverbal standard score either was unbiased or may overpredict achievement on all three criterion measures for Spanish-dominant Puerto Rican and African American children. The K-ABC Nonverbal standard score was determined to be an unbiased predictor of NASM ratings for the English-dominant Puerto Rican group.

Overall, in Glutting's (1986) multicultural sample of kindergarten children, only one of the 15 Potthoff comparisons showed a group difference toward biasing the predictors against minority children. African American children who scored low on the Mental Processing Component had underpredicted scores on the grade criterion. The author concludes that "school psychologists can use K-ABC IQs with kindergarten children to predict both achievement test scores and the more relevant criterion of classroom success" (Glutting, 1986, p. 232).

Criterion-Related Validity: Concurrent Validity

The last few pages discussed the K-ABC's ability to reliably predict a child's future academic performance (predictive validity). Concurrent validity is similar to predictive validity in that it is concerned with an instrument's relationship to a meaningful criterion. However, with concurrent validity, the relationship examined is between tests administered at approximately the same time, rather than with a long interval of time between them, as in predictive validity.

The *K-ABC Interpretive Manual* (Kaufman & Kaufman, 1983a) presents concurrent validity research with several different criterion measures. With the national standardization sample, two individual achievement tests were administered concurrently with the K-ABC: the Passage Comprehension subtests of the Woodcock Reading Mastery Tests (WRMT) and the Written Computation items on the KeyMath Diagnostic Arithmetic Test. The PPVT-R (Dunn & Dunn, 1981) was also administered to most children in the standardization and sociocultural norms samples of the K-ABC. Other individual achievement tests such as the PIAT, the Wide Range Achievement Test (WRAT), the Stanford Diagnostic Reading Test, and the complete battery of the KeyMath Diagnostic Arithmetic Test were also administered concurrently with the K-ABC, using smaller samples.

Most 6- to 12.5-year-old children from the standardization sample were tested on either the WRMT Passage Comprehension subtest or the KeyMath Written Computation subtests. The data were analyzed as a total sample and separately for whites, African Americans, and Hispanics (Kaufman & Kaufman, 1983a). Table 3.17 presents the data for Passage Comprehension, and Table 3.18 presents data for Written Computation.

When examining the three racial or ethnic groups, the correlational results between Passage Comprehension and the K-ABC mirrored that of the total sample. For African Americans, the correlations between all K-ABC Global Scores and Passage Comprehension ranged from (.48 with Sequential Processing to .78 with Achievement). For Hispanic children, the correlations ranged from .45 with Sequential Processing to .89 with Achievement.

In analyses with KeyMath Written Computation as a criterion measure, the highest correlation for the total sample was with K-ABC Achievement (.59). With the total sample, other correlations between K-

TABLE 3.17 Concurrent Validity: Correlations Between K-ABC Global Scale Standard Scores and Woodcock Reading Mastery Tests Passage Comprehension, by Race or Ethnic Group, for Normal Children

Race or Ethnic Group	Passage Comprehension Raw Score		Correlation Between Passage Comprehension z Score and K-ABC Global Standard Score				
	Mean	SD	Sequential Processing	Simultaneous Processing	Mental Processing Composite	Achievement Scale	Non-verbal Scale
African American (n = 100)	31.5	16.9	.48	.50	.56	.78	.51
K-ABC Mean			95.5	91.4	92.0	92.1	90.8
K-ABC SD			14.1	13.4	13.2	13.4	13.1
Hispanic (n = 33)	28.8	16.3	.45	.61	.70	.89	.91
K-ABC Mean			99.9	97.8	98.1	92.0	97.6
K-ABC SD			12.9	14.8	12.5	12.4	13.6
White (n = 445)	39.0	18.0	.52	.52	.60	.80	.56
K-ABC Mean			101.4	102.8	102.5	103.1	103.0
K-ABC SD			13.7	14.3	13.9	13.2	13.9
Total (n = 592)[a]	37.2	18.2	.53	.56	.63	.82	.58
K-ABC Mean			100.3	100.7	100.6	100.7	100.8
K-ABC SD			14.0	14.9	14.4	14.1	14.6

SOURCE: Adapted from Kaufman and Kaufman (1983a).

a. Total N included 14 children classified as "other" (e.g., Native American), for whom separate data are not reported.

NOTE: K-ABC = Kaufman-Assessment Battery for Children.

ABC Global Scales and Written Computation ranged from .34 to .47. These results were also similar for African Americans, Hispanics, and whites (Kaufman & Kaufman, 1983a). For the groups of whites and African Americans, Simultaneous Processing correlated slightly more highly with KeyMath than did Sequential processing. However, this was not true for the Hispanic group, in which the Sequential Processing correlated slightly more highly with written computation than did Simultaneous Processing (see Table 3.18). Kaufman and Kaufman (1983a) state, "The similar coefficients between K-ABC standard scores and performance on reading and arithmetic tests for the three racial or ethnic groups offer evidence for the differential validity of the K-ABC" (p. 126).

A systematic exploration of the differential validity of the K-ABC for whites, African Americans, and Hispanics was completed by Reynolds,

TABLE 3.18 Concurrent Validity: Correlations Between K-ABC Global Scale Standard Scores and KeyMath Diagnostic Arithmetic Test Written Computation Items, by Race or Ethnic Group, for Normal Children

	Written Computation Raw Score		Correlation Between Written Computation z Score and K-ABC Global Standard Score				
	Mean	SD	Sequential Processing	Simultaneous Processing	Mental Processing Composite	Achievement Scale	Non-verbal Scale
African American (n = 99)	14.8	9.5	.30	.45	.47	.54	.48
K-ABC Mean			97.2	92.1	93.3	92.9	91.1
K-ABC SD			13.8	12.1	11.8	12.5	11.6
Hispanic (n = 39)	18.5	9.0	.43	.38	.45	.62	.43
K-ABC Mean			97.2	99.3	98.1	92.7	99.4
K-ABC SD			15.0	16.0	15.8	12.9	15.0
White (n = 494)	18.8	10.3	.28	.39	.41	.54	.39
K-ABC Mean			102.5	103.9	103.7	104.6	103.9
K-ABC SD			13.3	13.9	13.1	13.2	14.0
Total (N = 544)[a]	18.1	10.2	.34	.44	.47	.59	.46
K-ABC Mean			101.1	101.5	101.4	101.5	101.2
K-ABC SD			13.9	14.4	13.8	14.1	14.5

SOURCE: Adapted from Kaufman & Kaufman, 1983a.

a. Total N included 14 children classified as "other" (e.g., Native American) for whom separate data are not reported.

NOTE: K-ABC = Kaufman-Assessment Battery for Children.

Willson, and Chatman (1983). They used Potthoff's (1966) statistical technique in their analyses with Passage Comprehension and KeyMath data. They concluded that there was no evidence that the K-ABC was biased toward minority groups.

Kaufman and Kaufman (1983a) present additional concurrent validity data using the PPVT-R as a criterion measure. The sample used to obtain the PPVT-R data was very large (Total N = 2,522) and therefore provides very stable and generalizable results. Table 3.19 displays the results of the correlational analyses.

Additional analyses with the PPVT-R were conducted with groups of whites, African Americans, and Hispanics. The results were similar across groups, with correlations between the PPVT-R and Mental Processing Composite of .53, .62, and .56 for African Americans, Hispanics,

TABLE 3.19 Correlations Between K-ABC Global Standard and Scores on the Peabody Picture Vocabulary Test-Revised (PPVT-R) for Various Samples

Sample	N	Mean	SD	Sequential Processing	Simultaneous Processing	Mental Processing Composite	Achievement	Non-verbal Scale
Normal[a]	2,522	94.2	18.7	.43	.57	.58	.75	.55
K-ABC Mean			100.0	92.1	93.3	92.9	91.1	
K-ABC SD			15.1	12.1	11.8	12.5	11.6	
Preschool	640	95.3	17.5	.33	.38	.45	.62	.43
K-ABC Mean			97.2	99.3	98.1	92.7	99.4	
K-ABC SD			15.0	16.0	15.8	12.9	15.0	
School-Age	1,882	93.8	19.1	.28	.39	.41	.54	.39
K-ABC Mean			102.5	103.9	103.7	104.6	103.9	
K-ABC SD			13.3	13.9	13.1	13.2	14.0	
African Americans	776	84.6	18.3	.34	.44	.47	.59	.46
K-ABC Mean			101.1	101.5	101.4	101.5	101.2	
K-ABC SD			13.9	14.4	13.8	14.1	14.5	
Hispanics	156	88.0	20.6	.50	.56	.62	.82	.52
K-ABC Mean			98.6	99.6	98.9	93.7	98.7	
K-ABC SD			14.3	15.1	14.5	14.5	14.0	
Whites	1,543	99.6	16.4	.43	.53	.56	.70	.52
K-ABC Mean			101.1	102.2	102.0	102.7	102.4	
K-ABC SD			15.0	15.0	14.7	14.3	14.8	

SOURCE: Adapted from Kaufman and Kaufman (1983a).

a. Data for the normal standardization sample and the sociocultural norms sample are reported for the total group and also separately by race or ethnic group and for preschool and school-age children. Forty-seven children classified as "Other" (e.g., Native American) are included in the total sample and the separate data for preschool and school-age children but are excluded from the analysis of race and ethnic groups.

NOTE: K-ABC = Kaufman-Assessment Battery for Children.

and whites, respectively. For each of the three groups, the correlations between the K-ABC Achievement and PPVT-R were the highest, ranging from .70 for whites to .82 for Hispanics. Kaufman and Kaufman (1983a) state,

> The most noteworthy finding . . . is that black children scored on the average a substantial 9 points higher on the K-ABC Achievement Scale than on the PPVT-R (mean of 94 versus 85); the difference was even

higher for preschool black children (97 versus 84) than for school-age black youngsters (93 versus 85). (p. 137)

Summary

After examining the research available on the use of the K-ABC with culturally different groups, the question remaining is whether the K-ABC is less culturally biased than comparable tests of intelligence. When considered in comparison to the actual lack of cultural bias found in most *well*-constructed standardized tests of intelligence, the K-ABC appears equally as culturally sensitive (Kamphaus & Reynolds, 1987). However, "the K-ABC is among the best" (Kamphaus & Reynolds, 1987, p. 172). Even Sternberg (1984, p. 271), one of the K-ABC's harshest critics, stated that in comparison to other existing instruments, the "K-ABC comes closer than most, if not all, existing instruments" to being culture-fair or representative of all groups in its norms.

4 The Learning Potential Assessment Device

An Alternative Approach to the Assessment of Learning Potential

REUVEN FEUERSTEIN
LOUIS H. FALIK
RAFI FEUERSTEIN

In 1979, the senior author, in a book entitled *The Dynamic Assessment of Retarded Performers,* presented the rationale for needed alternatives to conventional psychometric assessment, as well as a new approach to the assessment of learning potential, the Learning Potential Assessment Device (LPAD). The LPAD was, and continues to be, related to the development of the theory of structural cognitive modifiability (SCM) and its applied systems—both conceptual (Mediated Learning Experience; MLE) and programmatic (Instrumental Enrichment; IE). That formulation of the concepts and processes of what came to be generally described as dynamic assessment stimulated considerable research and clinical interest.

As early as 1981, Ramey and MacPhee, in a review of the Feuerstein (1979) book, identified the theory and approach as representing a new paradigm with regard to assessment, with particular impact on conventional psychometric practice. The shift from traditional assessment methods was, they said, impelled by disenchantment with the logical inconsistencies in the traditional system (theory and practice), by a recognition of the need to respond differently to specific segments of the population, and by the emergence of a new conception of learning and intelligence that spurs the development of a new "technology." That paradigm, presented by Feuerstein and his colleagues, stimulated great interest in the development of procedures and methodology to provide alternatives to a wide range of conventional practices.

This interest has been reflected in the development of a number of systems and approaches to assessment that have been identified as dynamic. They have been subjected to critical review and comparative analyses (see Campione, 1989; Jitendra & Kameenui, 1993) and have joined the LPAD in the pantheon of attempts to address the acknowledged need for paradigm shifts. Among the more systematically developed are Assisted Learning for Transfer (Campione & Brown, 1987), Testing the Limits (Carlson & Wiedl, 1978, 1979), the Continuum of Assessment Model (Bransford, Delclos, Vye, Burns, & Hasselbring, 1987); Learning Potential (Budoff, 1974, 1987); and Learning Tests (Guthke, 1992; Guthke & Stein, 1996). Each of these approaches has addressed aspects of the dynamic assessment paradigm, adding important dimensions to the definitions and processes of assessment, but—as we shall describe below—none goes far enough to implement changes in the process to fully meet what we believe are the critical and essential requirements of the assessment process. There is a growing literature, stimulated by our initial thinking and operational propositions but less closely related to our perspective, that considers the various elements, needs, methodologies, and research applications of alternative assessment processes that are to some degree categorized as dynamic in their nature and purpose (see Hamers, Sijtsma, & Ruijssenaars, 1993; Haywood & Tzuriel, 1992; Lidz, 1987).

The LPAD reflects a different view of human beings and their development. It represents a sharp departure from practices that are based on a view of human characteristics as fixed, immutable, and therefore subject to study by psychometric methods of measurement. In its underlying theory, in its structure of instruments, and in its development of procedures, the LPAD presents a radical alternative to the statistically based, normative comparisons and predictive goals of conventional assessment. In its simplest sense, the LPAD shifts the focus from what the individual is able to do (at a given moment in time) to what the individual *can become able to do* in the immediate time frame and in subsequent, future interactions. In the LPAD, whatever is done, through the process of assessment and stimulation of behavioral changes, cannot be considered as the limits of the individual's ability to benefit from the intervention or the examiner's activity. It is the limit of what can be done at the particular moment. Eventually, at some other time, with modified and adapted interventions, or in some other regions of functioning, further modifiability can be anticipated. It is this basic understanding—that we cannot reach all of the regions or potentials of knowledge about the other without an open, adaptive posture in our process and our instrumentation—that underlies the LPAD philosophy.

In this regard, it has become necessary to change some of our nomenclature. As the goal of the LPAD is to discover the hidden potential of the individual, which is not revealed by manifest levels of functioning, the use of the term *potential* has come to be somewhat ambiguous and used in a limiting and restrictive way. We have pointed out elsewhere (Feuerstein, Feuerstein, & Gross, 1996) that the construct of potential is as limiting as the concept of intelligence to a given quantity or even quality of the individual's functioning. We are therefore proposing the term *propensity* to denote qualities of power, energy, orientation, and inclination, so as to better reflect the individual's unrevealed innate capacities. Thus, the Learning *Potential* Assessment Device, which has had an active life of over 40 years in use, becomes the Learning *Propensity* Assessment Device to do greater justice to the mental construct of intelligence as a propensity to change and adapt.

The LPAD Process of Dynamic Assessment

The LPAD is designed to achieve goals that are substantially different from traditional, static psychometric assessment methods. The differences can be characterized according to the dimensions listed in Table 4.1. These dimensions require a theoretical conception that supports and guides these activities. The LPAD paradigm is based on the theory of SCM and on MLE. In addition, two operationalized theoretical constructs have been developed to guide the observation and decision making of the assessment, and they will be described here: the *deficient cognitive functions* and the *cognitive map*. The LPAD is thus "theory- and construct-specific," and users of the approach must be familiar with the philosophical belief system that holds individuals to be modifiable, as well as amenable to registering and detecting adaptive changes. The

TABLE 4.1 Comparative Assessment Methods

Standard	Dynamic
Looks for stages and progress in mental development	Seeks character and processes of mental development
Makes comparisons to normative groups of peers	Compares to individual's own performance at different times and under different conditions
Measures manifest levels of current functioning	Assesses indications of learning propensity and modifiability
Classifies through ranking and normative comparison	Searches for indices of modifiability based on samples of produced changes during assessment
Predicts future performance based on fixed and permanent characteristics	Searches for propensity and conditions of structural change

LPAD is a first step toward the goal of postulating definitions of the enhancement of human modifiability, setting theoretical conditions and giving legitimacy and direction to the intervention necessary to produce the desired and feasible changes (Feuerstein et al., 1996).

Structural Cognitive Modifiability (SCM): Human beings are viewed as having a unique propensity to change or be modified in the structure of their cognitive functioning, as they respond to changing demands of life situations. Changes occur in response to external stimuli and internal conditions. They are also a product of an active involvement in the process of learning and changing. Change is structural when (a) change in a part affects the whole to which the changed part belongs; (b) when the very process itself of change is transformed in its rhythm, amplitude, and direction; and (c) when the produced change is self-perpetuating, reflecting an autonomous, self-regulatory nature. SCM is assumed to occur when the changes are characterized by a certain degree of permanence and pervasiveness and when they are generalizable. Human beings are viewed as open systems, accessible to change throughout their life spans, and responsive to conditions of remediation, providing that the intervention is appropriately directed (in quantity and quality) to the individual's need.

Mediated Learning Experience (MLE)— Dimensions and Quality of the Interaction

Cognitive development occurs through an individual-environment interaction. This interaction is affected by certain characteristics of the organism (including those of heredity, organicity, maturation, and the like) and qualities of the environment (educational opportunities, socioeconomic status, cultural experience, emotional contacts with significant others). Changes produced by interaction between the organism and the environment happen through two modalities: (a) as a *direct* learning experience, immediately consequent to direct exposure to stimulation, and (b) through a *mediated* learning experience that requires the presence and activity of a human being to filter, select, interpret, and elaborate that which has been experienced. MLE theory holds that the organismic and environmental factors are *distal* determinants of cognitive development (causing differential responses to the environment), whereas MLE constitutes the *proximal* determinant that influences structural cognitive development and the potential for being adaptive to and modified by experience (see Figure 4.1).

For MLE to occur, an *intentional* human being must interpose himor herself between the stimuli and the learner's response, with the intention of mediating the stimuli or the response to the learner. This is mediational in the sense that the situation (stimuli and responses) are modified by affecting qualities of intensity, context, frequency, and order, while at the same time arousing the individual's vigilance, awareness, and sensitivity. The interactional experience may have the quality of repeating or eliminating various stimuli, relating events in time or space, or imbuing experience with meaning (see Figure 4.2).

MLE requires the presence of three parameters that are the object of planful attention on the part of the mediator: intentionality and reciprocity, transcendence, and meaning. In addition, situational variables in the encounter present opportunities to mediate for other important parameters of the experience: regulation and control of behavior, feelings of competence, psychological differentiation and individuation, sharing behavior, goal seeking/planning/achieving behavior, competence/novelty/complexity, self-change, optimistic choice of alternatives, and feelings of belonging. Each of these criterial parameters offers opportunities for the mediator to make planned and systematic choices to exploit the media-

DISTAL AND PROXIMAL DETERMINANTS
OF DIFFERENTIAL COGNITIVE DEVELOPMENT

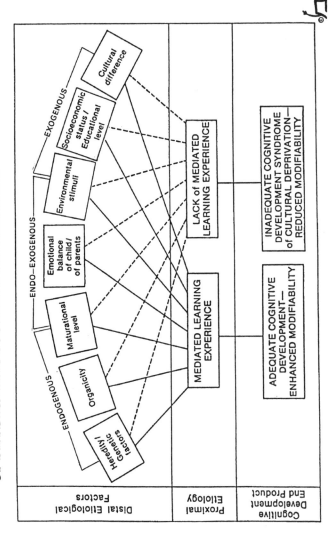

Figure 4.1. Distal and Proximal Determinants of Differential Cognitive Development
SOURCE: Adapted from Feuerstein and Rand (1994).

105

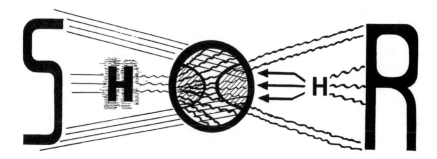

Figure 4.2. Mediated Learning Experience (MLE) Model
SOURCE: Feuerstein, 1979, 1980; Feuerstein & Feuerstein, 1991.

tional potential of the situation to encourage cognitive functioning and stimulate modifiability.

Mediation is different from other kinds of interventions, such as coaching, teaching, or testing the limits (which is one of the features of another approach to dynamic assessment; see Carlson & Wiedl, 1978, 1979). The mediator is animated by intentionality, and this is coupled with reciprocity, which engages the examiner in a process of actively changing the three partners in the mediational interaction: the mediator, the mediatee, and the message or content of the interaction. The mediational interaction creates a closed loop between the components. For example, the examiner emits a message—a stimulus. If the examiner does not make sure that the subject has indeed received it, then the mediational interaction has not been experienced. Intentionality requires the mediator to be alert, vigilant, and animated if the situation is to have all the necessary conditions to assure that the subject grasps the task and is ready to focus and interact with it. As meaningful changes are observed, the subject is encouraged to go beyond the strictly necessary to the areas and regions to which the recently learned has been applied successfully. The mediation of transcendence goes beyond the immediate content of the interaction. For example, in a matrices problem, when a subject must distinguish the two determinants of shape and color and responds with "green and black lines," that person is led to use the higher order concepts of color and shape because in subsequent problems those concepts will be needed to describe elements, differing from those previously experienced. When individuals are able to identify and describe various characteristics of the stimuli they experience, they acquire concepts that are not restricted to the immediate context in which they are learned but transcend immediate needs and are available to be applied to elements in a variety of situations. The mediational process therefore extends beyond a simple, task-oriented, product-oriented, coaching/teaching objective toward making the individual able to function independently of specific situations, and it renders the learner able to adapt to the new dimensions that he or she will confront.

The procedures and instruments of the LPAD are designed to enable this to occur to the highest degree possible. Detailed descriptions of the particular qualities and manifestations of the MLE parameters are available in a number of other sources (Feuerstein, 1979, 1980, 1995; Feuerstein & Feuerstein, 1991).

MLE significantly affects the individual's capacity to become modified structurally through direct exposure to stimuli. The more MLE acquired by the individual, the more benefit that person derives from direct exposure to learning; the less MLE received, the less a person is able to learn from direct exposure, and the less adaptive the individual will be. This is a central construct for the structure and application of the LPAD as an assessment methodology.

Deficient Cognitive Functions— Dimensions of the Individual

Inadequate MLE leads to cognitive functions at the input, elaboration, or output phases of the mental act that are undeveloped, impaired, or fragile in their presence and contribution to learning and cognitive behavior. The process orientation that is part of the LPAD creates conditions that elicit the appearance of deficient cognitive functions and determine their level, nature, and amenability to change—as an index of potential for structural cognitive modifiability.

These deficiencies do not necessarily appear in toto as a complete repertoire of the cognitive characteristics of the low-functioning individual (e.g., the culturally deprived, the learning disabled, etc.). Certain deficiencies may appear in a given individual whereas others may be absent. Accordingly, different individuals will need more or less investment in one function rather than another and be more or less resistant to change, according to the profile of modifiability that emerges from the assessment process. The presence of a deficient cognitive function, the pattern of both deficiencies and well-established and/or modifiable functions, and their saliency in the profile of the individual will determine the nature of the intervention, according to the amount of resistance encountered and the extent of the investment required to overcome it.

The cognitive functions are presented as deficiencies for the very important reason that we wish to focus on intervention, modifiability, and change. To do so, we describe the functions in terms of their absence or impairment to direct attention and effort toward needed and available interventions and strategies, as well as the propensity in the individual to be modified. There has been a tendency by some proponents of dynamic assessment to describe the cognitive functions from a positive perspective—that is, in terms of their presence in the behavioral repertoire of the individual. Although this can be viewed as the other side of the same coin, there is the danger that such an effort contributes to a fixed and static view of the individual's functional potential, which is contrary to the goals and philosophy of the LPAD approach to dynamic assessment.

The deficient cognitive functions can be analyzed as they manifest themselves in the three phases of the mental act: the input phase, the elaboration phase, and the output phase. The input and output phases can be described as peripheral compared to the elaboration phase, which is the core of the mental act. This orientation links deficient functions to the phases of the mental act and helps define the specific factors impairing successful mastery of the task, suggesting types of strategies for their correction. Although this division is somewhat artificial (in the sense that the mental activity within these phases is indivisible), it helps in both diagnosis and prescription. The interactions occurring between and among the phases are of vital significance in understanding the extent and pervasiveness of cognitive impairment. An additional dimension, the affective-motivational factor, has a significant effect on the three phases of the mental act.

The Input Phase: Deficiencies at the input phase include all those impairments concerned with the quantity and quality of data gathered by the individual in the process of solving a given problem or at early levels of appreciation of the nature of the problem. Some impairments at this phase include:

Blurred and sweeping perception

Unplanned, impulsive, and unsystematic exploratory behavior

Lack, or impairment, of receptive verbal tools that affect discrimination (e.g., objects, events, and relationships are not appropriately labeled)

Lack, or impairment, of spatial orientation and lack of stable systems of reference by which to establish organization in space

Lack, or impairment, of temporal concepts

Lack, or impairment, of conservation of constancies (e.g., size, shape, quantity, color, orientation) across variation in one or more dimensions

Lack of, or deficient need for, precision and accuracy in data gathering

Lack of capacity for considering two or more sources of information at once. This is reflected in dealing with data in a piecemeal fashion rather than as a unit of facts that are organized

These factors, acting either by themselves or in clusters, result in a condition of deficiency in *readiness for response*. The response will invariably be inadequate because appropriate data have not become available to the examiner. If we were to trace the response back to the premises from which it originated, we might find that sound elaborational techniques were employed for the processing of inadequate data. Impairment at the input phase may also, but not necessarily, affect the ability to function at the phases of elaboration and output.

The Elaborational Phase: Deficiencies at the elaborational phase include those factors that impede the individual's efficient transformation of the available data. In addition to impairments in data gathering, which may or may not have occurred at the input phase, these deficiencies operate to obstruct proper elaboration of whatever cues do exist:

Inadequacy in the perception of the existence of a problem and its definition

Inability to select relevant as opposed to irrelevant cues in defining a problem

Lack of spontaneous comparative behavior or the limitation of its application by a restricted need system

Narrowness of the mental field

Episodic grasp of reality

Lack of need for the eduction or establishment of relationships

Lack of need for and/or exercise of summative behavior

Lack, or impairment, of need for pursuing logical evidence

Lack, or impairment, of inferential, hypothetical ("iffy") thinking

Lack, or impairment, of strategies for hypothesis testing

Lack, or impairment, of planning behavior

Lack, or impairment, of interiorization

Nonelaboration of certain cognitive categories occurs because the verbal concepts are not a part of the individual verbal inventory at a receptive level, or because they are not mobilized at the expressive level.

Deficiencies in the elaboration of cues occur, often in combinations, with marked frequency in the culturally disadvantaged and retarded performing individual. It is the elaboration of cues to which we usually refer when we speak of "thinking." Inadequate or inappropriate data do not preclude an appropriate, original, or creative response. Elaborational processes may occur in situations where there is a perception of inappropriate elements, or where not all the elements are perceived and some must be deduced. Incomplete data may well be the cause of inadequate elaboration (reflecting dimensions of narrowness or episodic qualities of the mental field). The outcome may be either a personalized or bizarre response, an impoverished one using only the data meaningful to the respondent, or perhaps no response at all—a blocking in anticipation of complete failure.

The Output Phase: Deficiencies at the output phase include those that result in inadequate communication of final solutions. Even adequately gathered data and appropriate elaboration can result in inappropriate expression if difficulties exist for the individual at this phase. Specific difficulties include:

Egocentric communication modalities

Difficulty in projecting virtual relationships

Blocking

Trial and error responses

Lack, or impairment, of verbal or other tools for communicating adequately elaborated responses

Lack, or impairment, of need for precision and accuracy in the communication of one's responses

Deficiency in visual transport

Impulsive, random, unplanned behavior

LPAD examiners must be thoroughly familiar with the deficient cognitive functions to detect their manifestation in the performance of the examinee; they must also know the mediational interventions offered to correct such deficiencies. Sources of difficulties are identified, interventions are directed toward them, and the instruments are presented, manipulated, and interacted with to stimulate responses that elicit change and indicate that the change is structural. The reader will become familiar with what this process entails, as we further discuss the structure of the LPAD process and the nature of the instruments.

The Cognitive Map— Dimensions of the Task

To understand sources of cognitive impairment, it is necessary to analyze the characteristics of the task to which the individual is required to respond. The analysis is done with the help of the cognitive map, wherein critical elements require the individual to generate responses relevant to the demands of the tasks. These components of the task interact with the cognitive functions in the formulation and production of responses, which may be adequate, appropriate, and facilitative of learning and problem solving, or may combine to generate failing, inadequate, and inefficient performance.

The cognitive map includes seven parameters by which a task can be analyzed: content, modality, phase, operation, level of complexity, level of abstraction, and level of efficiency. Tasks thus require mastery of elements that in turn require adequate cognitive functions for efficient thinking to occur in a process-oriented approach.

Content: Each mental act can be described according to the subject matter with which it deals and the universe of content on which it operates. Experiential and educational background (e.g., prior learning that has been assimilated) and culturally determined saliency (the importance and value as a factor of an individual's cultural experience) lead to differential levels of competency in individuals.

If the content is strange to the learner—and indeed, people differ greatly as to the specific content they are exposed to and familiar with—or if facts, events, or details of the required performance are not within the individual's experiential repertoire, there will need to be an investment in acquiring mastery before the learner can be expected to focus on the cognitive operations that are the target of the assessment. Failure to respond, therefore, must be considered in light of the presence or absence of relevant content dimensions embedded in the task. Any attempt to evaluate the intelligence of the individual without considering content as a source of success or failure is doomed to do injustice to the individual.

Modality: Tasks may be presented in a variety of languages: verbal, pictorial, numerical, figural, or a combination of these and other codes, which range from mimicry and metalinguistic communication to conventional signs that are detached from the content they signify. Efficiency in use of specific modalities may differ among individuals because of their preferential modes or because of their differing saliency for particular socioeconomic, ethnic, or cultural groups. It is also a function of specific distal factors (such as neurological or sensory deficits, lack of exposure to specific teaching, etc.).

Functional impairment must be considered in light of the modality(ies) required by the task, as well as the range of cognitive functions present in the learner to make possible the reception of stimuli. Inadequate responding can be changed by shifting the modality of presentation of the task and its required expression of solutions. One cannot conclude that an operation is inaccessible to a learner simply on the basis of an inability to perform it in a specific modality. On the other hand, difficulty involved in using a particular modality must be understood in order to be bypassed or challenged, depending upon the goal.

The Phase of the Mental Act: The three phases of the mental act—input, elaboration, and output—may be differentially represented in a given task. When functioning is appropriate, it is difficult to clearly identify the contribution of each specific phase. With failure, however, it is necessary to isolate the responsible phase and understand its role in interfering with performance, as a basis for assessment and intervention. A task that places too much emphasis on input from the individual may disadvantage that individual in subsequent performance. For example, an individual's response may be inadequate because of incomplete, imprecise data gathering, which, even if elaborated properly, would lead to failure at the output phase.

As a dimension of the task, examiners must analyze the specific phase requirements or emphases embedded within it to understand failures in performance, and then link them more specifically to the cognitive dysfunctions that may be present in the individual. If, for example, the task requires primarily input or output phase functions, performance on the task may be more resistant to change than if elaboration is emphasized, and this may require more investment of time and energy or focus on structural interventions. The analysis of impaired performance in terms of phase helps to locate deficient cognitive functions and the source of difficulties and attribute a differential weight to success or failure. Thus, an arithmetical problem requiring the computation of 100 additions is measurably less difficult than one requiring four types of operations ordered in a given sequence.

Operations: A mental act may be analyzed according to the operations that are required for its accomplishment. An operation may be understood as a group of activities that enable information derived from internal and external sources to be organized, transformed, manipulated, and acted upon in a way that generates new information. In defining the nature of an operation, it is important to identify the prerequisites necessary for its generation and application. For example, classification, seriation, logical multiplication, or analogical, syllogistic, or inferential thinking are more complex in the demands they place upon the individual to use cognitive functions than recognition or comparison.

When the examinee's performance is impaired, the examiner must determine the component elements in the task necessary for the acquisition and/or application of the required elements and assess the presence or level of impairment in the related cognitive functions required to achieve the operation.

Level of Complexity: The level of complexity of a task may be understood as the quantity and quality of units of information required to be handled for its solution. However, this in turn is contingent on the quality of the information, its degree of novelty for the individual, and the level of conceptual organization. The more familiar the units, and the more organized, even if they are multiple, the less complex the act; the less familiar, or organized, the more complex the mental act. It is thus necessary to analyze the task from three perspectives: (a) the number of units of information contained in the task, (b) the degree of familiarity the subject has with the task and its component elements, and (c) the degree of organization, grouping, and categories that allows a reduction in the complexity of the task. Intervention and mediation is then directed toward these dimensions. As these elements are modified by mediation of organization, levels of complexity change, both within tasks and across tasks with similar structures or modalities.

Level of Abstraction: The level of abstraction is defined as the distance between a given mental act and the object or event upon which it operates. Thus, a mental act may involve operations on the objects themselves, as in sorting, or it may involve relationships between hypothetical propositions without direct reference to real or imagined objects and events. The level of abstraction as here defined becomes a source of interpretation of the difficulties the examinee has in acceding to higher levels of functioning, as well as the modification that occurs when such levels become accessible as a result of MLE.

Level of Efficiency: This parameter is qualitatively and quantitatively different than the other six, although it is determined or affected by them, singly or in combination. It is defined as the structure of the task requiring a certain degree of rapidity and precision in order to be solved. A third dimension is the level of effort experienced by the subject as needed to generate or sustain a given performance.

The relationship of level of efficiency to the other parameters may be observed, for instance, where a high level of complexity, attributable to a lack of familiarity, may lead to inefficient handling of a task. The inability to differentiate efficiency from capacity is an important potential source of error in assessment, resulting in faulty labeling and erroneous prognosis. The lack of efficiency, defined as slowness in response generation, reduced production, or imprecision (lack of accuracy), may be totally irrelevant to the propensity of the individual to grasp and elaborate a particular problem and may need to be analyzed from the perspective of other parameters of the cognitive map. Indeed, tasks may differ widely as to the efficiency they require from the performer.

With regard to the dimension of perceived level of difficulty, a variety of task-intrinsic and/or task-extrinsic factors may be present. These can be categorized as *affective-energetic* factors in performance, and they need to be carefully considered in the analysis of results (see discussion of Interpretation of Results later in this chapter). Fatigue, anxiety, lack of motivation, and the amount of required investment may all affect the individual in the performance of a task. In addition, the recency of acquisition of a pattern of behavior must be considered, as behavior not yet automatized or crystallized is more vulnerable to the impact of interfering factors and can thus be described as fragile.

Conventional test scores more often than not actually reflect efficiency in terms of rapidity and accuracy (the number of correct responses) without taking into account any other parameters of the mental act. Dynamic assessment, on the other hand, considers these parameters in conjunction with a careful analysis of the cognitive processes underlying performance, to provide a meaningful assessment of modifiability and to search for the most efficient and economical ways to overcome the barriers presented by the retarded performance.

The cognitive map as an analysis of the dimensions of the tasks to which the individual is required to respond is thus an important element in the process of dynamic assessment and the use of the LPAD. It influences the examiner's choice of the types and order of instruments to use in the assessment, the amount of time and extent of focus within an instrument, and the nature and type of mediation to offer in the interaction with the instrument(s). Together with a deficient cognitive function (describing the individual), the cognitive map describes the nature of the task and is crucial for the process of interpretation.

Using the LPAD in a dynamic manner requires a continuous interweaving of these elements, at levels of both theory and application. Effective processing and inclusion of these dimensions enable the LPAD examiner to orient the assessment toward seeking—through a process orientation—answers to critical questions that frame the relevance and purpose of the assessment process:

What are the observed obstacles to effective performance?

How amenable to change are the observed deficiencies?

How much change can be expected?

What is the nature of the investment required to produce the desired changes? (content areas, modalities of response, mental operations, etc.)

How much investment is required to produce the desired changes?

How much stability can one attribute to the desired change?
How much generalization can one achieve following MLE intervention?

The Instruments of the LPAD

We will here briefly describe the instruments developed that compose the LPAD battery of tests. A full description of the instruments, including specific procedures for administration, scoring, interpretation of responses, and their use in a clinical assessment process are presented in the *Revised Examiner's Manual* (Feuerstein, 1995).

An LPAD assessment consists of the administration of a battery of several instruments, selected to allow the examiner to observe and interact with the examinee. As the examinee responds, the examiner gathers information, develops ideas about the learner's needs and deficient functions, and uses these observations to guide further teaching to elicit and stimulate changes in performance, directed toward creating the profile of modifiability. Therefore, the time required for the assessment, and the number and range of instruments selected for the assessment process, can vary a great deal.

Instruments Focusing on Visual-Motor and Perceptual Organization

Organization of Dots

On this test, the subject looks at a model figure containing simple geometrical shapes, starting with squares and triangles and increasing in complexity with subsequent task demands to include shapes composed of both regular and irregular curvilinear and rectilinear forms. The subject is then asked to "find" the model shapes in frames filled with unstructured, visually amorphous clouds of dots. The task is to draw lines to connect the dots to produce the shape of the model, presented in many instances as overlapped, rotated, and superimposed in various ways. The subject must look for the relationships, plan and use information that must be internalized, and exercise eye-hand coordination to draw the connecting lines. As the subject completes the tasks, the examiner observes and mediates the development and use of cognitive strategies

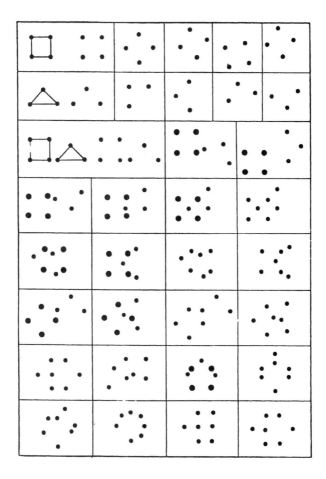

Figure 4.3. Organization of Dots, Training Sheet
SOURCE: From *Instrumental Enrichment.* Copyright Reuven Feuerstein and the Hadassah-WIZO-Canada Research Institute, Jerusalem, Israel. All rights reserved. Reproduction by permission.

such as planning, inferring, and regulating perceptual conflicts. (See Figure 4.3.)

The primary modality of the task is figural and grapho-motor. Operations included in this task include differentiation, segregation of overlapping figures, conservation of the figure across changes in its position, articulation of the field, and representation (interiorization).

Complex Figure Drawing Test

The Complex Figure Drawing Test is adapted from Rey (1959) and Osterreith (1945). The subject is asked to copy the Rey/Osterreith complex geometric design, looking at the model. The subject must use organizational principles to create an efficient production in the face of the complexity of the task. The great number of units of information becomes reduced by organization and awareness of the succession of steps to internalize the multitude of details. During the first reproduction phase, only minimal orienting mediation is offered. Following the first reproduction, and after a 3- to 5-minute latency period, the subject is asked to reproduce the design from memory (without looking at the model). Following the memory phase, and based on observations of the subject's performance, a mediation phase is conducted where the examiner reviews with the subject aspects of his or her performance, identifies errors and inefficiencies, and teaches organizational and design aspects. After mediation, the subject is asked to copy the design again from the stimulus model, and again from memory. Assessment is directed toward the initial performance (organizational approach, accuracy of motor skills and structural details, etc.) in reproducing the design and changes in the second copy and memory productions, following mediation.

The task requires functioning in a figural and graphic modality and measures both short-term learning and the persistence of perceptual organization difficulties. The mental operations involved in this test include discrimination, segregation of proximal elements, the articulation of a complex field, and reproduction, representation, differentiation, integration, and visual-motor coordination.

An additional phase is also available for this test, the Representational Organization of Complex Figures, in which the subject is presented with a template containing 10 designs, constructed in such a way that a central geometric figure is embedded in a set of adjacent or juxtaposed figures. The subject is asked to scan the first figure and indicate which part of the figure he or she would prefer to draw first, and the order in which all of the remaining parts would be drawn. The examiner then proceeds through the rest of the figures. No figure is actually drawn—the subject merely indicates the parts and sequence in which they "would" be drawn. This phase is useful for those subjects who present persistent difficulties in organizational aspects of the Complex Figure

Drawing and reveals the effects of mediation offered in earlier phases of the instrument. It removes from performance any difficulties the subject may have in the visual-motor modality.

Instruments Focusing on Memory, With a Learning Component

Positional Learning Test (5 × 25)

This test is adapted from the work of Professor Andre Rey. The subject is shown a grid of 25 squares, organized in five rows and five columns, with five positions (corresponding to one for each row and column) designated and indicated by the examiner using an auditory verbal and motor modality (saying "here" and pointing). After a short (10-second) latency period, the subject is asked to reproduce the indicated positions by marking them on the same grid. The procedure is repeated, with minimal mediation, until the subject can reproduce the pattern correctly three times in succession. If difficulty is experienced, mediation is directed toward the apparent source of the errors and toward establishing strategies that the subject can use. After the examinee learns one pattern, the procedure is repeated similarly with different patterns, enabling the examiner to observe learning of new patterns in the presence of previously learned and potentially confounding patterns. The learning on this instrument reflects a visual/motor and graphic modality and requires the subject to use the operations of encoding, sequencing, and reproducing a perceived set of positions.

Plateaux Test

This instrument is also adapted from the work of Professor Andre Rey. On this test, the subject is presented with a set of four plates, superimposed upon one another in the subject's view. Each plate contains nine buttons or pegs, arranged in three parallel columns or rows (a 3 × 3 design). Each plate has one peg that cannot be removed. The fixed peg is in a different position on each of the four plates. In the exploratory phase, the subject is asked to search for the fixed peg on the first plate by taking out the pegs and replacing them until the fixed one is located and to identify its position. The subject is asked to repeat the process for the

remaining three plates successively, being encouraged to develop strategies leading to learning the positions on each plate and discovering a
generalization—rule or principle—relating to the pattern of fixed positions. After the subject has learned the four positions (making three er-
rorless repetitions), the orientation of the plate is rotated, and the subject
is asked to identify the position of the fixed pegs following the rota-
tion(s). A second, representational phase is undertaken when the subject
is asked to draw the pattern of fixed pegs on paper, reflecting a two-di-
mensional transition and interiorization. This phase assesses the transition from the concrete position to the use of a memorized or internalized
representation from a three-dimensional experience to a graphical two-
dimensional plane—a substitution of learned reality. A third phase is
introduced in order to learn about the plasticity and flexibility of the
memorized data. In this phase, the well-established positions and their
successions are successively rotated by 90, 180, and 270 degrees, and the
examinee is required to represent schematically (on paper) the fixed pegs
in the new positions produced by the respective rotations. This phase
represents a higher-order cognitive operation than the simple reproduction of the positions and their initial graphic representations, reflecting
the outcome of rotations requiring shifting of learned positions.

Associative Recall: Functional
Reduction and Part-Whole

This test consists of two versions, similar in organization and objective but differing in stimulus presentation. The subject is shown a page
that contains a row of 20 simple line drawings along the top, selected for
their familiarity to the subject and the unambiguity of their figural pre-
sentations. In the first row, the objects are presented in their entirety, and
the subject is asked to name them (a labeling phase). In the second row,
on the Functional Reduction page, drawings of functional substitutes are
shown. On the Part-Whole page, a salient feature of the object is presented. In the third and fourth rows, there is a further stimulus reduction
and changes in order of presentation. The subject is asked to recall the
original labeled object on the top row from a visual inspection of the
reduced stimuli under the various conditions presented in the subsequent rows that are exposed, with the preceding rows concealed. The
Functional Reduction page is used with most subjects, and the Part-

Whole page may be used when the examiner feels further mediation is needed for repetition or crystallization of the functions learned on the Functional Reduction page, or when the subject's level of perceptual functioning suggests that restricting the task to a focus on structural details as the link to associative memory will yield more efficient and elaborative responses. Both pages also enable the assessment of immediate free recall and delayed free recall of the original 20 objects. The modality of this test is visual, auditory, motor, and graphic. It requires the subject to use the operations of encoding, symbolization, and the discovery of functional relationships.

16-Word Memory Test

This test consists of a group of 16 simple common words presented orally to the subject. The words are presented in a fixed but conceptually random order. The subject is asked to repeat as many as can be recalled following the presentation of the list and a latency period of about 10 seconds. The subject is told that the process will be repeated several times. No mediation is offered for the first three or four repetitions. The examiner observes the subject's spontaneous recognition and inclusion in memory of the four categories into which the 16 words can be grouped. After about four repetitions, mediation is offered, if needed to encourage the memory process, using a variety of cues, both mnemonic and cognitive, until the subject can recall all or a majority of the list using internalized memory functions and achieve accuracy and efficiency of response.

The modalities of this test are auditory and verbal, and the mental operations require the reproduction of an auditory set of stimuli, internalized controls, organization, and both encoding and decoding (representationally) skills.

Diffuse Attention Test (Lahy)

This instrument was developed by Lahy from the work of Zazzo (1964). It is used in the LPAD procedure to assess the subject's adaptability and flexibility, manifested in rapidity and precision on a task that requires visual scanning. The subject must maintain attention and focus on a visual/motor and repetitive process, learning a perceptual set, and either maintaining it over time or being able to learn a new set without interference from the learning. Three of the eight figures are designated as model figures, and these are isolated at the top of each section of the test page, which the subject learns to differentiate. The subject must then scan lines of 40 figures, including the 8 figures presented in a random order, and mark the three model figures when they are perceived and identified. The stimulus field is thus perceptually quite dense and requires the subject to scan carefully and work to maintain visual tracking and cognitive attention. There are two forms of this test, one having only one such array, and 24 lines of stimuli to scan. A second form has three sections, with three different sets of three model figures, thus enabling the assessment of retroactive inhibition—the effect of learning one set of differentiations on the subsequent performance on another set. Performance is observed in 1-minute intervals, yielding scores of the proportion of correct and incorrect inclusions and omissions within the segments. No mediation is typically offered during the performance on the task, but the task can be practiced and mediated in a variety of ways after performance and repeated after various practice experiences, to assess the changes with "over learning."

The modality of this test is visual-motor and graphic. The operations included are limited to the identification of differentiated cues (an encoding process) and the "re-cognition" of the model.

Instruments Involving Other Cognitive Processes and Mental Operations

LPAD Matrices: Raven Colored Progressive Matrices and Standard Progressive Matrices. Set Variations B-8 to B-12, Set Variations I, Set Variations II

The instruments used in the LPAD procedures are those of the published Raven's (1956, 1958) Colored (CPM) and Standard Progressive Matrices (SPM). Set Variations B-8 to B-12 are based on Raven's CPM items 8 to 12. Set Variations I is based on items from the CPM levels A, Ab, and B. Set Variations II is based on principles similar to SPM levels C, D, and E, but the items present greater novelty in the modality of presentation. The LPAD objective in the presentation of these problems to the examinee is to assess to what extent a rule and set of prerequisites acquired to solve a particular problem are adaptively used in variations of the task, and to what extent do the learned elements of the original task become the facilitating factor in adaptation to the new task.

The Raven's instruments are administered according to LPAD procedures, using a "test-teach-retest" approach. The Set Variations instruments are constructed and administered on principles similar to those of Raven's, with a sample problem for each set of variations that receives intensive mediation; then, independent performance is observed on a series of problems similar to but also becoming progressively more difficult than the mediational example. The tasks require the learner to look at a series of designs and complete the series by selecting a correct alternative from a number of choices. To choose the correct alternative, the subject must understand the relationship among the variables. The tasks progressively add variables and change the dimensions used to establish the relationships. What is assessed on these tasks is the subject's ability to think using analogies presented as figural (visual/perceptual) information and their response to the teaching of strategies to solve the problems. The operations involved are those of perceptual closure and discrimination; the generation of new information through synthesis, permutations, and seriation; inferential thinking; analogical thinking; deductive reasoning; and relational thinking. (See Figure 4.4.)

Representational Stencil
Design Test (RSDT)

The RSDT is based on the Stencil Design Test of Grace Arthur (1930), but it differs significantly in its structure and technique of application, primarily in its shift of the task away from the concrete, manipulative modality toward a representational, internalized modality. In the LPAD procedure, the design is constructed by the subject on a purely mental level. The instrument consists of 20 designs that the subject must deconstruct representationally by referring to a page of model "solid" and "cut-out" stencils that must be mentally superimposed upon one another. The problems increase in level of difficulty (on dimensions of form, color, and structure) and are organized so that mastering simpler problems leads to the ability to solve harder ones. The procedure of this test orients the subject to the stencil page, offers a test page of problems, and then provides a training page to mediate various processes and strategies according to what is observed during performance on the test page. A

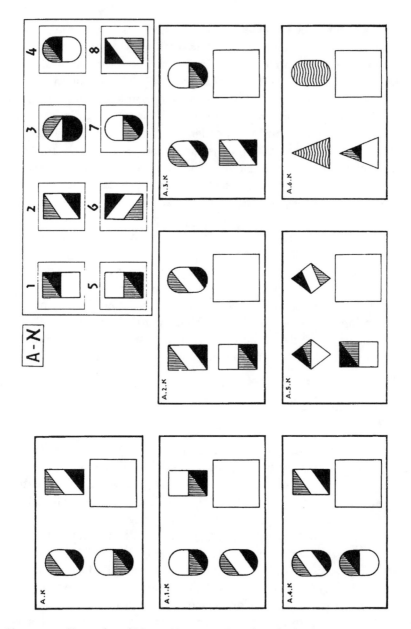

Figure 4.4. Examples of Matrix Variations Based on the Learning Potential Assessment Device model

Parallel Test is provided to be used following mediation. The instrument assesses the subject's ability to learn a complex task using internalized systems of organizing, and to use acquired learning to solve more complicated problems. Part of what is assessed in this instrument is how readily available the learner's inner (representational) processes are and how easily and adaptively they are used in subsequent problems of increased complexity and abstraction. The modalities involved are figural, numerical, and verbal. The operations involved in successful mastery of the tasks are segregation, differentiation, representation, anticipation of transformation, encoding and decoding, and generalization.

Numerical Progressions

This test assesses the subject's capacity to understand and deal with relationships, identify them as rules, and apply them to building new information, using numerical and graphic modalities. The task presents progressions of numbers, related to one another according to rules that must be deduced from the available information. At the end of a sequence of numbers, the subject is asked to supply the two missing numbers. A correct response suggests that the subject has understood how the numbers are related to one another. The format is that of a pretest, a learning phase, and two forms of a posttest. In the learning phase, the subject is encouraged to formulate and state the rule by which the answers were achieved. The examiner teaches relationships that are not understood and establishes strategies according to an analysis of needs (errors and performance on the pretest). Following mediation, a posttest is given to determine how well the subject has learned strategies for solving the problems. The parallel form of the posttest makes possible assessing the permanence and stability of what has been learned over time. The operations involved in this instrument are those of basic mathematics (addition, subtraction, multiplication, and division) and the more generalized mental operations of differentiation, segregation, inferential thinking, and deductive reasoning.

Organizer

This instrument presents the subject with a series of verbal statements consisting of sets of items that must be organized according to closed, logical systems. The task involves the subject placing the items (colors, objects, people, etc.) in positions relative to one another according to the determined attributes or conditions presented in the statements. A series of statements or premises is presented in each task. Each premise permits the extraction of only a part of the needed information required to determine a full and precise placement of the items. Thus, the subject must gather available information, develop and test hypotheses with succeeding information given, and generate information that is not immediately available in the given propositions. The tasks become more complex because of more units of information and the level of inference needed to solve them. What is assessed in this instrument is the subject's ability to gather new information through the use of inferential processes, formulate hypotheses and test them according to new information or assumptions generated, and apply strategies for discovering relationships. The instrument consists of pretest, learning, and test phases.

The modality is verbal, with a numerical subcomponent. The operations involve decoding, encoding, representation, inferential thinking, transitive thinking, propositional reasoning, negation, with a heavy loading of mnemonic (memory) functions.

Other Instruments Associated With and Sometimes Used in the LPAD

Two other instruments have been used in the LPAD battery and may be included by various dynamic assessment practitioners and LPAD trained examiners. They are the Test of Verbal Abstracting (TVA) and the Human Figure Drawing (administered according to LPAD procedures). The reader can find complete descriptions in the first edition of the *LPAD Examiner's Manual* (Feuerstein et al., 1996) and in the *Revised Examiner's Manual* (Feuerstein, 1995).

The Structure of the LPAD

The LPAD represents a shift from a static to a dynamic goal of assessment, notably from searching for stable characteristics to determining the potential for modifiability of the individual. This requires changes in four dimensions of the testing conditions:

1. The structure of the test instruments
2. The nature of the testing situation and procedures
3. A shift of emphasis from product to process
4. A change in the interpretation of results

The Structure of the Instruments

The objective of assessing the modifiability of functions requires a more or less radical restructuring of the test instruments. Conventional psychometric tests are shaped by the belief in the fixity and stability of intelligence and its measurement. There are a number of aspects of instrument construction that manifest this conceptualization, all of which lead to the search for reliability, and ultimately for predictability. For example, items that are known to produce unstable results are eliminated because they are too sensitive to the changes that the individual's cognitive function may undergo. There is often little or no inherent relationship from one item to another as long as they are statistically correlated and prove their predictive capacity. There is little or no provision for feedback of previous performance to the examinee, so that the examinee is not prepared for handling subsequent items. Even tests such as Raven's (1947, 1956, 1958) Progressive Matrices, which makes an attempt to present items that prepare the subject for subsequently more difficult items, fails to foster learning when presented in the standardized manner, as explanations are permitted only for the easiest items. Thus, the failure to perform on tasks oriented in the manner of conventional psychometrics is usually interpreted as a limited capacity to handle higher mental processes. This has been used by Jensen (1969) in describing his concept of Level I intelligence, and others (see Herrnstein & Murray, 1994) to justify supposed innate deficiencies in thought processes and intelligence for certain classes of individuals.

The LPAD instruments are designed to overcome the limitations inherent in the conventional psychometric approach. We have developed a model that serves as the basis for the construction of a number of different kinds of tests, presenting an array of tasks, all of which are oriented to assessing fluid rather than crystallized intelligence. As noted above,

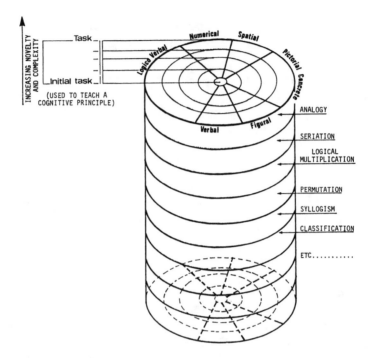

Figure 4.5. Learning Potential Assessment Device (LPAD) Model
SOURCE: Feuerstein, 1979. Reprinted by permission.

these instruments present a sharp departure from the goals usually set
for assessment. Figure 4.5 illustrates the LPAD model by which the instruments are constructed, reflective of the goals described above. The
very small circle at the top center of the cylinder represents a problem,
task, or situation first presented to the examinee for solution and mastery. As the subject responds the problem, the examiner explores with
and/or teaches the individual to use or employ appropriate given principles through the application of relevant cognitive operations. The examinee is given the training necessary to enable the solution of this initial
problem. Once mastery is achieved, the examinee is then presented with
additional tasks that represent more complex modification of the initial
training task, represented in the model as moving outward from the center, as the diverging, concentric circles indicate. This movement entails
varying the novelty, difficulty, and complexity, which simulates the

adaptational requirements that often confront the individual in real life. The progressive novelty, difficulty, and complexity are produced by changes in one or more dimensions inherent to the solution of the task. One can change the objects or the situation; one can change the relationship between objects or their specific functions with regard to one another; or finally, one can change the cognitive operations that are required to solve the problem. The radial lines that divide the top of the cylinder into sections indicate that the task selected can be presented in different modalities, indicated as spatial, pictorial, concrete, figural, verbal, logical-verbal, or numerical. Variations in modalities of presentation are also presented to the examinee, both within the same level of novelty, complexity, and difficulty, and as the demands on these dimensions are increased.

Thus, one may keep the operation constant while changing objects and relationships, or keep the objects and relationships constant while only varying the operations. Novelty can then be observed by considering the number and nature of dimensions introduced in the problem, as compared with those of the initial task used for training purposes. The specific operations required by the problem represented by the center small circle and by the diverging tasks introduced following initial training can be presented to the examinee in a variety of modalities or "languages." A third dimension of the model represents a selection of mental operations relevant to the task, such as analogies, logical multiplication, permutations, syllogisms, categorization, seriation, and so on, reflected in the vertical layers of the cylinder.

By using instruments constructed according to this model, one may gather data relating to the following critical dynamic assessment criteria:

The readiness of the examinee to grasp the principle underlying the initial problem and to solve it

The amount and nature of investment required in order to teach the examinee the given principle

The extent to which the newly acquired principle is successfully applied in solving problems that become progressively more different from the initial task

The differential preferences of the examinee for one or another of the various modalities of presentation of a given problem

> The differential effects of different training strategies offered to the exami-
> nee in the remediation of functioning, involving the criteria of novelty-
> complexity, language of presentation, and types of mental operation

The use of this dynamic approach in assessment assumes that the individual represents an open system that may undergo important modifications through exposure to external and/or internal stimuli. However, the degree of modifiability of the individual through direct exposure to various sources of stimulation is considered to be a function of the quantity and quality of MLE. It is the MLE that sensitizes the human organism to specific characteristics of the stimuli and establishes sets and modalities for grasping and elaborating reality, vital for the appropriate integrated use of new experience.

Static measures completely neglect separate assessment of the dimension of modifiability because they equate the measure of manifest functioning with the true, fixed, and immutable capacity of the individual. The dynamic approach does not deny the fact that the functioning of the individual, as observed in the level of achievement or general behavior, is low; but by considering this level as pertaining only to the manifest repertoire of the individual, it takes into consideration the possibility of modifying this repertoire by appropriate strategies of intervention.

The tasks in the LPAD instruments are shaped in such a way as to provoke the appearance of the deficient cognitive functions viewed as responsible for the failure of the individual to master the task and adapt to a variety of life and learning conditions. It is the objective of the various instruments to tease out the types of deficiencies and, through the analyses of the process, observe what is causing success or failure. The tasks are therefore selected and constructed according to the dimensions of deficient cognitive functions and the cognitive map. In the RSD instrument, for example, we try to figure out the type of perception of the individual, the capacity to analyze, to create cardinal order, to represent what is perceived abstractly. Each task, in this and all other instruments, is presented to permit addressing certain conditions of cognitive functioning that are related to functioning in other areas—modalities of responding, academic areas of performance, and the like.

An additional goal determining the structure of the LPAD tasks is the search for indicators of even the most minimal changes in the functioning of the individual, to be used as representative samples of modifiability. For example, increased speed of formulating responses, or expressions of certainty or energy in responding, often signify the establishment of changes at a structural level and give the examiner cues for further or different interventions.

The Nature of the Testing Situation and Procedures

Changes in the instruments are not by themselves sufficient to fully elicit and assess the modifiability of the individual, even though they are a most vital component in a more adequate system of assessing the retarded performer. The testing situation itself must be changed in a way parallel to changes in the instrumentation in order to reach the dynamic goals set by the LPAD.

Conventional psychometric tests are characterized by uniform, standardized, and controlled sets of procedures from which no deviations are permitted. When the purpose is to rank an individual in terms of the manifest level of performance according to a set of established norms, such an approach is not only justified but is also a condition of the comparability of the test results to others examined. However, this comparability is not the purpose of the LPAD; consequently, the procedures governing the assessment must be adjusted. Not only is the purpose of the assessment to evaluate the individual's ability to learn, but it is also designed to yield information regarding the manner and modality through which learning is best achieved. This necessitates a highly flexible and individualized approach in which the role of the examiner is to produce change—to prod and explore for signs of modifiability and also to attend to the functions that appear to impede the progress of the individual.

Two distinct aspects of the testing situation, although strongly interdependent, must be considered separately: (a) changes in the examiner-examinee interaction and (b) the introduction of training (teaching) as an integral part of the assessment process.

Examiner-Examinee Relationship

The motivation of a low-performing and/or culturally deprived examinee in the conventional test situation is usually low because the tasks included rarely have appeal. A reduced level of curiosity is only one reason for a lack of motivation. Another is that the perception of novelty necessary to elicit an orienting reflex and an arousal followed by an exploration is not always present. Perception of novelty depends upon cognitive functions such as comparative behavior, analytic perception, and a capacity to grasp relationships and their transformation within a constant framework. The lack of task-intrinsic motivation is then further aggravated by the negative valence with which the presented task may be endowed, provoking an avoidance reaction in the individual, who associates the task with repeated experiences of failure. Failure experiences become the source of deeply ingrained feelings of intellectual insufficiency that further increase the negative reaction evoked by the novel tasks.

The examiner must therefore orient the relationship toward this condition of reduced motivation about the test situation, paying particular attention to three distinct determinants: (a) lack of curiosity resulting from deficiency in the prerequisite cognitive conditions, (b) lack of a need system that endows successful performance with specific meaning, and (c) the existence of a negative component—an avoidance reaction to tasks that have been associated with repeated experiences of failure, which leads to deeply ingrained feelings of intellectual inadequacy.

Given the lack of positive task-intrinsic motivation and the presence of aversive qualities, one can understand that the specific weight of emotional factors in determining the outcome of the conventional test situation is much greater than one is led to believe by the casual mention usually made of the meaning of the examiner-examinee relationship and the maintenance of the rapport established between them. The presence of a neutral, even sympathetic, and yet basically unresponsive examiner who limits the interaction with the examinee to issuing dry, standardized instructions cannot but add a further negative valence to the test situation. The examinee's possibly fragmentary grasp of the instructions, as well as a potential lack of motivation toward the task, will lead either to a correspondingly vague or imprecise way of dealing with the problem at hand, accompanied by a low level of anxiety and a "tuning-out" of the examiner, or—to the contrary—to a high level of anxiety, involving a feeling of great threat and low expectation of success. Thus, the lack of manifest interest on the part of the examiner, prescribed by the standardized test procedure, is potentially interpreted by the examinee in two different ways, both leading to negative reactions. First, "if it doesn't matter to you, why should I be concerned with it?" This is then followed by a tuning-out by the examinee, who no longer pays much attention to the task and proceeds to respond in a random or casual manner. Second, the examinee may interpret the neutrality of the examiner, even if basically benevolent, as a manifestation of hostility and an expectation of performance failure. This reduces efficiency by lowering motivation to cope or by energizing a countering hostility that interferes with any cognitive process that might otherwise have emerged.

The LPAD technique not only allows but intentionally creates the conditions for a radical change. This is accomplished by a shift in the roles of examiner-examinee into the relationship between teacher (the mediator) and pupil (the mediatee). What follows is an elimination of the neutral, indifferent role of the examiner in exchange for the active cooperative role of the mediator, who is vitally concerned with the maximization of the success of the pupil. It is through this shift in roles that we find both the examiner and the examinee engaged in the same task, in a common quest for mastery of the material. Thus, the examiner constantly intervenes—questions, orients, makes remarks, interprets results, and gives explanations whenever and wherever they are necessary, asks for repetition, sums up experiences, anticipates difficulties, warns the examinee about them, and creates reflective insightful thinking in the individual, not only concerning the task but also regarding the examinee's reactions to it. To accomplish all this, the examiner must be alert to each reaction of the individual, and in the course of behaving this way, the examiner acts radically different than the usual psychometrician. The examiner is vibrant, active, and concerned instead of aloof, distant, and neutral, giving the examinee the feeling that the task is important, difficult, yet quite manageable and that the examiner is committed to the examinee's success.

With the establishment of such an interactive process, we usually observe a sharp increase in motivation. At the beginning, it is purely extrinsic, with the major motive of the examinee being to please the examiner. At this stage, any manifestation of reduced or discontinued interest on the part of the examiner is followed by a marked decrease in the efficiency of the trainee. Later, as the teacher-trainee relationship develops, and includes the task as a part of it, turning the dyad into a triad, we invariably observe a shift from extrinsic to intrinsic motivation. That is, the examinee begins to delight in the task itself, having grasped the deeper meaning of his or her own activity and the successful mastery of the task.

This shift is basically produced by two factors. One is directly linked to the capacity of the individual to perceive the nature of the problem by having integrated a series of criteria, at the end of which the solutions that are confronted become problems. Here, the TOTE (Test Operate-Test Exit) model is relevant in explaining the growing interest in the task itself, following the establishment of internal standards through previous experience (Hunt, 1961; Miller, Galanter, & Pribram, 1960). The second factor has to do with the development of a positive approach to problem solving through increased mastery of tasks, especially when the sequence of tasks follows the LPAD model of progressively increasing difficulty. Such mastery immediately raises the need in the individual to repeat the experience. This repetition has functional value in that it consolidates and crystallizes a successful pattern of behavior in a way similar to the circular reactions described by Piaget, and at the same time, it raises the level of aspiration and the achievement motivation of the examinee. At this point, it is the task that becomes the center of interest and motivation of the examinee, and no longer is motivation solely aroused by the examiner.

This shift in motivation, achieved by assigning meaningfulness, giving encouragement, and ensuring the experience of success, will not suffice to make the examinee's problem-solving behavior successful and efficient. For this, it is necessary to provide the examinee with a constant, fine-grained feedback of this interaction with the task that transcends the task itself and uses a variety of communicational modalities. In the usual psychometric model, feedback is often considered valueless or deleterious to either the examinee, to the standardized testing procedures, or to both. It is considered deleterious if the individual is told of his or her failure, without helping and permitting correction in a meaningful way. Even if correction is allowed in certain tests, it does not take the form of a thorough feedback strategy, focused on helping the examinee to master the present material in order to enable more effective performance on future test items. In tests whose structure does not involve interitem dependency, the task-bound feedback is considered to have negative instead of positive implications for future test items. The individual learns only that failure has occurred, but not how or why. Even if the examinee should be shown how or why, little or nothing is gained that will help the individual cope with subsequent items because they will be very different. No wonder the psychometrist conventionally limits the amount of feedback interaction with the examinee. The usual static test is structurally not suited to the use of feedback procedures.

In the case of the dynamic LPAD procedures, the feedback fulfills a variety of functions. It is used as a constituent part of the training process. The examinee is informed of the nature of the product (his/her responses) in a differentiated way, allowing for an immediate correction of incorrect responses or permitting generalization of the specific behavior employed if the response was adequate. In both cases, there is neither an increase in anxiety nor a reduction of the optimal motivation needed to maintain interest in further accomplishment. Successes are acknowledged through the conveyance of exuberance, interest, and pleasure, intended to communicate the meaning of the experienced success. Failure, on the other hand, is acknowledged in a tone that, although it diminishes the importance of the failure, still includes the challenge to do better. In other cases, behavioral patterns leading to one or another result are analyzed and explained, thus rewarding certain types of behavior as differentiated from other facets of the response.

In summary, the personal interaction between the examiner and the examinee on the LPAD has as its basic outcome an increase in the test-taking motivation of the examinee by the fact that the examiner (acting as a teacher-trainer) conveys to the examinee (responding as the pupil-trainee) the meaning of the task, the importance of mastering it, the capacity to do so, and finally, by a process of feedback, an ability to select the appropriate behavior leading to success. This process is also intended to produce a shift from extrinsic to intrinsic motivation in the examinee, thus engendering more independence and, to a certain extent, more reality orientation. We feel that in this kind of testing the personal relationship, which entails the change in interaction patterns as described, is a necessary condition for the appropriate assessment of the modifiability of culturally deprived and low-functioning individuals. This has implications leading to an emphasis on individualized testing, with one-to-one relationships, careful focus on mediational strategies, and much care to preserve the critical characteristics of the interactional models described above. However, it is possible to extend the process to group situations (see below) and to other modalities of interaction, such as programmed learning systems that may or may not be computer based. However, in such extensions, one must argue for extreme caution and vigilance, not only as to the application but even more so as to interpretation of the results, lest the mediational and interactive aspects essential to the approach be lost or so diluted as to become counterproductive.

The Training Process Integral to the Test Situation

Here we describe the examiner-examinee interaction in the LPAD procedure, which aims at inducing the cognitive prerequisites for the examinee's successful confrontation with the testing task. It should be understood that this training is not merely oriented toward a specific content but includes the establishment of the prerequisites of cognitive functioning for a wide array of behavioral patterns and the repertoire necessary for problem-solving behavior. The six areas on which mediation focuses are:

Regulation of behavior through inhibition and control of impulsivity, as well as the initiation of appropriate responsive behaviors

Correction of deficient cognitive functions and activation of available but fragile functions

Enrichment of the repertoire of mental operations

Enrichment of the task-related content repertoire (e.g., labeling of relationships such as up, down, equal to, etc.)

Creation of reflective, insightful thought processes

A shift from reproductive to productive, creative information-generating activity

A Shift in the Goals of Assessment From Product to Process—Profiles of Modifiability

Dynamic assessment requires a shift from a product-oriented to a process-oriented approach. Rather than simply registering, summarizing, and computing the obtained results and comparing them to existing scales, the major effort is directed to the understanding of the processes involved in their evolvement. This will require a special intervention on behalf of the examiner/mediator, modeled largely on the clinical method employed by Piaget in his interviews and observations. As indicated earlier in this chapter, the shift demands both theoretical/philosophical changes and new conceptual and methodological structures. There are many specific implications of these changes, in the constituent conceptual framework and in the clinical application to individuals and groups. An important aspect of the shift is, therefore, the creation of modalities of observation and registration of indices of the processes responsible for the outcome of the assessment. Here again we remind the reader that the ultimate purpose of dynamic assessment, from the perspective of the LPAD, is to create samples of change by which one may identify the propensity (of cognitive change) and to describe that change in such a way that subsequent learning and cognitive interventions will be identified and recommended.

Toward this end, the two conceptual formulations described above (the cognitive map and the deficient cognitive functions) are used in an integrated way in the establishment of what we refer to as the *profile of modifiability*. It must be made clear that these profiles are not to be considered as the ultimate traits and characteristics of the individual, but rather they refer to the process that has been set in place by the mediational interaction, a process that will result in a continuous set of changes based on the modifiability demonstrated and observed. We emphasize that the profile is a process and not a product. The structure of the profile reflects the special nature of the LPAD as a dynamic assessment procedure inasmuch as it releases the examiner from the more fixed and prescribed patterns of scores and other similarly rigid prescribed statistical and comparative portrayals. Moreover, the LPAD directs the summary and analysis to comparisons *within* the individual rather than to comparisons *among* individuals. Finally, the LPAD creates a structure that serves as a point of departure in consultation between the examiner and the relevant professionals and significant others (parents, spouses, relatives) in the life of the subject. As a tool of dynamic assessment, the structure for conveyance of results and recommendations must comprise dynamic qualities—flexibility, descriptiveness, multidimensionality, and forward-thrusting—leading to its use as a road map for subsequent activities.

The LPAD profile represents a conceptual tool that permits the examiner to organize, describe, and systematically interpret changes produced in the examinee through the LPAD assessment. The use of the profiles to describe and evaluate modifiability goes beyond the mere registration of the absolute magnitude of observed changes in performance, extending to include a series of qualitative characteristics of these changes as well as the examiner's assessment of their functional meaning. The functional meaning of the observed changes is determined in particular with regard to their predictive value for the accessibility of the individual to additional changes, as well as the preferential interactions and environmental conditions that make such changes possible.

Dimensions of the LPAD Profile

The LPAD profile is based on three dimensions that the examiner relies on to produce the specific assessment of the functional meaning of the change. The first of these dimensions is the area in which the change has been observed, considering (a) changes in certain contents of the repertoire of functioning of the individual's concepts, operations, and strategies; (b) changes in cognitive functions; (c) changes in the affective, energetic aspects of behavior; and (d) changes observed in the individual's efficiency of functioning. Incorporating these as dimensions of the profile requires a conceptual, descriptive development and the examiner's familiarity with how they operationally manifest themselves in performance (see Feuerstein, 1979, 1995). The second dimension deals with the qualitative nature of the produced changes. The extent to which they are of a structural nature is observed on the parameters of (a) retention/permanence, (b) resistance, (c) flexibility/adaptability, and (d) generalizability/transfer (see description in Criteria to Evaluate Change below). The third dimension focuses on changes in the amount and nature of the required mediational intervention that was necessary, first to produce, and then subsequently to sustain the given results. An additional variable that must be considered in the eventual interpretation and conveyance of results is that of the magnitude of change, considered with reference to information obtained with the referral, other baseline data, and the changes observed and registered within the assessment itself.

The LPAD examiner, integrating the concept of the profile into the assessment process, is called upon to consider the given and produced evidence of specific changes within these three dimensions. The examiner seeks to specify the types of interventions that may have to be offered to the examinee, as well as the accessibility of the examinee to specific changes that may have to be considered and developed to enable the reaching of autonomous-independent functional potential.

The LPAD profile represents a break with tradition in two interrelated ways. The first of these is that it is based on the assumption that the qualitative aspects of the observed changes are as significant—if not more so—than the quantitative aspects, especially for estimating the functional predictive meaning of the observed changes for modifiability of the individual. The second is the way in which the profile breaks with the conventional role attributed to the examiner: The examiner is called upon to exercise the subjective judgment of a well-trained professional who has in-depth knowledge of the processes being assessed and is thereby able to interpret the phenomena observed.

The source of these differences lies in the focus of the LPAD upon assessment rather than measurement. Measurement, which means the application of a standard gauge to a stable element with reiterated and uniform results, may be useful in particular situations and with certain types of data that conform to physical laws. However, in light of the considerable degree of flexibility and plasticity of human mental and emotional characteristics, as well as their great complexity, the utility of measurement as a means of evaluating human cognitive capacities is very doubtful. The problem is exacerbated when measurement is accompanied by the conviction that the obtained results truly reflect fixed and immutable characteristics of the observed phenomenon behavior. The issue of the use of standard measurement practices becomes even more critical when the obtained results are considered to reflect linear, one-dimensional rather then multidimensional projections or, in other words, to reflect predictable rather than divergent conditions.

Because the focus of the LPAD is on assessing the modifiability of the cognitive structure of the examinee, and then on intervening to modify that structure, its main focus and findings relate to the very process of change rather than to the numerical benchmarks and the differences between the two static poles of an examinee's baseline and end-product performance. Even more than the magnitude of the observed change, it is the process of change itself—its rhythm, amplitude, and direction—that is the LPAD's major concern. A qualitative change whose effect may be insignificant quantitatively may still be of great interest and value when it is seen as a process that is emerging within the examinee, and that may orient his or her cognitive behavior in directions different from the present course of functioning.

The Role of the LPAD Examiner

In the attempt to modify the examinee in the course of dynamic assessment, a great variety of techniques and strategies must be used to first produce and then detect changes. What is required is a highly refined MLE interaction in conjunction with the use of the LPAD instruments. In addition, the examiner must have an operational familiarity with the dimensions of the tasks (cognitive map) and the nature of the cognitive functions as they are reflected in the subject's task performance. The process of dynamic assessment aims at manipulating the various conditions under which a given state can be modified, and then registering and describing the optimal conditions by which the modified response can be elicited and maintained. Any attempt to interpret the meaning of an examinee's functioning at any point in the interaction—at the stage of either baseline, intervention, or subsequent performance—must rely on tools that permit the gathering and conceptualization of data that are relevant to the process of change. In an interpretation, a differential weight must be ascribed to the various sources of observed function and dysfunction, and areas pertinent to the dysfunction must be located and intervened upon to affect the examinee's performance in the desired direction (toward adequate functioning).

The contribution of the examiner is crucial to the proper interpretation of the process of change. The dynamic approach of the LPAD is based on a transactional model that affects the nature of the interaction in a multitude of ways. It considers the assessor no less responsible for the produced change than the characteristics of the subject being evaluated. Expanding the frame of reference from the individual who is being assessed (the examinee) to include an active and involved diagnostician changes the emotional and motivational attributes of both parties in the transaction. The LPAD examiner is highly motivated to have the subject succeed in overcoming difficulties because doing so reflects upon the capacity and investment of the examiner. This will have a reciprocal effect on the responsiveness of the examinee.

To be effective in diagnosing modifiability, the LPAD examiner must be skilled in the ways in which changes in functioning are produced. The examiner must consider (a) why the change has happened and (b) how to make it happen again, or (c) how to keep changes from happening if they are undesirable. In the LPAD, the examiner's responsibility for a subject's success becomes a potent force for a radical alteration in the examiner-examinee interaction, as compared with testing situations in which an examiner only measures and registers certain (presumed) objective, stable, continuous, linear phenomena.

The LPAD examiner establishes an attitude that specifically questions and ultimately reframes the meaning of success and failure. Success is not always indicative of the existence of some potential, and failure is not always indicative of a lack of potential. Both success and failure may have innumerable possible reasons. Simply challenging failure by attempting to modify it, without seeking its real cause, does not permit any conclusions regarding the effect of such failure on the adaptational capacity of the person. To determine the real meaning of success and failure, the LPAD examiner must carefully and precisely observe the interaction of the examinee with the instruments (the tasks). The analysis of the task according to the parameters of the cognitive map is necessary to identify determinants that may be crucial, both in explaining the reasons for various responses and subject performance and in processing the rich repertoire of potential mediational interventions out of which optimal strategies will be selected to solve an observed difficulty in the examinee. Finally, all of these elements must converge in the interpretation of results, an interpretation that must also suggest operational modalities by which to modify a person's deficiencies meaningfully and permanently for his or her better adaptation. The LPAD profile is the structural and process vehicle to make this possible.

The Interpretation of Results

The interpretation of results differs in the LPAD in a number of ways. Absolute numbers derived from the individual's initial performance (at what can be called baseline) or following intervention—or from both— may be of indicative value. However, except for instances of great success (where they certainly constitute evidence of the individual's capacity to acquire and apply learning), the absolute numbers are not informative about the changes that can be produced in the individual. In situations of lesser success, no success, or negative performance, absolute numbers can be misleading at best or can obscure change potential at worst.

Regardless of the level of efficiency reached by the examinee during the assessment, the LPAD examiner is called upon to detect and make as accurate an assessment as possible of the conditions preventing the individual from functioning at higher levels and to describe the amount, type, and nature of intervention that is needed to overcome them. The LPAD profile, therefore, focuses on a number of qualitative characteristics of the examinee's performance to help the examiner in this task.

As emphasized throughout, the LPAD is a process, and the design of its instruments and its procedures for administration creates the conditions to stimulate and elicit changes in the subject. The most important information generated in this specially structured interaction does not refer to what an examinee *can do* during the assessment experience, but it refers rather to the changes that have to be produced, and can be produced, to permit the examinee to accede to higher levels of functioning, and to maintain and elaborate them. The LPAD is thus an assessment of the propensity to change, and of the modifiability of this very condition. The gathering of data and conveyance of results as an outcome of this process must, therefore, be richly reflective of the change processes structured into the approach.

The data produced by the LPAD should not be considered as evidence of immutable and fixed traits (of modifiability). Even the examinee's modifiability cannot be considered stable. To the contrary, the indicators of modifiability obtained during the assessment constitute a reduced form (with regard to range and extent) of what can be expected with further investment. It therefore follows that the "rate" of observed change may undergo meaningful change in the direction of a higher, a more rapid, or a slower rate of modifiability following intervention. In other words, the recency and fragility of the examinee's acquisitions in the context of a comparatively brief, albeit intensive, dynamic assessment may produce evidence of modifiability that will become more enhanced with consolidation, crystallization, and habit formation, which may be achieved with subsequent interventions over a period of time following the assessment. This may produce a meaningful further enhancement of the individual's modifiability, making the examinee increasingly accessible to both areas and levels of functioning that could not be directly and specifically observed and predicted from the initial assessment of learning potential.

External Sources of Baseline Data

External sources may be implicit, as in a global index of cognitive development, which permits inferences regarding the presence or absence of certain cognitive functions; or explicit, as when some functions or mental operations are singled out to describe or illustrate a more general, implicit assumption about the subject of assessment. All baseline data must be considered in terms of their reliability, meaning, pervasiveness, and direction.

Baseline data of this type can come from parents, teachers, and professionals. They may be the product of direct, prolonged observation by parents, with varying degrees of systematicity; of a focused assessment by an experienced psychologist; or of an interaction with the observed child by a classroom teacher in a variety of situations. The information from various sources may converge when it refers to the same areas and conditions of functioning; however, it may also be divergent both in the description and interpretation of the subject's behavior. Incompatibilities and divergences that appear (and their appearance should be encouraged and paid attention to) may yield important information about a person's capacity above and beyond the manifest level of functioning. Without negating reports from one or another source of information, divergences may point to failure or success as being situationally determined. The interpretation of results differs greatly from conventional static models inasmuch as normative comparative bases are not used, but rather the significance is derived from an analysis of the performed tasks, the errors made, and the nature of the components of the mental acts responsible for functioning (phases, the cognitive map, etc.). For example, a psychologist may describe a child as being incapable of abstract thinking, pointing as evidence to the child's IQ of 55. The psychologist's opinion is offered in spite of the fact that the child has mastered reading, writing, and the basic mathematical operations. The psychologist might interpret the incompatibility as being due to the child's strong motivation, rather than as a sign of the possibility that the conclusion regarding the alleged incapacity is unwarranted. Incompatibility on the baseline level should lead the examiner to question certain assertions stemming from the manifest level of functioning. Thus, for example, descriptions of a short attention span may be challenged by observations in particular situations in which the same child persists in attending beyond what the child is requested or permitted to do. In this instance, any attribution of stable and pervasive neurologically based conditions must be questioned in favor of a more differential task-specific reactive response.

Information from external sources should therefore be carefully collected. Opportunities should be sought to identify contradictions, incompatibilities, and divergences, which can then be interpreted as reactions to specific conditions. An attempt must be made to reconcile controversial data, not only to understand the specific conditions under which they were obtained and the dynamics in which certain phenomena appear, but also in order to challenge them (in the assessment process). A way must be sought to correct stereotypic, limited perceptions of the subject, thereby providing evidence against established assumptions.

The baseline data gathered from external sources will often include a global evaluation in the form of a label, or a diagnostic category with psychological meanings from which a number of inferences follow. These inferences often limit the perception of functional adequacy of the individual. Thus, labeling someone as profoundly retarded usually implies a lack of symbolic functioning on a verbal level and—even more so—on the lexic level. Certainly, inferential, abstract, and representational thinking are considered nonexistent and not compatible with such a diagnostic label. Referring to someone as severely retarded implies the possibility (although not necessarily the actuality) of some minimal verbal functioning. No representational, symbolic, or abstract thinking is considered within the available repertoire of functioning. When describing an IQ within the educable mentally retarded (EMR) range (e.g., 50 to 75 IQ), verbal communication and a certain amount of simple, lexic function is assumed to be present and possible. However, the propensity to use thought processes requiring the elaboration of data and the generation of new information as a derivative of such organization is considered inaccessible. The LPAD examiner, who is familiar with the assumptions underlying such labeling and categorization, and who understands the underlying theory of SCM, will attempt to challenge these assumptions by orienting the search of the LPAD assessment toward the inferences directly derived from them. External sources of information that define a person by IQ, as an example, and other similar indices of manifest functioning do not guide the LPAD examiner in the direction of searching for confirmation (a relatively easy task), but conversely in the direction of seeking invalidation of the label; or at least toward the attempt to understand more precisely and intimately the reasons for the low manifest level of functioning.

Sources of Baseline Data Within the LPAD

Baseline information is gathered during the dynamic assessment in two ways. The first is by confronting subjects with tasks without training or prompting, in which they must show their capacity to cope spontaneously with tasks. The "objective data" thus derived are then used as a target for remediational processes and for change. Although such baseline data are easily gathered in this way, both in individual and especially in group administration formats, the examiner should be extremely cautious about depending on or emphasizing this method in individual, clinical assessment situations. Beyond the tendency to lapse into psychometric assessment styles, the subject's frustration, which may be created by such practices, will not be easily dissipated at later stages of the examiner/examinee interaction, and may limit the extent of the changes the learner can generate. It is of great importance to note that failure experiences risk raising certain resistance to more adaptive ways of functioning, which then may be ascribed to a preference to remain with the familiar—even if unsuccessful—pattern of functioning. A more pervasive consequence is that whenever limited or deficient cognitive processes are used, there is a readiness and propensity to repeat a previously given response, which results in the preservation of failure, rather than stimulating change. A second possibility is establishing baselines of subjects' manifest behavior by inferred information. This is preferable to producing data based on some degree of failure experience, with all that entails regarding the subject's potential lack of confidence. We have observed a tendency to repeat and perseverate in producing failing answers even after feedback leading to correction, as if the error has received some legitimization and is chosen because it has become familiar and easily accessible for retrieval. Indeed, the atmosphere engendered by an objective baseline, as described above, is not the type of examiner/

examinee interaction fostered and encouraged in dynamic assessment, where the examiner offers the mediational prerequisites for successful mastery of the task.

Observation-Derived Baseline Data

A more desirable way of establishing a baseline of intact and deficient functions, mental operations, affective and motivational factors, and efficiency is by the examiner's direct observation during the LPAD session as the subject performs. The examiner searches for the reasons underlying difficulties experienced by subjects in solving certain problems. This search is guided by the parameters of the cognitive map (see above). The deficient cognitive functions that are evidenced by the subject's performance must be carefully observed and registered, and then elaborated by mediation. The effects of this mediation on the development of adequate modes of coping with problems are then available for observation by presenting the subject with similar tasks to see if the deficiency revealed in the initial performance will produce another failure, or if—in subsequent tasks—the deficiencies have been corrected and no longer negatively affect the subject's functioning. In later stages of the assessment, the LPAD examiner must bear in mind those areas whose correction was attempted in the mediation phase.

Group LPAD Assessment

Our experience over the past several decades, in both clinical and experimental settings, suggests that with careful consideration for the theory and practice of the LPAD, and with well-organized procedural conditions, the LPAD can be effectively and usefully administered in a group setting (see *Revised LPAD Examiner's Manual*, Feuerstein, 1995).

Goals of Group LPAD Testing

The major goals and objectives of the LPAD, administered in a group setting, remain the same as those of the individual LPAD: to assess the propensity of individuals to modify their cognitive structures. When

concern is directed at the cognitive functions of individuals as they perform in groups, for example, in classrooms, a dynamic group assessment
procedure provides a modifiability profile as it may occur in the regular
condition. In a general sense, the dynamic approach applied in this context enables the examiner to describe the expected changes in the conditions of educational processes. It must be emphasized, however, that the
condition of group dynamic assessment does not offer the individual the
optimal conditions of mediation.

The essential focus of the LPAD in a group format is unchanged from
that of individual assessment. Here are some advantages of the group
format.

1. Information can be collected on students in situations that are
similar to the real learning experience of students, where variables can
be observed that are not available in the one-to-one interaction. These
include the subject's attending to instructions and explanations, the
maintaining of performance when direct monitoring is not being provided, response to distractions, self-control and behavioral monitoring
in situations of independent work formats, the effect of peer social relationships, and the like.

2. On the basis of information collected on the group, relevant interventions for the group as a whole can be developed. Observations of
group performance, response to mediation, and the emergence of learning and didactic strategies can be formulated into interventional suggestions that can be transmitted to teachers for implementation. In addition,
the development of individual programs derived from and relevant to
group performance becomes possible.

3. Because group assessment requires a more standard and structured set of initial procedures, the procedure is more amenable and useful for research purposes. The individual LPAD varies from examinee to
examinee, from examiner to examiner, and from session to session. This
lack of consistency makes comparisons difficult, even within the same
subject. The group LPAD assessment procedure is of necessity more
structured, with less variability in the mediation, scoring, and examiner

interventions, making the baseline data available more appealing for research-oriented applications, but less clinically rich and revealing.

4. Group testing is more economical in that it enables the evaluation of groups of subjects simultaneously. Individual LPAD is potentially a lengthy and extensive process, and it is therefore often viewed as beyond the resource capacities of schools or other institutions. Under proper conditions, group LPAD can be used as an initial screening, to answer some of the first questions regarding student functioning and classroom pattern variables, with the identification of later interventions emerging from the "first picture" offered by the group procedure.

Target Populations and Essential Conditions for Group Testing

Group testing is not intended to replace individual assessment in those cases where the focus is on the difficulties experienced by the specific individual. The group LPAD assessment is appropriately employed with children, adolescents, and adults who are either functioning at a low level, or where general levels of functioning need to be explored, and among those who are able to function adequately in a group setting. The purpose of group testing under these conditions is to gather evidence regarding abilities and functioning that are not readily observed in manifest behavior.

Group testing is also an appropriate tool for assessing changes in learning ability and cognitive structures of students who have experienced special programs, as in a research paradigm. For example, it is often paired with Instrumental Enrichment (Feuerstein, 1980) as an indicator of pre- and posttreatment outcome effects. It can also serve to identify deficient cognitive functions in those learners who are performing at higher levels but have specific learning difficulties.

The group testing procedure of the LPAD can be considered appropriate and useful and complementary to the individual test format, subject to two critical conditions:

The "Mediational" Condition: Mediational intervention is necessarily more restricted in the group procedure. It is obviously not possible to individually mediate all members of the group. The procedure thus requires modified and limited mediation and less than fully responsive interactions during the subject's "independent work" responding to the tasks of the instruments. Therefore, the results obtained by the individual on the group test are considered meaningful to the extent that they demonstrate that the examinee is able to successfully use the training (mediation) provided in the test situation. In this respect, success is defined by the level of functioning achieved by an examinee on the criterion measures. A baseline of the individual's actual level of performance may be established, either on the criterion levels themselves or by data from other criteria and performance measures. The fact that an individual is able to achieve an adequate level of performance, or demonstrates changes in levels of performance, under the constraint of the limited interaction that occurs in the group LPAD must be regarded as a positive achievement, indicative of an ability to function in situations that provide only limited personal involvement. In a school classroom, for example, such an ability is necessary for adaptation, and hence, adequate performance on the LPAD in the group situation suggests a positive prognosis for adjustment to a school environment.

In the case of an individual who fails to perform adequately on the group LPAD, great caution should be exercised in the interpretation of the results. No decision concerning an individual's true potential to be modified should be made until evidence based on an individual assessment is available. Poor results on the group LPAD may occur because the training required by a particular individual is not provided or the group administration format, with its reduced opportunities for directed feedback, does not meet the individual's specific needs at that point. Whatever the reason for lack of response, individual assessment is mandatory to identify the deficiencies responsible for poor performance, further teaching needs, and capacity for modifiability.

The "Procedural" Condition: The second condition requires that the training phase be presented in a manner that will ensure the maximum possible efficiency. Despite the limitations imposed by the group situation, training must still be oriented toward the correction of deficient functions that are required by the specific tasks, as they are manifest in the various phases of the mental act: input, elaboration, and output. This orients to logistical procedures in the presentation of materials to the subjects (posters or transparencies to display attributes of sample tasks), structures the orientation to initial tasks and mediational phases of tasks, defines specific objectives to orient the examiner during the independent work on instruments, and includes debriefing procedures with the group following the completion of the independent work but prior to the re-testing phases. There are other considerations of logistics that are critical to achieving the objectives of the procedures. Among them are providing differentially structured scoring and data registration procedures, orienting the examiners in their use, and assigning sufficient examiners and/or assistants to monitor the processes and ensure maximal controlled intervention when required.

The Group Test Battery

As the result of many years of experimental and clinical experience, the following instruments have been used in the group LPAD format: Organization of Dots, Raven's Progressive Matrices, Complex Figure Drawing Test, Set Variations B-S to B-12, Set Variations I, Set Variations II, Representational Stencil Design Test, Positional Learning Test, Organizer, and Numerical Progressions.

A group assessment selects some, but seldom all, of these instruments for inclusion, subject to the considerations of time, needs of the students, and institutional structure variables. Order of presentation is also determined by the exigencies of the situation. Researchers, incorporating the LPAD battery into their programs, have also experimented with other instruments, some traditionally associated with the individual administration format (such as Word Memory, the Diffuse Attention Test, and Associative Recall), and other instruments not associated with the LPAD (e.g., standardized tests in cognitive functioning, assessment of academic skills, etc.).

Differentiating LPAD From Other Dynamic Assessment Methods

At the outset of this chapter, we indicated that the LPAD currently represents one among a number of approaches that are identified as dynamic in nature and structure. Although we cannot exhaustively differentiate and elaborate the reasons why we believe that the LPAD remains the approach that most completely fulfills the essential characteristics and requirements of a dynamic approach to assessment, we will here outline some of the more salient points on which the LPAD responds to the dynamic paradigm. It is our intent to deal with these issues much more systematically in forthcoming publications.

Some essential points that need to be addressed to understand the LPAD in the larger context of dynamic assessment are as follows:

1. Basic assumptions regarding the nature of intelligence
2. The types of changes that can or should be produced
3. The means to produce such changes
4. The criteria to evaluate changes
5. The nature of interventions
6. The structure of tasks
7. The role of the examiner
8. The relation to academic content and tasks

Assumptions About the Nature of Intelligence

The theory of SCM conceptualizes human intelligence as characterized by the option, possibility, and propensity to become meaningfully changed by experience, to be transformed by the production of new structures that were previously nonexistent or not efficiently used in the behavioral repertoire of the individual. This includes new ways of thinking and acting, as well as the generation of new need systems themselves. These structures can emerge in individuals in ways that may even be discontinuous for the individual, causing disequilibrium and stress. Contrary to some aspects of Vygotsky's (1978) concept of the zone of proximal development, the theory of SCM considers the possibility of producing cognitive structures that would not emerge in the individual without MLE.

Thus, SCM defines intelligence as the propensity of the organism to modify itself when confronted with the need to do so, in order to better adapt to increasingly new, complex situations of its existence. Intelligence is thus a state of the organism, in constant readiness for change

and adaptation, rather than a trait that has immutable and fixed properties. This definition places emphasis on the process of modifiability, opposed to other definitions that view intelligence as an object (cf. Spearman's g factor, which continues to receive contemporary attention
[Perkins, 1995], Gardner's 1993 concept of multiple intelligences, and
Sternberg's triarchic intelligences, 1985a).

The LPAD imposes the concept of process on the assessment of intelligence, as crucial element, first in understanding the essence of intelligence, and then in making possible the modifiability necessary for human adaptability. This quality of adaptational intelligence rests on the
experience of distance in dealing with the content of interactions with
the world. We contend that specific learning is of little value if it is not
accompanied with the processes necessary to transform specific content
experiences into sources of generalization, and that the generalization
must become transferable to the newly generated contents; with both
transformations dependent on process (Feuerstein, Feuerstein, & Shur,
in press). This elevates the importance of process-oriented activity of the
mind, which allows the individual to operate on the world to create temporal and spatial distances that are the sources for creation of mental
operations needed for more complex, richer, and multidirectional learning. A critical comparative dimension, across a number of parameters, is
therefore the extent to which the assessment procedure is either content-
or process-based, and thus the extent to which the content of the assessment tasks allows for or stimulates the needed modifiability that we hold
to be central to the process of defining and assessing intelligence.

Types of Changes Produced

At a basic level, the question can be posed as to whether the changes
produced are peripheral to the activity, or whether the changes represent
adaptations in the nature and structure of the adaptation of the organism.
We hold that the assessment process must look for (create the conditions,
stimulate, and elicit) types of changes that are related to the evolvement
of new strategies, new structures not immediately present in the repertoire of the individual but readily acquired and used, given appropriate
conditions. In this regard, the LPAD is not interested in changes in products (indices of performance), but rather in processes that become the
targets for change (see discussion of content and process above). Thus,

the major goal of the LPAD is to produce changes in the process and structure of functioning and to extrapolate from those changes to potential for modifiability and further adaptation.

The Means to Produce Changes

The changes produced by the assessment process are a function of several important conditions: the design of the procedure, the nature of the tasks presented to the examinee, the nature of the intervention structured into the procedure, and the role of the examiner in the assessment process. The LPAD has been explicitly designed and developed to reflect these variables in the observation and elicitation of the sample of changes reflecting structural cognitive modifiability. The basic structure of the LPAD procedure is designed to create the process-oriented approach necessary to produce samples of SCM, through the application of MLE. Interactions that are limited in their mediational flexibility, such as graduated prompting (Bransford et al., 1987; Campione & Brown, 1987) or the testing the limits approach of Carlson and Wiedl (1978, 1979) will not make possible the detection of the microchanges which can be produced in the individual on a variety of levels. We hold that dynamic assessment requires a "tight-knit net" that will catch even the smallest elements, at the same time it lets in the biggest. In the LPAD, we create the conditions for the individual to change in the largest sense of the term, but we do not want to lose the slightest indications of change as a sign of the existence of the propensity for modifiability. This means that it is important for dynamic assessment to find ways of going beyond and beneath the manifest levels of functioning.

Criteria to Evaluate Change

The evaluation of changes in performance and functioning is interrelated with a number of other variables: a definition of intelligence and capacity, the nature and structure of tasks, the kinds of interventions permitted by the procedure, and a framework for summarizing and interpreting the results (e.g., the product-oriented vs. process-oriented approach). In the LPAD, we add another important variable: whether the change is peripheral to the organism or affects the cognitive structure of the individual.

The four criterial indicators of the presence of structural change are:

1. *Retention/Permanence:* The maintaining of changes under similar task or stimulus presentation. This is manifested in reduced impulsivity, greater control of behavior during latency periods, and higher levels of sustained motivation for continued performance. Individuals who experience permanence in their cognitive structure sustain attention longer, suffer from less immediate fatigue, and seek continued opportunities to perform.

2. *Resistance:* The maintaining of change in situations that differ in time or space. This element describes the sustaining of the change in the face of situational or affective changes in the individual's experience with task or performance.

3. *Flexibility/Adaptability:* The opposite of resistance, in that the individual is able to modify or adapt previously learned structures to accommodate substantively different conditions, while retaining crucial elements previously learned, which are appropriately applied to the new situation. This element, the plasticity of changes, is applied to situations that present altered conditions.

4. *Generalizability/Transformability:* Acquired structures are applied to a broad set of situations and tasks, reflecting an abstract, representational function of the act. They can be specific to context, as in what can be termed *near transfer,* or related to a more generalized, abstracted aspect of the task, *far transfer.* The ability of individuals to manifest this element in their responses to learning exposure suggests the propensity for higher, formal mental operations. This can be observed in task performance and responses. For their further manifestation in learning tasks and subsequent performance, they must be structured into the dynamic assessment process in order to assess the presence of structural cognitive change.

The degree to which these criterial elements, or as they have been called elsewhere (Feuerstein, 1995) *qualitative parameters of change,* are present in the functioning of the subject is an important indicator of the subject's modifiability in a structural, rather than peripheral, manner. In the LPAD, changes in specific task performance are continuously—at the outset and throughout the assessment process—assessed in relation to changes in generalized, higher-order thought processes. Indeed, the mediational interventions offered the learner are designed to build in some of these changes so that they can be observed in subsequent performance.

The LPAD is designed to provide information so that changes in performance are observed, described, and analyzed within domains of functioning (related to a delineation of the cognitive functions) and along parameters of meaningful performance. When scores are obtained, they are used as descriptive of change, from baseline to various degrees of postintervention performance. They are not meant to be considered normative or comparative, which we consider to be external to the performance of the subject being assessed. It is in this context that we express our concern that to the extent that approaches to dynamic assessment focus on task performance, attempt to preserve psychometric properties of the assessment, and limit the mediational interventions, they will inevitably limit the creation of conditions for structural cognitive change, with restrictions on criterial elements for observation and assessment. This is reflected in the model, design, and implementation of the LPAD.

The Nature of Interventions

Providing mediational intervention to clarify and elaborate a subject's performance is considered a central aspect of the dynamic assessment process. In the LPAD, mediation is designed to be flexible, adaptive to the responses of the subject, and directed toward producing structural change. Intervention is oriented to observing change as the subject responds to further similar and somewhat different tasks, and it is required to generalize from the task to underlying cognitive concepts. This requires the examiner to be flexible and willing to invest and interact with the subject, to encourage, stimulate, and merge with the subject, on cognitive as well as emotional and affective levels. Any approaches that constrict or script the interventions to fit within predetermined standards (see references to *graduated prompting, testing the limits* above) or control feedback within the task structure (see, for example, Guthke's 1992 "learning test" approach, also in Guthke & Stein, 1996) will not provide the conditions to elicit the full propensity for modifiability within the individual.

The Structure of the Tasks

To achieve the goals of dynamic assessment, the tasks must be selected and built into the instruments with careful regard to the nature of the functions to be observed and mediated, as well as methodological and philosophical considerations. This has been described in earlier sections of this chapter.

The Role of the Examiner

The LPAD examiner must possess an extensive and varied repertoire of cognitive as well as affective responses, formulated as modalities of intervention to be used in response to observed deficiencies in cognitive functions and mental operations, according to the parameters that have been identified and described above. The LPAD instruments are vehicles for the production of change, but the examiner uses the instruments to adapt, modify, and innovate to pursue potential change or teach a requisite skill that can facilitate a mental operation and contribute to a potential structural change.

Relation to Academic Content and Tasks

A question has been raised in cognitive education regarding the extent to which the tasks of assessment should be closely related to the specific academic or functional task dimensions to which the subject is expected to respond in the world of school or work—which has been termed *domain specific*. This has been contrasted to a focus on tasks and functions that are more generalized, presumed to be common to all processes and to be related to mental operations and generic cognitive functions. We have addressed above what we consider to be the critical need for the creation of distance in the cognitive learning experience of the individual, to facilitate the development of higher-order mental processing and the uniquely human and creative capacities of the individual. It is our view that selecting tasks from a domain-specific perspective minimizes the experience of cognitive distance for the learner and thus restricts the learning experience and the ability of the assessment procedure to clearly identify crucial elements of cognitive functioning and modifiability. The tasks of the instruments composing the LPAD are therefore designed to assess generalized prerequisite mental operations and modalities of functioning; they are only secondarily or inferentially related to specific academic or other content. Any attempt to make dynamic assessment contingent upon crystallized products of educational and instruction process will of necessity and unavoidably limit the open and flexible assessment of cognitive and functional modifiability, as the experience with the process will be restricted to static curriculum models and performance expectations.

Current and Future Problems for Study

The development of the LPAD is a dynamic process, with the instrument undergoing continual refinement, extension, and elaboration. We will briefly identify several of what we consider to be critical concerns for current activities and the future development of dynamic assessment:

Application of Dynamic Assessment to the Needs of Developing Countries: The paradigm of dynamic assessment needs to be considered in dealing with the rapid technological developments impinging on many nations and cultures, where assessment and evaluation methods must be developed to identify individuals' propensity and eligibility for higher levels of functioning. Static measurement dooms the individual to being considered on the basis of present levels of skills, of existent modalities of problem-solving behavior, and it creates great areas of inadequate information. The LPAD presents opportunities to develop and use tools to reveal the true capacities of the individual and the propensity of individuals to acquire prerequisites of functioning in newly developed areas of technological and cultural adaptation. We have observed the relevance of this issue in a variety of studies and projects with Ethiopian immigrants adapting to Israeli culture and life. There is great potential for these applications in many other areas of the world, both technologically advanced and developing.

Expansion of the Battery: The battery of instruments has expanded and developed since the first publications on the LPAD (Feuerstein, 1979). We have made possible the broader and more precise assessment of cognitive modifiability and improved the linkage from the assessment process to the identification of and focus on prescriptive and remediational strategies. This development includes elaborating instruments in the logico-verbal and numerical modalities, using a variety of operations in accordance with the LPAD model.

Upward and Downward Extensions of the Instruments: Initial instruments and techniques were designed for use with culturally deprived adolescents, regardless of the distal etiology for their manifest levels of functioning. Over more than two decades of development and clinical experience, the LPAD approach has been expanded to apply to a wide range of populations and age ranges: (a) to populations experiencing clinical, psychopathological difficulties, as in schizophrenia; (b) to preschool and primary school-age children and to university students and adults; (c) to populations as diverse as those requiring physical and developmental rehabilitation, those experiencing severe disability due to genetic chromosomal differences, occupational change, and adjustment in adults, and to individuals adjusting to cultural and societal discontinuity; (d) for higher range cognitive functioning as represented at college level and advanced occupational adjustment, and for the general enhancement of intellective production and performance.

Preferential Modalities: An area of significant interest requiring further research is the determination of individual preferences for learning through specific modalities and mediation. That individuals differ in their optimal use of specific modalities of information processing is well-known and understood. Our current efforts are directed toward the development and expansion of profiles of modifiability to address this question, with particular emphasis on studying the influence of various conditions of MLE on modifiability.

Affective-Energetic Factors: Although the LPAD is focused on the study of the cognitive structure and functions, we in no way neglect the interaction between affective and cognitive elements in the behavior of the individual. There is a growing appreciation (see Goleman, 1995) of how self-image and affective, motivational, and other factors interact with cognitive behavior to achieve a more precise prescription of remediation strategies. Our work, and the work of many others—in particular referring to MLE—continues to be directed toward an understanding of the specific weight of such factors and how they must be recognized within the dynamic assessment process.

Validity Studies: One of our early concerns was the question of in vitro versus in vivo validity. There is no question that during the test sessions, changes occur in response to mediational interventions. Examinees who become modified within the test situation quite obviously leave the concrete and task-bound level and are able to function with an abstract, internalized, representational conceptual thinking that was inaccurately and unjustly considered inaccessible to them previously. But to what extent and under what conditions will modification achieved within the test situation predict later performance in academic and real-life settings? The question of whether the LPAD procedure can attain degrees of reliability and validity might be answered by asking another question: Under what conditions can and should one test for validity? We continue to study this issue and search for relevant and meaningful answers.

Summary and Conclusions

The LPAD is a needed and necessary alternative to traditional psychometrically based assessment practices. It was a first, initially modest beginning to address complex issues connected to the core of human functioning in educational and social contexts. After many years of clinical experience and experimental study, it remains a well-articulated and focused technique and process to continue the exploration into better alternatives for assessment, placement, intervention, and consultation.

The first area that benefits from a dynamic assessment of cognitive functions is the study and deeper understanding of the widely used constructs of intelligence and capacity. The nature of these constructs is as much in dispute today as it was 60 or more years ago. It is only when we view these concepts and processes from the perspective of changes that may be produced in the nature, quality, and quantity of mental processes under specific conditions of manipulations and intervention that we gain needed clarity. It is under such search and scrutiny that the components of the mental act and their prerequisites for mastery become evident. The limits imposed by age, structure, and the state of the human organism may be better understood as to their central or peripheral nature. Such a philosophy challenges many of the established conceptions and permits the dissipation of many stereotypes prevalent today in developmental and differential psychology. Thus, from this perspective, we define and treat intelligence as a state rather than a stable and fixed set of traits. It is for this reason that we have shifted the emphasis in aspects of our theoretical focus from potential to propensity and reflect this in the changed name of our procedure—the Learning *Propensity* Assessment Device.

Because the examiner—as mediator—is the one to produce samples of change in the cognitive structure, he or she must be in possession of an extensive and varied repertoire of cognitive concepts, tools, and operations that will serve to better understand the functioning of the examinee. A thorough mastery of the list of deficient cognitive functions, manifesting themselves in the failure of the individual to solve problems; the use of the cognitive map to analyze the characteristics of the task; and the rich and varied modalities of mediation aimed at producing the desired changes all become necessary parts of the LPAD as a dynamic assessment process.

Another area of contribution is a better understanding of culturally determined differences between groups, as revealed by cross-cultural studies. These studies, which mainly use static measures for the description of differences, may bring more relevant information to active consideration once they add a dynamic dimension, focusing on the problem of how such differences could and should be leveled by a process of modification. This is especially necessary considering the rapid changes occurring in societies where development requires adaptation to modalities of functioning that are uniformly based on conceptualized, abstract, and efficient operational thinking. The LPAD has the potential of providing information regarding the extent to which changes are necessary or desirable, the preferential modalities by which a given cultural subgroup may best be modified, and the amount and kind of investment necessary to attain this goal. A most desirable product of such an approach would be how such changes could take place without altering dimensions, attributes, and characteristics vital for and inherent to the cultural identity of the subgroup.

Finally, dynamic assessment, provided through the methodology and procedures of the LPAD, as presented in this chapter and available through well-described and detailed publication and training processes, becomes a source of direct and immediate help for all individuals whose current level of functioning is the basis for far-reaching decisions, of import to the individual him- or herself and to the society in which that individual may contribute. It is not too much to say that such decisions are crucial to both individual and group destinies. It is here that dynamic assessment, and all that it entails, has the potential for systemic impact when it is developed further, implemented in broader and more integral ways, and disseminated to those constituencies in need.

At the outset of this chapter we referred to Ramey and MacPhee, who, in 1981, proposed the question as to whether the LPAD represented a new paradigm for assessment, based on a new conception of learning and intelligence. The development and further implementation of the LPAD, and the years of clinical experience on a worldwide basis, now permit us to say yes, it can and does—if and when it is given the chance. The conditions can be created, and the tools are available.

5 Linking Assessment to Intervention With Instrumental Enrichment

YVETTE JACKSON
JOHN E. LEWIS
REUVEN FEUERSTEIN
RONALD J. SAMUDA

Analysis of achievement scores suggest that a large percentage of our students in urban areas exhibit symptoms of inadequate performance on academic tasks and the new demands of the workplace. Two groups compose this pool of "at-risk" students: those identified as requiring special education services and those whose achievement declines to total academic failure. Although both groups arrive at this situation due to different causes and may exhibit different pathologies, they share the misfortune of lacking the skills and adaptive behavior necessary for academic achievement and productive citizenship. These students are deemed to represent the lower end of a "normal" distribution of intelligence and achievement.

Students classified at the lower end of the intellectual spectrum are often labeled dysfunctional, and the educational system then attempts to provide them with the kind of curriculum that would lead to limited growth in performance, justifying low expectations and concomitant separate, lower-level instruction. However, such instructional programs do not address the causes of the dysfunctions identified by the tests, resulting in an incongruence between assessment and instruction. The incongruence is a result of the tests themselves, because they yield limited information about the learning process, teaching treatment, and student potential (Hilliard, 1982). In summary, the standardized tests themselves are insufficient and inappropriate in such situations.

162

There has recently been a movement by the federal government to reform the entire assessment process and its relationship to instruction as a means of improving student learning (Applebome, 1997). This movement is requiring changes in the beliefs of teachers, clinicians, and other support staff regarding the development of potential and in assessment procedures for identifying and documenting potential; the focus of instruction must move from content acquisition to the learning process itself.

The groundwork for this reform has been most profoundly developed through the work of Reuven Feuerstein, whose theory of cognitive modifiability provides the radical shift from a static to a dynamic process for mediating the intellectual performance of students. This line of research emerged from Feuerstein's pioneering enterprise with Down's syndrome children. The implications of his findings are that with mediation, *all* children can succeed at intellectually demanding tasks.

Two approaches form the foundation of Feuerstein's methodology, namely, the Learning Potential Assessment Device (LPAD), a test-teach-test process where assessment is transformed to engage the student in a learning/testing process that demonstrates the potential for learning (instead of what the student has failed to learn); and Instrumental Enrichment (IE), the instructional mediation program that addresses the deficient cognitive functions identified through LPAD. This program provides a reflective process for the learner to acquire skills and strategies for self-correction and intrinsic motivation.

The development of the LPAD has made it possible to isolate and identify the nature of deficient cognitive functions at the core of reduced cognitive performance. The LPAD is designed to be much more than an assessment method. It also serves as a diagnostic tool by which specific cognitive deficiencies are pinpointed. Identifying specific cognitive functions allows one to use a planned, directive intervention strategy focused on the needs of the individual. This intervention strategy, IE, is based on the application of the theory of Mediated Learning Experience (MLE) and serves to generate cognitive modifiability, thereby improving an individual's performance on cognitive tasks. The theoretical basis for IE is the same as for the LPAD: MLE can produce structural cognitive modifiability.

The systematic use of the IE program can improve or fill in the cognitive gaps that were discovered during the dynamic LPAD assessment.

The findings concerning the learning propensity of individuals assessed by the LPAD provides the basis for IE. The program is designed to attack directly cognitive deficiencies that are responsible for low performance on the LPAD or other assessment measures. This linkage between the LPAD and IE is predicated on various elements in the teaching-learning process that are common to both LPAD test and IE lesson situations. These common elements, or mediational processes, encompass improvement of deficient cognitive functions; preparation for higher order learning through the establishment of prerequisite functioning; behavioral regulation; development of reflection, insight, and analytical thinking; teaching of cognitive operations and content; provision of performance feedback; and the establishment of appropriate communication skills. The main goal of IE is to increase the capacity of individuals to become modifiable by: (a) exposing them directly to stimuli and experiences provided by encountering life experiences and (b) involving them with formal and informal learning situations.

A description of the IE program constitutes the focus of this chapter. In addition, the principles outlined lead to an overview of how the program can be applied. An example of such an application is presented by examining the use of an IE program in the Atlanta, Georgia, school system.

Instrumental Enrichment

IE consists of predominantly figural and symbolic exercises divided into categories called instruments. A teacher acts as a mediator and interacts with students to guide and interpret the processes carried out in the exercises. These interactions allow the teacher to dynamically assess students' difficulties or learning changes, which are demonstrated as the students apply problem-solving processes to perform the tasks.

Teachers mediate learning in several ways. First, teachers expose students to dimensions of experiences important for more complex and long-term aspects of their development. Second, teachers provide an understanding of the instructions so that the students realize that they are not just carrying out commands but are actively involved in the reasoning process. Third, teachers select stimuli that are meaningful and establish patterns of attention to ensure appropriate focusing behavior, the capacity to efficiently register and correlate relevant data. Fourth, teachers schedule the appearance and disappearance of stimuli/material to develop significant temporal factors (e.g., concepts of time/temporal distance and temporal order). Teachers also mediate positive or negative anticipation as an outcome of a student's own experiences. They provide models that students can imitate so that their capacity to become affected and modified through direct exposure later in life will be greater. Teachers, also, provide specific culturally determined material important for growth and orientation in a student's search for new elements in the learning experience. Teachers develop the need to share and communicate new perceptions and experiences. They also repeat and vary educational processes so students' interactions become more voluntary and innovative. They guide individuals to incorporate past and possible future sources of information to enrich and expand their own experiences. Finally, teachers develop comparative behavior through verbal interaction.

The interaction around the IE instruments encourages the development of the cognitive functions to enhance learning situations throughout life. These include: isolating problems, redefining a problem to ensure accuracy, using a systematic search for information, creating visual transport (mental images), forecasting, solving a problem and interacting for verification, comparing, evaluating relevant and irrelevant information, testing hypotheses, orienting things in space, proving, synthesizing information, analytic perception, and labeling. These functions are focused on throughout the instruments.

The instruments are organized into three categories: (a) nonverbal, (b) limited vocabulary/reading skills, and (c) verbal, independent reading skills. Nonverbal instruments include Organization of Dots, Analytic Perception, and Illustrations. Instruments requiring limited vocabulary and reading skills include Orientation in Space, Family Relations, Comparisons, Classifications, Numerical Progressions, and Representational Stencil Design. Instruments requiring independent reading include Temporal Relations, Instructions, Transitive Relations, and Syllogisms. Each instrument has a specific task and focus.

Organization of Dots

Task

The instrument consists of paper-and-pencil exercises designed to identify and outline several geometric shapes hidden in an amorphous array of dots. The spacing of the shapes, their position, and the amount and type of distracting elements become progressively complex and remain challenging even for the most astute learner. The objective is to teach and provide specific practice in projecting virtual relationships. A sample page is shown in Figure 5.1.

Focus

To identify shapes, learners must be able to use a number of cognitive processes. These include finding the relationship among objects (dots) that are in themselves discrete entities. To accomplish this task, learners must take an active role. They must be motivated to seek out relationships and meanings that are not obvious as important characteristics of the stimuli. This task develops a need to organize and make meanings among stimuli that may initially appear unrelated. Learners come to realize that the object remains the same, although its placement or position in relation to other items may have changed. Learners scan the model, represent it visually, and transport the visual image from short-term memory to the stimulus field. It must then be evaluated, overlapped, and compared with what is in the field. This cognitive process helps to determine where it fits. Learners must identify the precise dimension, size, and parallelism of the figures. In addition, an identification of the parts that are essential to the formation of the figure is necessary. Learners must then filter out elements that may be similar, yet do not correspond exactly to the criteria of the figure and must be able to separate elements that are overlapping or close together but do not belong to the same figure. Finally, to complete the task successfully, learners must formulate a strategic plan for completion, one that restrains impulsivity. This instrument provides opportunities for the performance of several cognitive operations: differentiation, segregation, organization by restructuring the field, and hypothetical as well as inferential thinking.

Orientation in Space I, II, III

Task

Orientation in Space consists of three levels of paper and pencil tasks where learners must differentiate between the spatial frame of reference and other criteria and toward the introduction and demonstration of the

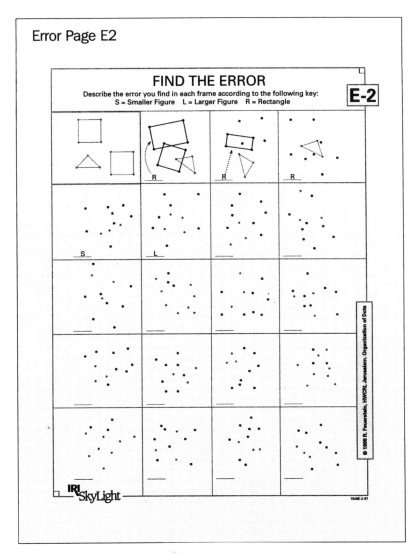

Figure 5.1. Teacher's Guide to Organization of Dots
SOURCE: Feuerstein (1995). Reprinted by permission.

relativity of certain systems as contrasted with the stability of others. The objective of the three levels is to provide a stable, albeit relative, system of reference in order to describe spatial relationships.

First, learners must identify the relationship between the position of objects (front/back, left/right) and the figure of a boy in a picture. The task becomes more abstract as it moves away from concrete figures to symbolic representations. In the second level, concepts such as up, down, between, and beside are added to describe the orientation of an object. In addition, learners must also produce statements describing the object's position from different points of view. In the third level, the four constants of north, south, east, and west are introduced as stable coordinates that can be used in describing the position of an object in space. These coordinates are then related to the directions learned in level I. Next, the body's internalized relationship in space and the fixed interrelationship of the points of the compass is reinforced. In the final sections of the instrument, learners are required to use several sources of information to follow or plot movement itineraries. A sample page is shown in Figure 5.2.

Focus

Through this modality, learners begin to develop an understanding of the relativity of perception and perspective, that these are dependent upon position in space. The main purpose of Orientation in Space is to correct the limited use of articulated, differentiated, and representational spatial dimensions. To master the tasks presented in this instrument, learners must be able to perceive objects and movement without having their own body as the point of reference. Learners must be able to perceive the environment from the perspective of another person or object. They must, in addition, become flexible by differentiating between stable/fixed and flexible/relative relationships. They must come to understand that the relationship between location and object is relative to the point from which the object is being perceived. Learners must use both stable and relativistic frames of reference, as well as internalized and representational movements to plan and conceptualize the outcome of each task. In addition, they must exercise the skills developed in the Organization of Dots, in particular, defining the problem, projection of virtual relationships, and conservation of constancy.

Overall, the Orientation in Space instrument aims to develop spatial orientation, ability to use multiple sources of information, ability to verbalize and follow specific instructions, and the flexibility required to con-

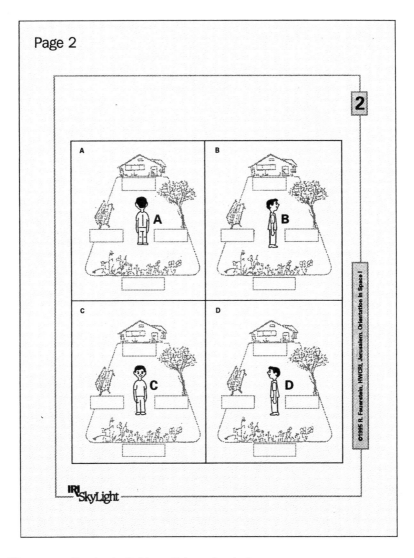

Figure 5.2. Teacher's Guide to Orientation in Space
SOURCE: Feuerstein (1995). Reprinted by permission.

sider various aspects of the environment from differing points of view. The cognitive processes developed through this instrument also have social implications. By learning to consider another perspective, learners are drawn away from egocentricity and become potentially capable of empathy.

Comparisons

Task

The objective of this instrument is to develop comparative behavior. A sample page from this instrument is shown in Figure 5.3. The instrument consists of exercises that require learners to analyze a set of items and determine the most critical similarities and/or differences among them. The tasks initially require comparison on the basis of single, discrete dimensions such as shape, quantity, and temporal and spatial placement, to those of abstract attributes such as function and composition. These tasks progressively lead to more complex comparisons requiring the consideration of stimuli on several dimensions simultaneously. These comparisons are based on classification by class and superordinate category.

Focus

To make comparisons, learners must mentally superimpose one stimulus on the other, identify the aspects of the stimuli that are identical in all possible dimensions, and determine the locus and direction of difference among any divergent elements. To complete the task, they must determine the most salient similarities and/or differences between the stimuli and then verbalize these differences using precise, exact wording. Learners must be able to thoroughly and systematically scrutinize all aspects of the stimuli, paying close attention to all details, to obtain relevant information for analysis. They must be able to discriminate, perceive, and formulate the differences among characteristics of the stimuli along dimensions of equal-unequal and similar-dissimilar. They must organize the results of the analysis into categories from the most broad to the most specific. Last, learners must decide which categories are most characteristic of the relationship between the stimuli in order to plan and produce the correct response. They also must formulate hypotheses about the relationships among stimuli sets, consider the stable and rela-

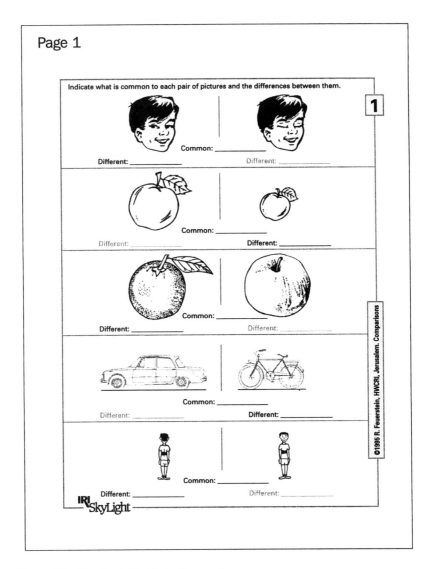

Figure 5.3. Teacher's Guide to Comparisons
SOURCE: Feuerstein (1995). Reprinted by permission.

tive attributes of the items, simultaneously consider several sources of information, and produce definitive verbal responses.

Internalized automatic use of comparisons is one of the methods by which we are able to learn from direct exposure to stimuli. Making comparisons hones the perceptual skills of the person, enabling a more precise and detailed awareness of the environment. Comparative behavior allows for the deduction of relationships between seemingly unrelated objects or events, enabling the learner to become aware of and comprehend the rules that govern various social and environmental relationships.

Categorization

Task

The goal of this categorization is to engender spontaneous categorizing behavior. To assimilate and accommodate information to preexisting schemas, learners must be able to identify and process the rules most critical to the schema and new stimulus. Without comprehension of the rules that govern various phenomena, the ability to alter, transform, and apply existing information to a novel situation, or the ability to create knowledge, is impaired.

The instrument consists of exercises where learners must progress from categorizing and labeling objects according to set membership, to categorization based on predefined and self-defined principles. Learners must also progress from assigning the same object to diverse categories based on various sets of rules to presenting the information in diagram form. A sample page is shown in Figure 5.4.

Focus

This instrument demands that learners use a reflective style of thinking, rather than responding to the immediate sensory aspects of the stimuli. Learners have to compare objects and categories, identify the invariant aspects of the categories and subsume the objects within a category based on shared underlying characteristics of seemingly unrelated entities. They must use abilities such as precision, systematic labeling, comparison, and discrimination among stimuli, consideration of multiple sources of information, selection of the most relevant information, hypothetical and analytical thinking, virtual projection of relationships,

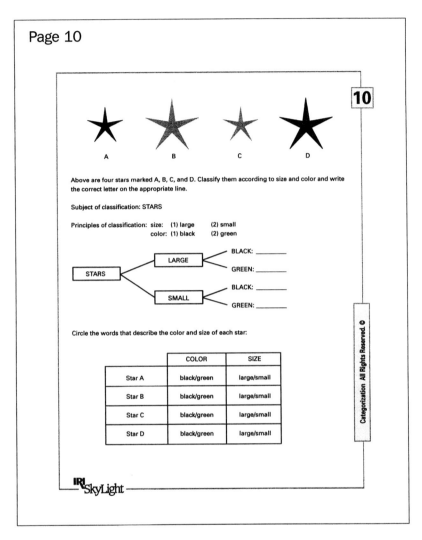

Figure 5.4. Teacher's Guide to Categorization
SOURCE: Feuerstein (1995). Reprinted by permission.

planning, inhibition of impulsive behavior, and organized representation of responses in a verbal or diagrammatic format.

Analytic Perception

Task

The objectives of Analytic Perception focus on the teaching of strategies for articulation and differentiation. In addition, the teaching of integration and synthesis is provided. The exercises require learners to use inductive and deductive reasoning. They are required to dissect a whole into its component parts, to identify the parts belonging to a specific whole, and to compose a whole out of parts. A sample page is shown in Figure 5.5.

Analytic Perception uses perceptual processes to develop a variety of cognitive strategies that lead to attitudinal and motivational changes. Individuals learn to differentiate themselves from their context and develop an internal frame of reference. The establishment of an internal frame of reference fosters an individual's ability to structure and restructure situations on his or her own.

Focus

This instrument focuses on learners' abilities to hypothesize about relationships between objects and to comprehend that the nature of any given relationship is flexible, defined by, and dependent on, the context within which the relationship is being considered. Furthermore, learners must come to understand that the parts themselves, as they relate to the whole, may be perceived and defined as required by the given situation. To master the tasks in this instrument, learners must be able to (a) divide a whole into its component parts; (b) determine a relationship between a set of objects to construct a whole object; (c) systematically compare, (d) categorize, and (e) define problems; (f) formulate hypotheses; (g) plan and carry out strategies; (h) orient in space; (i) use precise labels; (j) consider multiple sources of information simultaneously; and (k) control impulsive behavior. Overall, Analytic Perception attempts to modify the processes by which learners perceive their environment and understand reality by developing a flexible, perceptual, and organizational processing style.

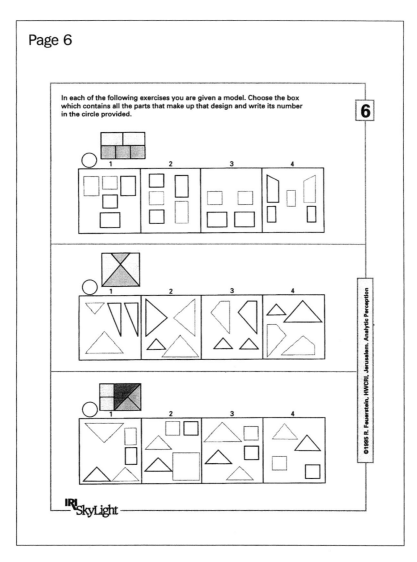

Figure 5.5. Teacher's Guide to Analytic Perception
SOURCE: Feuerstein (1995). Reprinted by permission.

Family Relations

Task

The purpose of this instrument is to use kinship as a vehicle for teaching conceptualized relationships. A sample page is shown in Figure 5.6. The exercises in this instrument require individuals to identify the relationships that exist within the family, using graphic representation. The format of the instrument resembles a genogram. This instrument determines the role of one individual within a family pattern, then identifies and determines the multiple roles one individual may have within the family. It permits learners to recognize and use the concepts of symmetrical and asymmetrical relationships in perception and organization of the family and to express the logical reasoning upon which these relationships are based.

Focus

Like Analytic Perception, Family Relations focuses on the exploration of the relativity and flexibility of objects and relationships. To successfully complete the exercises, individuals must be able to use precise definitions and labels; orient in space and time; work in a systematic fashion; identify and define the specific problem; plan out and enact a course of action; project horizontal, vertical, symmetrical, asymmetrical, and hierarchical relationships; search for and use relevant information; categorize; formulate hypotheses; make inferences; consider multiple sources of information simultaneously; and express the solution verbally, through logic-based statements. In particular, learners need to overcome an episodic grasp of reality by projecting relationships between two or more elements. Overall, this instrument, through relating analytical and flexible thinking to the familiar context of family relations, serves to further engender within learners a flexible, analytic, perceptual processing style and to transform passive, unwilling learners into active critical participants within their world.

Temporal Relations

Task

This instrument develops learners' need and ability to use temporal concepts to describe and order their experiences. It contains five sections,

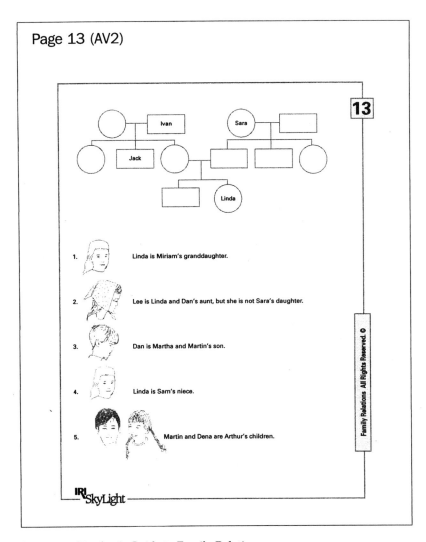

Figure 5.6. Teacher's Guide to Family Relations
SOURCE: Feuerstein (1995). Reprinted by permission.

or units, each concentrated on a particular aspect of temporal relations. A sample page is shown in Figure 5.7. The first section deals with time as a stable system of reference and distance as a situationally defined system. It concludes with velocity, or the expression of the relationship between time and distance. Learners must identify, isolate, and discover the relationship between the three factors.

In Unit 2, the objective measures of time (i.e., hours, days, seasons) are presented. Learners are required to categorize increments of time in a hierarchical and serial fashion and to identify and define the relationship between different time units. In Unit 3, learners must further work with the concept of temporal sequence and its relative status within an overall stable system of reference. They are required to identify the direction and historical placement (past, present, future) of an event, including the relationship to their own life.

In the fourth unit, the skills of Analytic Perception and Family Relations are used by presenting the possibility of a subjective view of an objective phenomenon (time span). Learners are required to use concepts of early, late, before, and after and to explore the affective ramifications of these concepts as they relate to time. In the final unit, synchronous and asynchronous events, along with cause and effect relationships, are explored. Learners are required to determine whether the possibility exists that a given set of events entails a cause and effect relationship.

Focus

The Temporal Relations Instrument is geared toward correcting any deficits in the perception of relationships, particularly deficits in orienting to time. Learners must manipulate abstract concepts, using operations such as summative behavior, quantification, comparison, ordering, and categorization. They must be able to perceive the need for identifying and gathering all possible relevant sources of information, to define, describe, and express information precisely, to consider multiple sources of information simultaneously; to use symbolic representation of relationships; to use logical, hypothetical, and divergent thinking to make inferences and predictions of outcomes; and to move between and identify relationships among different systems of reference. Learners must also distinguish between what is necessary and what is sufficient, seek precise information, and express hypothetical relationships and conclusions through logical, verbal statements.

Numerical Progressions

Task

In Numerical Progressions, a new dimension is added to the conceptualization of relationships. This new dimension focuses on the rules and

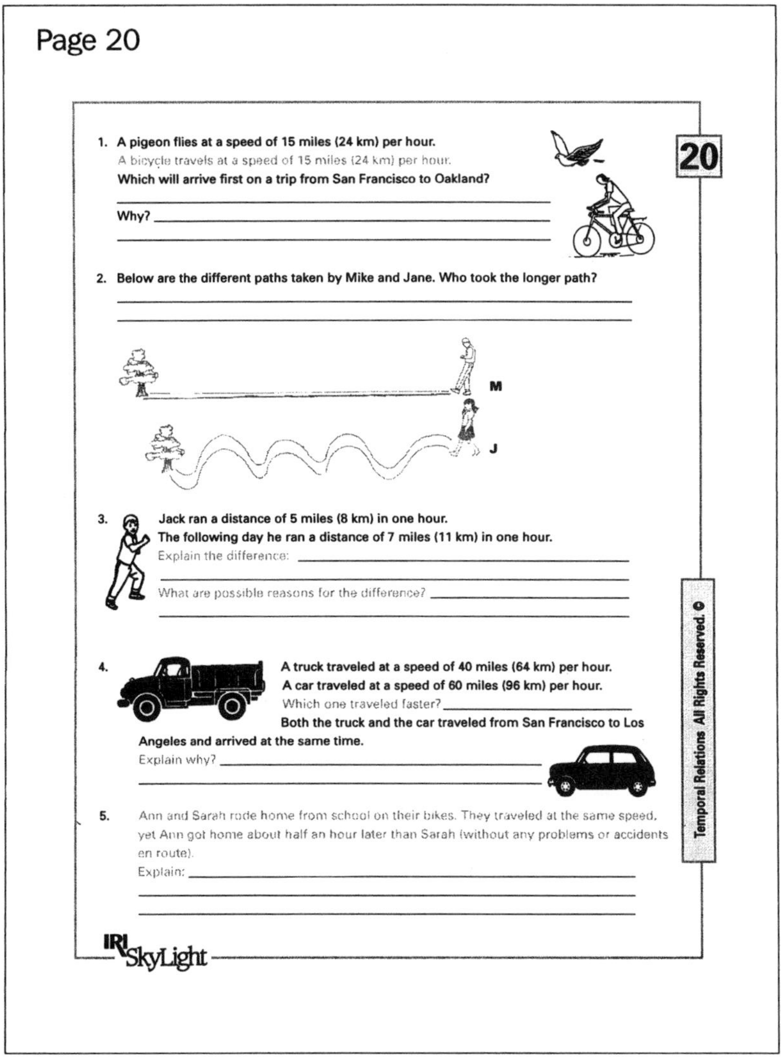

Page 20

1. A pigeon flies at a speed of 15 miles (24 km) per hour.
   A bicycle travels at a speed of 15 miles (24 km) per hour.
   Which will arrive first on a trip from San Francisco to Oakland?
   _____
   Why? _____

   20

2. Below are the different paths taken by Mike and Jane. Who took the longer path?
   _____

   M

   J

3. Jack ran a distance of 5 miles (8 km) in one hour.
   The following day he ran a distance of 7 miles (11 km) in one hour.
   Explain the difference: _____

   What are possible reasons for the difference? _____

4. A truck traveled at a speed of 40 miles (64 km) per hour.
   A car traveled at a speed of 60 miles (96 km) per hour.
   Which one traveled faster? _____
   Both the truck and the car traveled from San Francisco to Los
   Angeles and arrived at the same time.
   Explain why? _____

5. Ann and Sarah rode home from school on their bikes. They traveled at the same speed,
   yet Ann got home about half an hour later than Sarah (without any problems or accidents
   en route).
   Explain: _____
   _____
   _____

IRI SkyLight

Figure 5.7. Teacher's Guide to Temporal Relations
SOURCE: Feuerstein (1995). Reprinted by permission.

rhythms that govern relationships. The main objective of the instrument is to develop the need to perceive separate objects and events as being linked in a relationship that can be deduced. A sample page is shown in Figure 5.8.

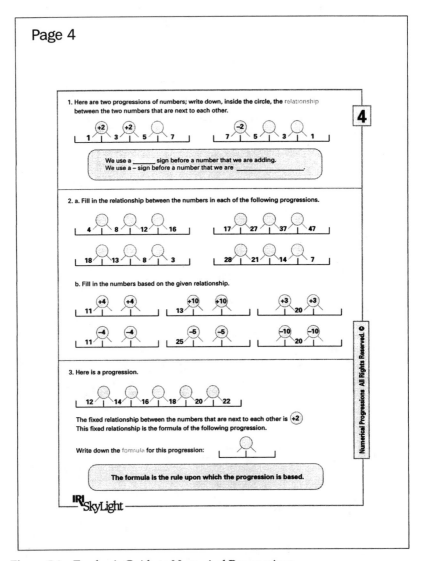

Figure 5.8. Teacher's Guide to Numerical Progressions
SOURCE: Feuerstein (1995). Reprinted by permission.

This instrument requires learners to establish a relationship and sub-sequently a rhythm or pattern. This pattern produces a repetition of the relationship between events. Learners must identify and verbalize the rule by which the pattern is generated in the entire set of events. They must then construct or complete a set of events based upon that rule.

Focus

The focus of the Numerical Progressions is to counter an episodic grasp of reality and help a person to understand that it is possible to deduce the link or relationship between discrete entities. Learners must have a basic grasp of numbers and be able to identify the problem, formulate hypotheses, and search in a systematic fashion for the relevant characteristics that may reveal a rule common to all objects. They must be precise in their definitions and hypothetical statements and must be able to discriminate, compare, and reserve judgment until all of the information has been gathered and considered. Learners must be able to use the newly identified rules to generate original data. They must also recognize higher order relationships and encode them, use multiple sources of information simultaneously, and compare and draw conclusions based on logical evidence.

Overall, this instrument helps to develop a sense of empowerment. Learners perceive that it is possible to generate information and discover the rules governing relationships. Through careful data gathering and systematized hypothetical information processing, learners are taught that they are capable of figuring out the rules governing most interactions in their world, through observation and analysis of events. Knowledge of these rules will enable them to actively control events rather than being passive recipients.

Instructions

Task

This instrument has as its main objective decoding and encoding. Written instructions are decoded, elaborated, and translated into a graphic modality. This instrument is one of the few that require intensive verbal work and verbal communication. It contains verbally oriented exercises where learners are required to carefully read an instruction and carry it out. A sample page is shown in Figure 5.9.

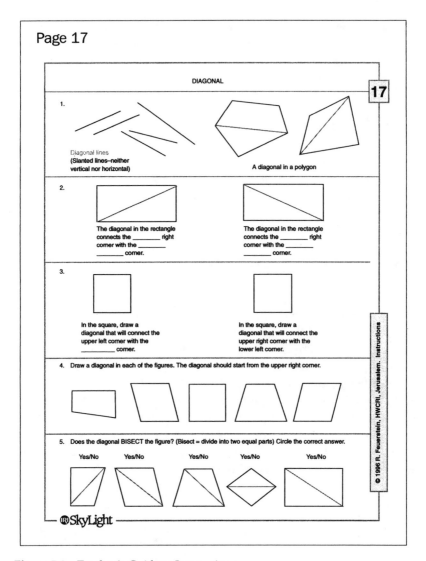

Figure 5.9. Teacher's Guide to Instructions
SOURCE: Feuerstein (1996). Reprinted by permission.

Focus

Planning behavior, restriction of impulsivity, and thorough, systematic working through of problems is enforced. Learners must be able to read the instructions, gather and attend to all relevant aspects of the information provided, and organize and sequence information required in relationships. They must actively seek out relevant information contained in the instructions, label all objects precisely and accurately, formulate a plan of action, and systematically carry out that plan.

Learners must be able to orient in time and space, use representational processing, make comparisons and inferences, encode visual stimuli and decode verbal instructions, follow through on a sequence of behaviors, and differentiate the rules governing several overlapping relationships. Learners must also be able to discern the need for precision, clarification, and elimination of ambiguities in gathering information and carrying out any other interactions. Overall, the goal of Instructions is to strengthen the systematic processing of information throughout the three phases of cognition (input, elaboration, output) by the development of controlled planning behavior and hypothetically representational processing.

Illustrations

Task

Illustrations is a collection of discrete exercises that require learners to perceive, recognize, and solve specific problems requiring the use of cognitive processes developed through the other instruments. The instrument is a collection of situations in which problems leading to disequilibrium must be perceived and recognized. An attempt is then made by the learner to restore equilibrium by solving the problem. The exercises consist of cartoon illustrations similar to those found in comic strips. A sample page is shown in Figure 5.10.

Focus

The humorous and often absurd nature of the illustrations produces a disruption in the cognitive equilibrium of the person, creating an internalized need to identify and solve a problem. To generate explanations for what makes the illustrations humorous, as well as to produce the solutions appropriate to each illustration, learners must focus their perception, attend to details, use relevant cues, and make inferences about relationships and behaviors. In addition, they must understand

Page 7–The Weightlifter

Figure 5.10. Teacher's Guide to Illustrations
SOURCE: Feuerstein (1995). Reprinted by permission.

the difference between the goal and the actions necessary or available to reach that goal. Learners must understand concepts of constancy and conservation and make spontaneous comparisons. They must search for and detect the transformations that occur from one frame of the illustration to the next and make inferences about the changes to some elements that have occurred between the episodes depicted in the frames. They must grasp the concepts of objective and subjective reality and the impact of affect on these concepts. Overall, Illustrations attempts to correct the tendency to use an episodic rather than a continuous reasoning process and is designed to strengthen hypothetical and inferential processes.

Transitive Relations

Task

Transitive Relations deals with formal operations and logico-verbal reasoning. It encourages high-level abstraction and inference. Throughout the instrument, learners are given the opportunity to learn rules and apply them. They learn to infer new relationships from existing ones through the process of deduction. The information in this instrument is composed of ordered sets and signs. The signs signify the order of relationships. These signs describe the differences between the set members in terms of *greater than, less than,* and *equal to.* Learners are asked to coordinate two propositions to reach a single conclusion regarding unknown relationships. A sample page is shown in Figure 5.11.

Focus

This instrument uses verbal, numerical, pictorial, graphic, and symbolic modes to enable learners to clearly perceive information, attend to directionality and sequence, and use several pieces of information simultaneously. In addition, the individual is required to define problems, compare, categorize, and hypothesize. In so doing, the individual develops the ability to project virtual relationships, encode responses, and restrain impulsivity.

Syllogisms

Task

This instrument has similar goals to those found in Transitive Relations. Both focus on logico-verbal reasoning and formal cognitive operations. Both infer new relationships from existing ones through induction

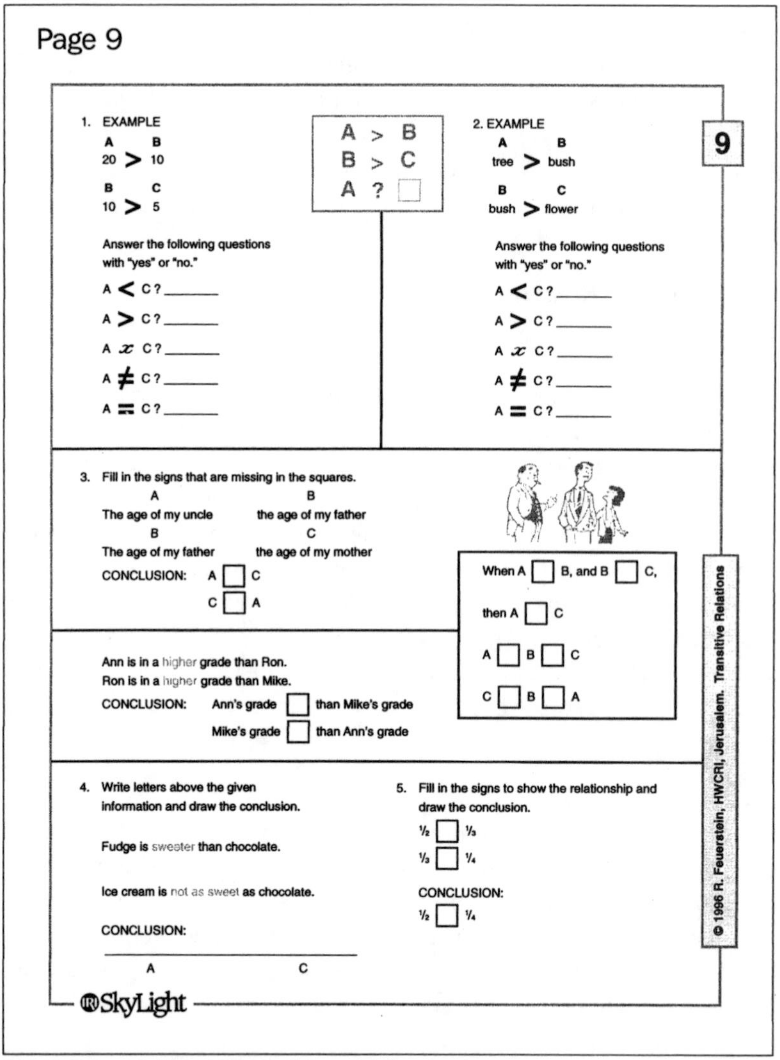

Page 9

1. EXAMPLE

A	B
20 > 10	

B	C
10 > 5	

$$A > B$$
$$B > C$$
$$A \; ? \; \square$$

Answer the following questions with "yes" or "no."

A < C? _____

A > C? _____

A x C? _____

A ≠ C? _____

A ≊ C? _____

2. EXAMPLE

A	B
tree > bush	

B	C
bush > flower	

Answer the following questions with "yes" or "no."

A < C? _____

A > C? _____

A x C? _____

A ≠ C? _____

A ≡ C? _____

3. Fill in the signs that are missing in the squares.

A	B
The age of my uncle	the age of my father

B	C
The age of my father	the age of my mother

CONCLUSION: A ☐ C
              C ☐ A

When A ☐ B, and B ☐ C,

then A ☐ C

A ☐ B ☐ C

C ☐ B ☐ A

Ann is in a higher grade than Ron.
Ron is in a higher grade than Mike.

CONCLUSION: Ann's grade ☐ than Mike's grade

              Mike's grade ☐ than Ann's grade

4. Write letters above the given information and draw the conclusion.

Fudge is sweeter than chocolate.

Ice cream is not as sweet as chocolate.

CONCLUSION:

_____
A   C

5. Fill in the signs to show the relationship and draw the conclusion.

½ ☐ ⅓

½ ☐ ¼

CONCLUSION:

½ ☐ ¼

®SkyLight

© 1996 R. Feuerstein, HWCRI, Jerusalem. Transitive Relations

Figure 5.11. Teacher's Guide to Transitive Relations
SOURCE: Feuerstein (1996). Reprinted by permission.

and deduction. Syllogisms deals with formal propositional logic. It focuses on having learners analyze their own proposition and premises for truth. They learn to discriminate between valid and invalid conclusions.

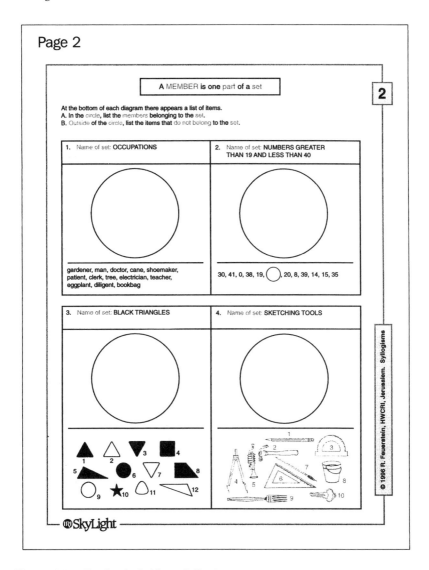

Figure 5.12. Teacher's Guide to Syllogisms
SOURCE: Feuerstein (1996). Reprinted by permission.

The content of this instrument is a series of relationships presented in terms of formal propositional logic. A sample page is shown in Figure 5.12.

Focus

This instrument facilitates the acquisition of clear perception, systematic exploration of data, discrimination, and synthesis. In addition, it encourages spontaneous comparative behavior, reduction of an episodic grasp of reality, comparison of several pieces of information simultaneously, summative thinking, and hypothetical thinking. The instrument helps to curb impulsivity and encourages the projection of relationships.

Representational Stencil Design (RSD)

Task

This instrument capitalizes on cognitive functions acquired in previous instruments and allows the application of previously learned concepts in situations that require complex representational internalized behavior. RSD consists of tasks in which learners must mentally construct a design identical to a colored standard that is presented, without using motor manipulation. A sample page is shown in Figure 5.13. Learners must be able to complete a complex sequence of steps. They must analyze a complex figure, constructed of shapes and colors, and identify various components of the figure that are transformed by superimposition.

Focus

Learners are required to observe systematically, perceive clearly, restrain impulsivity, and work systematically. They also must compare, categorize, use several pieces of information simultaneously, and use hypothetical thinking skills.

Using the Instruments

The teacher-student interactions and cognitive functions nurtured through IE transform basic curriculum to one that develops adaptational behavior. The key to this adaptation is the bridging process. After completion of the exercises by the student, the teacher introduces concepts from the instruments and bridges these concepts to appropriate content

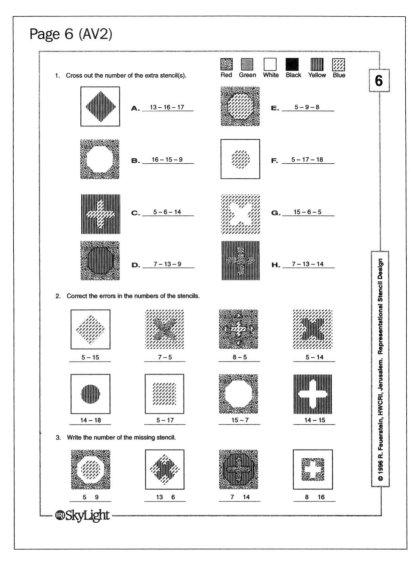

Figure 5.13. Teacher's Guide to Representational Stencil Design
SOURCE: Feuerstein (1996). Reprinted by permission.

topics. This bridging activity is performed by the teacher in the role of prime mediator. The goal is to enable students to make their own bridges to support their own learning. Through this process, connections are made between cognitive skills and content materials.

IE is a 2- to 3-year intervention program designed to strengthen cognitive functions through interactions that motivate and enhance the learning process. Instead of instructing students in what to think, it guides students in *how* to think. The role of mediation has several functions. First, mediation attempts to correct cognitive weaknesses and behaviors as identified on the LPAD. Second, it focuses on the use of learners' cognitive strengths rather than deficiencies. Third, it focuses on motivational interaction, guided by a mediator/teacher who believes in the individual's ability to increase learning propensity. Finally, mediation incorporates methods designed to equip learners with multiple strategies for solving problems. The dynamic interaction between the teacher and the student facilitates changes in behaviors indicative of learning and necessary for achievement.

These features of the mediation process are illustrated in a systematic project that took place in Atlanta, Georgia. This study is now described in detail.

The Atlanta Project

Research for this study began in the late 1970s in a Title I school in Yonkers, New York. The student population was predominantly from low-income African American and Hispanic families. The administrator of the school wanted to institute a "gifted" program to challenge the high-achieving students. The school had not been selected to have a district-sponsored gifted and talented program. The Title I status (determined on the basis of poverty and remedial needs identified on standardized tests) precluded its eligibility for the district program.

Identification of the students' potential was cited in the *Report on Education of the Disadvantaged* (U.S. Department of Education, 1980b) as a problem resulting from the following:

1. Remedial programs excluded students from curricula that developed cognitive skills assessed on standardized tests.
2. Standardized tests were unable to assess either the scope of gifted behaviors or the strengths of the students.

The implication of this report was the recognition that within the category of Title I schools, there were students who had the potential to achieve at much greater levels than had been determined on standardized achievement tests. This recognition formed the basis for research to address the hypothesis that low achievement of disadvantaged students could be reversed with a program that could strengthen cognitive weaknesses as well as increase cognitive functions indicative of high intellectual aptitude.

The setting identified for the research was Atlanta, Georgia, where the coordinator of the Title I Math program adopted IE for all the Title I schools. Here, as in Yonkers, students in this status were assigned to remedial programs to address identified deficiencies. After participation in the remedial program, many of the students continued to demonstrate weak cognitive functions and experience a *cumulative deficit* in their rate of learning. IE was selected as an alternative to the remedial programs offered; the plan was to investigate whether the program would correct cognitive weaknesses, strengthen cognitive functions and behaviors associated with giftedness, and increase the rate of learning of a significant number of the identified students. It was hoped that as a result of the program, changes in the cognitive functions of many of the students would be demonstrated to such a degree that they could be identified as potential candidates for the district's gifted and talented programs.

The goal for this program was to improve math achievement by substituting remedial training with IE bridged to mathematics skill development. The program included about 800 African American students in the fifth through seventh grades who had been identified as needing remediation in mathematics as a result of scores that fell below the 26th percentile on the Mathematics Concepts and Applications sections of the California Achievement Test. The implementation of IE in Atlanta made two considerations important in designing the study: (a) the impact of bridging IE to mathematics on achievement gains and (b) the correlation between the achievement gains resulting from participation in IE and the eligibility criteria for the gifted and talented program.

The Impact of Bridging IE to Mathematics on Achievement Gains

IE was designed to address cognitive functions that must be applied in all basic subject areas. Bridging IE to mathematics to create achievement gains indicative of giftedness was viable because: (a) IE focuses on the analytical skills that enhance development of the formal operational stage associated with scientific and formal math reasoning (Rand, Tannenbaum, & Feuerstein, 1979) and (b) math-related skills are influenced by particular cognitive functions associated with gifted performance (i.e., reasoning, analysis, synthesis, and evaluation) (Adler, 1968).

The Division of Evaluation and Data Processing for the Atlanta Public Schools conducted an evaluation of IE to determine the feasibility of instituting it as a Title I program. Standardized achievement scores after first- and third-year participation of fifth and seventh graders in IE were reviewed for comparative analysis. Three groups were compared to the IE group: students in the regular mathematics program, those in the two other Title I programs (Prescriptive Learning Center and Curriculum Development Association Program), and those in the eclectic program. Analysis of the scores indicated that the IE students either exceeded or equaled the gains of students in all the comparison groups except those Title I students involved in an eclectic program. In addition, analysis indicated that the achievements of the IE group exceeded those of all the comparison groups with an average gain of 1.6 years, whereas all the other programs averaged gains of 1.3 years. These math achievement gains confirmed the positive impact of IE when bridged to mathematics, warranting a closer look at the rate of growth as a possible indication of giftedness.

Data Analysis

Regression analysis was used to compare predicted gains after participation in IE in Grades 6 and 7. The hypothesis was that if IE had no significant impact on achievement levels, the student scores should be approximately equal to the achievement level predicted before IE. Conversely, the impact of IE would be demonstrated if achievement levels exceeded levels predicted if the students had not participated in IE.

The predicted scores from the regression procedure were compared to the actual scores, using a *T*-test (computed on the gains in each grade) and a nonparametric Sign Test. Predicted scores were also compared to national norms. The average IE student in Grade 6 obtained an actual end-of-year grade equivalent score of 5.4, compared to the predicted level of 5.3, with 14 of the 25 students demonstrating positive gains. The normal curve equivalent gain was a +.8. However, at the end of Grade

7, the average IE student obtained a grade equivalent of 7.4, or 1 year 6 months over and beyond the predicted level of 5.8 that would have been achieved if there had been no participation in IE. All but one demonstrated achievement levels superior to levels predicted, and 11 of 25 students performed at or above grade level. The average gain was 12.9.

IE is designed as a 3-year program and could not be expected to illustrate its full impact until the third year of implementation was completed. Therefore, although partial implementation of IE had no significant impact on mathematics achievement in Grade 6, the impact of full implementation in Grade 7 was highly significant, with achievement in mathematics approaching the level of performance of non-Title I middle school students. Such an increase in achievement of the Title I students, in spite of the disadvantaged factors, indicates the immense growth these students would be capable of, given the proper learning supports (in school and out of school). This belief was even more strongly justified by confirmation of the hypothesis that some who participated in IE would demonstrate an increase in achievement that would make them candidates for the gifted program. About 20% had achievement gains of at least 1 year above grade level in mathematics (meeting the program criteria of performing at significantly higher level than average, considering disadvantaged factors), with one student demonstrating superior performance with a final score of 12.5 at the end of Grade 7, or 3.5 years above level. This achievement was significantly higher than predicted and much greater than the gains of those who did not participate in IE.

The pattern of student gains, from small achievement increments the first year of IE participation to a markedly increased achievement in the third year, was indicative of (a) an initial lack of teacher facility in program instruction (the program began prior to the completion of teacher training, resulting in the third and final year being the most productive in terms of teacher ability and student performance) and (b) the cumulative effect of IE (reversing the cumulative deficit experienced by disadvantaged students).

Research Summary

The scope of achievement gains and behavioral characteristics after participation in IE was clearly impressive. Only 12% of the students were performing at grade level in Grades 5 and 6. By Grade 7, 44% were performing at or above grade level. About 32% went from performing below grade level to performing at or above grade level. About 20% were at least 1 year above grade level. One had a gain from the 37th percentile in Grade 5 to the 99th percentile in the seventh grade.

Such statistics illustrate that IE resulted in the magnitude of gains on student achievement considered indicative of a very effective program (Joyce & Showers, 1988). Used as an intervention program with Title I students, IE not only reversed learning dysfunctions so that intellectual potential could be demonstrated, but it also illustrated that within the pool of remedial students, there were a sizable number who became eligible for screening for the gifted program.

The results of this study were remarkable but not surprising. They illustrate the possibilities for assessment that can be realized from teacher-student interactions based on high expectations and a belief in the modifiability of intellectual performance. The hypothesis that a remedy for altering the low academic achievement of disadvantaged African American students was a cognitive skills program that addressed weaknesses as well as strengths was confirmed through IE.

The success of IE can be attributed to four factors. First, the use of figural and symbolic materials (reduced verbal content) allowed the teacher to highlight the strengths of disadvantaged students. This method of using strengths to correct weaknesses and introduce new information increases understanding, reduces misinterpretation, and facilitates development of thinking skills necessary for achievement on standardized tests. Second, higher levels of student thinking were encouraged by focusing on analytical skills that produce understanding of concepts and operations. Third, the success is due to the reflective teaching applied to the identification of concepts for bridging the instruments to specific content. Finally, teacher-student interactions that motivate learning and stimulate an intrinsic need for the learner to improve cognitive functioning contributed to the success of the IE intervention.

Refocusing the Goal for Assessment and Instruction

"Addressing the needs of potentially gifted students so as to guarantee instruction commensurate with their abilities presents a serious problem to every school system" (Dranesfield, 1953, p. 11). Administrators in low-achieving schools in urban areas are faced with the double enigma: Can there be potentially gifted students within their Title I population? And if so, what type of instructional program would best equip these students to demonstrate this potential?

Through the research in this study, IE has demonstrated its potential to have major impact on the achievement of students who experience disadvantages resulting from limited opportunities for mediated learning experiences. The tragedy remains for those students who continue to be denied the learning experiences that identify and nurture their potential. They continue to be considered dysfunctional and are expected to experience marginal growth in performance. Low expectations perpetuate narrow curricula, which creates educational inequities and, moreover, fails to develop the aptitudes that many students possess (Eisner, 1994).

The element integral to the success of IE is the shift from the usual focus on product, or knowledge of content, to the focus on intellectual processes and learning. The most salient feature of IE, which reflects its focus on learning, is the dynamic interaction between teacher and student, which allows assessment to be a component of the instructional process. This feature is founded on the beliefs that (a) intelligence is not stagnant, (b) learning can be motivated, (c) cognitive characteristics (deficits and strengths) affected by ethnicity and environment can affect learning and must be considered and addressed, (d) assessment should address the modifiability of intelligence through cumulative and ongoing procedures, (e) teachers can acquire and integrate the instructional techniques of IE to increase learning, and (f) teachers can be trained to assess student strengths and rate of growth.

Applying IE Dimensions for Reforming Assessment and Instruction

Reform of assessment and instruction to reverse the decline in achievement of urban students requires methods of assessment that elicit hidden strengths and reflect the curriculum and instruction experienced by the students (Jones, 1994). The following dimensions of IE are significant as guides for districts committed to identifying and nurturing the potential of their students: (a) a correlation between assessment and instructions, (b) structures and procedures for collaboration among all staff responsible for the instructional program, (c) strategies for addressing the factors that impede intellectual performance and learning, (d) strategies for cognitive skills development that reflect the characteristic strengths of the students, (e) activities in cognitive processes that are considered indicative of intellectual giftedness (e.g., critical and creative thinking, reasoning, problem solving and decision making), (f) curriculum that integrates more divergent questioning and mediating techniques to elicit divergent responses and higher level thinking, (g) strategies for assuring student understanding, (h) activities that allow students to demonstrate their understanding, (i) interactions between teacher and students that bridge concepts to the content and activities through changes in thinking, and (j) extensive training in reflection and mediation for all staff responsible for the education of identified students. The dimensions focus on the learning process, providing strategies for developing cognitive functions and opportunities for assessment. When these dimensions are incorporated into the reform process, comprehensive and integrated instruction result.

Summary

Feuerstein contends that deficiencies identified through conventional psychometric tests are the result of low motivational and emotional components, which do not necessarily reflect deficient learning capacity. Eisner (1994) supports this theory through his work on concept formation, illustrating the interdependence between affect and cognition as part of the same reality in the learning process. This study illustrated the capacity of this problem for improving the cognitive functions of low-achieving African American students to the degree that performances indicative of giftedness were identified. This study confirmed the hypothesis that in the pool of students considered dysfunctional, there is the promise of great achievement. This pool is vast. It is our obligation as a society to create the assessment and instructional opportunities to recast this pool of dysfunction into a sea of achievement.

6 All Intelligence Testing Is "Cross-Cultural"

Constructing Intelligence Tests to Meet the Demands of Person × Task × Situation Interactions

ROBERT STERNBERG

On the planet Velda, adaptation to the environment depends on a person's ability to play a single game that is much like chess (Devet & MacLean, 1958). Because you, the reader, do not know how to play the game, you would probably not fare well on Velda. Fortunately, you do not live on Velda, and neither, to my knowledge, does anyone else, as the planet and the game are both fictional. But the story "Second Game" makes the point that what it takes to adapt in one situation may be quite different from what it takes to adapt in another, and that which is valued as adaptive behavior can differ radically from one place to another.

One does not have to travel to Velda to see the differences in what constitutes adaptive behavior across cultures. There are plenty of examples from cross-cultural research on Earth. Gladwin (1970) has pointed out that, to adapt successfully in the Puluwat culture, one needs to develop skills of navigation without using what most of us would recognize as any discernible landmarks. Kearins (1981) and Wagner (1978) pointed out that the strategies (in the case of Kearins) and content (in the

AUTHOR'S NOTE: The work reported herein was supported under the Javits Act program (Grant No. R206R50001) as administered by the Office of Educational Research and Improvement, U.S. Department of Education. The findings and opinions expressed in this report do not reflect the positions or policies of the Office of Educational Research and Improvement or the U.S. Department of Education.

case of Wagner) that facilitate memorization differ from one culture to another. Cole, Gay, Glick, and Sharp (1971) showed that sorting behavior that is considered to be intelligent in one culture may be considered to be foolish in another. Similarly, Greenfield (1997) has even shown that the very act of taking a test may itself be viewed differently from one culture to another.

If what is viewed as "intelligent" in the sense of adaptation to the environment differs from one culture to another (and, in fiction, from one planet to another), is it possible that there are differences not only across cultures, but across subcultures as well? Okagaki and Sternberg (1993) addressed this question in a study of conceptions of intelligence in parents of children of various ethnic groups in a California school. They found, in comparing Mexican (first-generation), Mexican American (second-generation), Cambodian, Laotian, and Anglo groups, that there were differences in parents' conceptions of what constituted intelligent thinking and behavior in their children. Some groups emphasized the cognitive-competence aspects of intelligence more, whereas other groups placed more emphasis on the social-competence aspects of intelligence.

Of course, the children's teachers in school had conceptions of intelligence as well, and these conceptions emphasized the cognitive aspects of intelligence. The conceptions affected the teachers' evaluations of the children's performance in school. The more the parents' conceptions of intelligence matched those of the teachers, the better the children of those parents performed in school. In other words, within a single school, different children were performing with different success in part as a function of match versus mismatch of what was considered to be intelligent behavior. When these children become adults, arguably, the social competence aspects of intelligence will become more important. However, the teachers were looking for what mattered for adaptation in their classroom, not for what would matter for adaptation later on in life.

If various national cultures as well as ethnic subcultures value different aspects of thinking, and if different aspects of thinking are adaptive in specific situations, is it possible that there are differences even within ethnic subcultures, say, among professional groups? Indeed, there are. Sternberg (1985b) asked professors of physics, philosophy, business, and art, as well as laypersons, to characterize the ideally intelligent person. The individual groups produced distinct prototypes of intelligence that reflected the demands of their profession. For example, the physicists more heavily emphasized thinking quantitatively and with physical systems, whereas the art professors emphasized creativity with materials and artistic envisioning. These results make sense in terms of the differing demands of their jobs, as well as in terms of the differing demands of training.

Although I have discussed the aspects of intelligence that vary across groups of people, tasks (such as those found in different jobs), and situations, not everything about intelligence is variable. According to my triarchic theory (Sternberg, 1985b), intelligence comprises an aspect that is constant across various kinds of groups but also an aspect that varies across such groups. To adequately measure intelligence, one would need to take into account both the fixed and the variable aspects. For example, the need to recognize when one confronts a problem, to define what the problem is, to formulate a strategy to solve the problem, and to monitor and later evaluate the solution to the problem is fixed—it is constant across groups. One could not adapt to the demands of any group of people, any task, or any situation without taking into account these kinds of demands. But the particular behavior that is adaptive within these constraints could easily vary across groups of people, tasks, and situations. For example, the strategy that one would use to please one's teacher would probably be different in at least some fundamental respects from the strategy one would use to please one's lover. Likewise, what would be considered a good solution to a problem of physical systems might or might not be practical in a business setting.

The Thesis

The main thesis of this chapter is that, in measuring intelligence, we need to take into account people, tasks, and situations, not only in cross-cultural or multicultural measurement, but in *all* measurement. The conventional model has been that one constructs a test of intelligence, and then, if one wishes to use it in new ways, one adapts it, with such adaptations usually being remarkably superficial. For example, a test of intelligence will simply be translated, or at best, some of the informational content (if it is a test of crystallized abilities) will be modified to suit the culture in which the test is to be given. But this kind of modification is largely cosmetic. We need to think much more carefully about our goals in a given measurement situation; and moreover, we need to think about them not only in cross-cultural measurement, but in all measurement.

In short, rather than constructing a global test of intelligence that is supposed to measure the whole of intelligence but typically measures only a small part of it, we can think in another way. Here, we think in terms of constructing much more targeted tests that meet the constraints of the people, tasks, and situations involved. This is the approach we have taken in the work described below.

In the remainder of this chapter, I will give eight completed examples and two examples in progress of how we have created targeted tests of intellectual abilities in order to generate measures that were appropriate, to the greatest extent we could make them, for the people, tasks, and situations relevant to our measurement. The first test was based on implicit theories of intelligence, the rest, on an explicit theory.

The Prototype-Based Test of Intelligence

The Goal

A prototype-based test of intelligence is a test that reflects the implicit theories, or conceptions of intelligence, of a given group of individuals. Thus, the goal of this test (Sternberg, Conway, Ketron, & Bernstein, 1981) was to (a) reflect the modal conceptions of intelligence of U.S. adult laypersons, (b) measure intelligence in a way that would take into account typical (rather than maximal) performance, (c) be nonstressful to those who took the test, and (d) provide a measure that would possess acceptable psychometric properties.

Test Construction

A first group of laypersons was asked to list behaviors that they believed would characterize an ideally intelligent individual. Those behaviors that were listed by at least two individuals were then collected into a questionnaire. A second group of laypersons assessed, for each of these behaviors, the extent to which the behavior was characteristic of the ideally intelligent individual. These ratings were then factor analyzed, revealing three principal factors: practical problem solving, verbal ability, and social competence. Note that only one of these abilities, verbal ability, is directly measured by most intelligence tests, and that another of these abilities, social competence, is typically not measured at all. Social competence corresponds to the ability mentioned above in the Okagaki and Sternberg (1993) study that was not emphasized in teachers' conceptions of intelligence. Then, a third group of individuals was asked to rate themselves for the extent to which each of the same behaviors that had been on the previous list was characteristic of them individually.

The test was scored by correlating the profile of ratings people in the third group gave to themselves with the profile of ratings people in the second group gave, on average, for the ideally intelligent person. Note that, because a correlation coefficient was used, the absolute level of the ratings had no impact on the score that a given individual received. Merely rating oneself higher in terms of a behavior would not give one a higher score. Rather, the score was represented by a correlation coefficient and was a function of profile match between the individual's self-ratings and other individuals' ratings of the profile for the ideally intelligent person.

The Results

We found that there were extensive individual differences in the correlations that were obtained. Moreover, when these correlations were themselves correlated with scores on conventional tests of psychometric abilities, the resulting correlations were at the .5 level. In other words, people's self-characterizations moderately predicted their performance on psychometric tests. One would not predict any more than moderate correlations, because the prototype was based on implicit theories, was of typical performance, and was assessed by self-characterization. However, these results suggest that prototype-based measures can provide a useful converging operation to measure intelligence, supplementing more conventional measures, especially when there is reason to believe that scores on conventional tests may be partially or even wholly invalidated by (a) a difference in the prototype of a group from what it is that conventional tests measure, (b) the stress of taking the conventional test, or (c) the use of a maximum performance measure if what one prefers to focus on is typical performance.

In a follow-up study, we asked people to rate the intelligence of fictitious people described in mock "letters of recommendation." The behaviors referred to in the letters of recommendation were taken from the behaviors listed as characterizing intelligent people. Some of the behaviors were more characteristic of intelligence than others, and by averaging the characteristicness ratings (from the second group of participants) in the letters, one could obtain a prediction of how a new group of participants would rate the intelligence of the people who were described. The correlations between the predicted ratings (based on characterizations of an ideally intelligent person) and the observed ratings (based on characterizations given in the letters of recommendation) was .99. In other words, people not only have prototypes of intelligence, they also use them in making evaluations of others.

The prototype-based measure of intelligence is based on a theory of intelligence, but an implicit one (i.e., one in the heads of the individuals being tested). The remaining tests are based on the triarchic theory, an explicit theory of intelligence (Sternberg, 1985a). According to this theory, intelligence consists of a set of information-processing components that are applied to relatively novel tasks and situations in order to adapt to, shape, and select environments. Three kinds of abilities are key to the composition of intelligence: analytical, creative, and practical. People vary in their levels and profiles of these skills. And different groups of people, tasks, and situations may require different profiles of these abilities in order for a person to be viewed as adapting successfully to the environment.

The Sternberg Triarchic Intelligence Test

The Goal

Students' abilities are evaluated and rank-ordered largely on the basis of analytical abilities. Typical psychometric tests measure memory and analytical abilities in greater or lesser degree, but creative and practical abilities are rarely assessed. This one-sided emphasis is problematic because often the abilities required for success in a given career do not match the abilities required for success in schooling for that career. For example, creative or practical intelligence may be far more important for success as a scientist or a business executive than they might be to success in graduate school or business school. Yet, predictions of future success are made on the basis of assessments of abilities and achievements that do not match those that later will be required.

The goal of the construction of the triarchic test was to produce a test of intelligence that would measure a broader range of abilities than conventional tests would measure. The test would (a) be based on the triarchic theory, assessing analytical, creative, and practical abilities; (b) measure the triarchic abilities in several different content domains and by at least two different modalities of testing (multiple-choice and essay); (c) be very liberally timed, so that power rather than speed of processing was emphasized; and (d) be appropriate for students at the high school level.

Test Construction

The test comprises 12 subtests. Four of the tests emphasize analytical processing, four creative processing, and four practical processing. In addition, one of each kind of test is multiple-choice verbal, multiple-choice quantitative, multiple-choice figural, and essay. Thus, this test is somewhat more likely to identify a person as having intellectual strengths than would a typical test, because people are allowed more ways in which to show their strengths.

Construction of actual subtests was an interactive process (see Sternberg, 1993; Sternberg, Ferrari, Clinkenbeard, & Grigorenko, 1996). Some subtests proved to be too easy, some too hard, and others of insufficient validity. Eventually, a set of test items was attained that was adequate for the purpose of distinguishing six groups of individuals: (a) those relatively high in analytical ability only, (b) those relatively high in creative ability only, (c) those relatively high in practical ability only, (d) those relatively high in all three abilities, and (e) those relatively high in none of the three abilities.

The Results

The test was used to divide students into groups in a study that examined the effects of matching versus mismatching ability patterns with instructional conditions. More specifically, we placed high school students into sections of an introductory psychology course that either matched their ability pattern (e.g., highly analytical students in an analytically oriented section) or mismatched their ability pattern (e.g., high-analytical students in a creatively oriented section). Achievement of all students was evaluated for memory learning, as well as for analytical, creative, and practical manifestations of learning. We found that (a) all three kinds of tests—analytical, creative, and practical—significantly predicted performance in the psychology course, (b) the analytical (most conventional) test provided the best prediction, (c) in multiple regressions predicting various kinds of course grades (homework, exams, independent project) from abilities, at least two of three kinds of tests always provided a statistically significant prediction; and (d) students who were matched performed better than students who were mismatched. Thus, the test accurately predicted performance, and the results showed that students perform better in a course if it is taught, at least in part, in a way that is compatible with their pattern of abilities.

Tests of Analytical Intelligence

The Goal

It is the analytical aspect of intelligence that conventional tests measure almost exclusively. Yet, our goal, especially in some of my early research (e.g., Guyote & Sternberg, 1981; Sternberg, 1977, 1980, 1981, 1983; Sternberg & Gardner, 1983; Sternberg & Weil, 1980), was to show that it was possible to measure the analytical aspect of intelligence in a way that would provide more information than a conventional test would. These tests are based in particular on the componential subtheory of the triarchic theory of human intelligence, which specifies the information-processing components used in the completion of various kinds of cognitive tasks.

In particular, we tried to design tests that would identify (a) the components of information processing used in various kinds of tasks employed to measure intellectual abilities, such as analogies, classifications, series completions, and linear, categorical, and conditional syllogisms; (b) the latencies of these components by how long it took to execute each of the components; (c) the probability of each component's leading to an error in the solution to the problem; (d) the strategy into which the components were combined to solve the problems; and (e) the form of mental representation used in the solution of the problem. To accomplish these goals, we first formed information-processing models of task solution; next, we recognized these models as mathematical models; and then, finally, we constructed tests that would enable us to estimate parameters of the mathematical models, usually through multiple regression (linear or nonlinear).

The Results

In general, we had success in accomplishing the above goals. Typically, our information-processing models accounted for 80% to 95% of the variation in the group item-latency data. Accuracy for individual test takers was somewhat lower, as one would expect, given the greater amount of error that one would find in the data of a single participant as opposed to group-averaged data. We found that a number of the components of information processing correlated with scores on conventional psychometric tests of abilities. Somewhat disappointingly, however, the highest correlation was often between these ability tests and the constant component in the regression equation. In other words, the information processing that was common across all the items was the best predictor of psychometric test performance, rather than the information processing that was isolated from problems of particular kinds.

We found that there were individual differences in strategies on some kinds of problems, such as linear syllogisms, making group averaging of data hazardous at best. Also, we found that even when participants were told to use a certain strategy, they would often use the strategy that came most naturally to them. We also found that there was not a simple relationship between latency and psychometrically measured intelligence. For most components, shorter latencies were associated with higher mental-ability test scores, as one would predict. But for some kinds of components, such as encoding of stimuli, in certain instances, and global planning for solution processing, the correlation was the reverse. The people who took longer actually did better on the psychometric tests, showing that it is time allocation rather than just time that is important for intelligent information processing.

Tests of Creative Intelligence

The Goal

Because creativity is so important to survival in today's rapidly changing world, and because it is rarely measured by conventional tests of intelligence, we have put somewhat of a priority on developing tests of creative intellectual abilities (Sternberg, 1981; Sternberg & Lubart, 1995, 1996). The tests we have used have been of two kinds: convergent and divergent. The convergent tests have a preferred keyed answer; the divergent tests do not, and hence they require rating of the quality of the products produced. In both cases, we wished to produce tests that would (a) measure the creative aspect of intelligence, (b) be designed in a way that would ideally be engaging for the examinee, (c) use tasks that would be meaningful and thus related to creativity in real-world settings, and (d) measure creativity in a psychometrically strong assessment.

Test Construction

Convergent Tests. The convergent tests have generally involved the timed solution of relatively novel kinds of problems. For example, one such test is a measure of *conceptual projection* (Sternberg, 1981, 1982). In one variant of this kind of test, examinees are taught about two new colors, based on Goodman's (1955) new riddle of induction: *grue,* which means green until the year 2000 and blue thereafter, and *bleen,* which means blue until the year 2000 and green thereafter. In the task, examinees are given partial information about objects both in the present and in the future and have to identify them as being either green, blue, grue, or bleen. In another variant of the task, examinees are taught about the planet Kyron, where there are various kinds of beings, such as ones who are born young and die old, as on Earth, but also ones who are born young and die young, are born old and die old, and are born old and die young.

In another convergent task, examinees are timed while they solve verbal analogy problems. Verbal analogies, of course, do not measure a nonentrenched form of reasoning; however, the problems we used did because they were preceded by a premise that could be either conventional (e.g., "fish swim in the water") or unconventional (e.g., "sparrows play hopscotch"). The examinee then had to solve each of the problems as though the supposition were true (Sternberg & Gastel, 1989a, 1989b). In yet another kind of convergent task (Davidson & Sternberg, 1984; Sternberg & Davidson, 1982, 1983), examinees were given mathematical insight problems, such as "If blue and brown socks are mixed in a drawer in a dark room in a ratio of 4 to 5, how many socks does one need to take out of the drawer in order to be assured of having two socks of the same color?"

Divergent Tests. The divergent tests, too, measured thinking in novel kinds of ways but required the production of products (Lubart & Sternberg, 1995; Sternberg & Lubart, 1995). We tested creative intelligence in four different domains. In the story domain, examinees had to write two very short stories, basing their stories on a selection of titles, such as "The Octopus's Sneakers" or "2083." In the art domain, examinees had to draw two sketches, again selecting from a variety of titles for compositions, such as "Earth From an Insect's Point of View" and "The Beginning of Time." In the advertising domain, examinees had to create two interesting advertisements for very boring products, such as bowties and doorknobs. Finally, in the scientific domain, examinees had to solve unusual scientific types of problems, such as one asking them how we might detect who among us were extraterrestrial aliens if these aliens were purposely seeking to escape detection.

The Results

The convergent tests proved to be reliable and to conform well to the predictions of the underlying information-processing models. More important, they suggested the locus of creative functioning, at least for these particular kinds of tasks. For example, on the conceptual-projection task, a number of components of information processing were correlated with scores on conventional psychometric tests, but the component most highly correlated with the more nonentrenched conventional tests was the one that measured the latency for switching between conceptual systems. In other words, flexibility in switching, say from "green-blue" to "grue-bleen" thinking and back again was what appeared to be most essential to the creative aspect of the enterprise. Note that a useful feature of the componential approach was that it was not only possible to isolate this and other components, rather than just to have a composite score that included within it the creative aspect of processing, but also to isolate, in a confounded fashion, other aspects of processing as well. In the analysis of insightful problem solving, we were able to decipher distinct kinds of insightful thinking, namely, selective encoding (distinguishing relevant from irrelevant information), selective combination (putting together information in a nonobvious way), and selective comparison (seeing the nonobvious relations between old and new information).

The divergent tests proved to be moderately domain-specific. In other words, performances across domains correlated with each other, but only moderately. Performances within domains were somewhat more highly correlated with each other. Perhaps more important, from the standpoint of our own theory, scores on these tests were related to scores on tests of the attributes of intelligence knowledge, thinking styles, personality, and motivation, which we theorized were relevant to creative intelligence. For example, a person with a legislative style (Sternberg, 1988, 1991, 1997), someone who likes to come up with his or her own ideas, produced more highly creative products than did a person with an executive style—someone who prefers to be told what to do.

We also found a tendency for those who were willing to take greater risks to be regarded as more creative. This finding was supported in the art domain, but not in the short stories, a fact that unveiled a further interesting point about the measurement of creativity. When we saw that we did not get a significant difference between the low and high risk-taking groups in the story domain, we decided to look at the very short stories of the greater and lesser risk-takers. What we found was that the greater risk-takers did seem to have written what we believed to be more creative stories, but the evaluators had apparently penalized some of them for taking unpopular points of view with respect to politics, religion, and other issues of the day. The point is that the measurement of creativity can only be as good as are the people who are doing the evaluations.

Tests of Practical Intelligence

The Goal

Practical intelligence is the kind of intelligence that is needed to adapt to, select, and shape environments. Much of dealing with life requires practical intelligence, such as getting along with friends and colleagues, making a sale, managing people, buying a house, or whatever. Therefore, we believe that conventional tests of intelligence fail to accurately measure the practical aspect of intelligence (Sternberg, 1985a). We have thus attempted to construct tests of practical intelligence that would be (a) psychometrically sound, (b) construct valid in the sense of truly measuring the practical aspect of intelligence, (c) domain-relevant, and (d) based on the idea of tacit knowledge.

Tacit knowledge is practical, procedural knowledge that is needed for adaptation to real-world environments but that typically is not taught explicitly or even verbalized. It is usually acquired simply from being in an environment, although people in a given environment vary as to how well they acquire this knowledge. Thus, we have tried to construct tests that would measure such knowledge as it applies to real-world adaptations (Sternberg, 1985a; Sternberg & Wagner, 1993; Sternberg, Wagner, Williams, & Horvath, 1995; Wagner & Sternberg, 1985, 1986).

Test Construction

We have developed a procedure for assessing the tacit knowledge that is relevant in a given setting. The particular settings we have looked at are those of the college professor, the college student, the business executive, and the salesperson. First, we interview experts in a given field as to the critical incidents they have confronted that they believe have required practical intelligence. We then extract from these interviews the tacit knowledge necessary for adaptation on the job. Next, we construct scenarios based on our interviews, which incorporate this tacit knowledge. We then have a test in which examinees are presented with tacit-knowledge (and, in one case, performance-based) scenarios in which the examinees are asked to rate each of a set of possible solutions to a problem for the quality of the solution for confronting the problem at hand.

For example, a business executive might be given a scenario about selecting a contractor, whereas a college professor would receive a scenario about writing up articles for publication or teaching a class.

The Results

Over the course of our research, we have elicited a number of potentially useful findings regarding the nature of practical intelligence as measured by tests of tacit knowledge. First, tacit knowledge tends to increase with experience, but it is how much an individual profits from the experience, rather than the experience itself, that is crucial to the development of tacit knowledge. Second, scores on tacit knowledge tests generally do not correlate significantly with IQ. Of course, this lack of correlation is within the range of abilities of people who normally pursue a given occupation. With enough range—say from retarded to gifted—it is more likely that there would be a correlation. But the truth is that there are not that many, if any, mentally retarded people in the occupations we have examined, such as college professors and business executives. Third, scores on tacit knowledge tests generally do not significantly correlate with the subtests of the Armed Service Vocational Aptitude Battery (ASVAB) either. In other words, the lack of correlation with conventional tests applies not only to so-called general ability, but also to subtests measuring group factors of intelligence as well.

Fourth, scores on tests of tacit knowledge appear to predict job performance as well as, or better than, conventional psychometric tests do. Thus, tests of tacit knowledge can be useful in conjunction with conventional psychometric tests for predicting job performance, because they both have criterion validity and are not significantly correlated with each other. In one study, we used hierarchical regression to predict performance on a managerial simulation at the Center for Creative Leadership in Greensboro, North Carolina, a center primarily for the training of middle-level managers. Of all the various kinds of intelligence, personality, and styles tests that were used, the tacit knowledge test was the best single predictor of performance on the managerial simulation; moreover, it provided significant incremental prediction even after all of the other predictors were entered first into a regression equation.

Finally, tacit knowledge tests appear to show moderate correlations across domains. Even within domains, different aspects of tacit knowledge, such as managing self, managing others, and managing tasks, tend to correlate. Thus, although tacit knowledge does not correlate with conventional kinds of test scores, it does correlate across its various manifestations.

Tests of Social Intelligence

The Goal

We have looked, in a series of experiments, at one aspect of social intelligence, namely, decoding of nonverbal cues (Barnes & Sternberg, 1989; Sternberg & Smith, 1985). Our goal was to measure the extent to which people could infer socially based information from photographs of people in interaction. As always, we wanted tests that were psychometrically sound and, here specifically, that would tap into skills that would be relevant in day-to-day social interactions. Thus, inferring information from nonverbal cues is important because gestures, facial expressions, body lean, and the like often contain as much information as, or even more information than, do the words that accompany these nonverbal cues.

Test Construction

We took photographs of pairs of people under two kinds of circumstances: (a) supervisors and supervisees, and (b) real and fake couples. In the former case, the examinees had to indicate which of two people in a naturalistic photograph was the supervisor of the other. In the latter case, the examinees had to indicate which of the photos showed real couples and which showed people who were merely posing as couples.

The Results

There were large individual differences in performance, with a range of scores from about chance to almost perfect. Performance in the two domains, as well as correlations with conventional psychometric tests, were weak. Correlations with other tests of social intelligence were also weak, but higher than the correlations with the tests of cognitive intelligence. Perhaps most interesting, we were able to construct decision models that would predict the difficulties of the items on the basis of the kinds of cues the examinees used. Thus, photos that contained more or more obvious cues were easier than photos that contained fewer or less obvious cues. Therefore, this approach required us to identify the cues that the examinees were using in making their judgments.

Survey Tests of Intelligence

The Goal

At times, survey-taking institutions such as the U.S. government would like a measure of intelligence of the individuals who are being surveyed. For example, one might be interested in knowing whether low intelligence is a risk factor for contracting certain kinds of venereal or other diseases. However, survey takers could not possibly administer conventional intelligence tests. First, it is extremely unlikely that many participants in the surveys would agree to take such tests. Second, the tests simply take too long, are too cumbersome, and require too much training to administer. Rather, survey takers need measures that are (a) relatively brief, (b) relatively easy, (c) fun to take, (d) easy to administer, (e) face valid, and (f) psychometrically reliable and valid.

Test Construction

We sought to create tests that would meet the constraints described above (Sternberg, Dennis, & Beatty, 1996). Basically, the creation of such tests requires a large amount of trial and error. Some tests will prove to be too easy or too hard, or not to be fun for the examinees, or to be psychometrically unsound. Ultimately, we designed a battery that addressed these issues with gamelike tasks, such as finding words in strings of letters.

The Results

We administered our survey tests, along with conventional psychometric tests for comparison. In a preliminary sample, we found that our tests were rated by the examinees as more interesting and fun to take, as well as less stressful, than were the conventional psychometric tests, but our tests were equal in perceived validity to those tests. Moreover, the correlational structure looked promising. Our tests were as highly correlated with the psychometric tests as the latter kinds of tests were with each other. Factor analysis confirmed that the tests clustered into factors by the kinds of content and mental processing involved, rather than by whether they were from the survey battery or the conventional test battery. Thus, our battery appears to hold some promise for use in future surveys, and we are currently developing it further.

A Levels-of-Processing Intelligence Test

The Goal

Children who are infected with moderate to heavy loads of intestinal parasites tend to perform worse in school than do children who are uninfected or who are infected only with a low load. Why? There may be many reasons, but one reason that has seemed plausible is that parasitically infected children may manifest certain deficits in intellectual processing that are not manifested by children who do not have such infections.

Our goal was to construct a battery of intellectual ability tests that would sample various levels of intellectual performance to answer two questions: First, at what level of processing do deficits in cognitive functioning occur? Second, do the deficits tend to be acute or chronic (Sternberg et al., 1995)?

By levels of processing, we refer to perceptual, memory, and reasoning processes, which we view loosely as successively higher levels of processing (at least in a traditional bottom-up model of information processing). By longevity of deficit, we refer to whether the deficit, if the parasitic infection were to be removed, would also immediately be removed (acute), or whether the deficit has accumulated over time and thus could be removed only with substantial cognitive remediation (chronic). For example, influenza results in an acute deficit. People suffering from the flu will probably not perform at their best on difficult cognitive tasks, but as soon as the flu has ended, so will the deficit in their information processing. In contrast, long-term debilitating illnesses such as polio can potentially result in lost time in school and other activities that develop thinking and thus require remediation in order for the afflicted person to catch up.

Test Construction

We constructed a levels of processing-based test that contained subtests measuring selective attention, vigilance, forward digit-span and backward digit-span memory, free recall, classification, and analogical reasoning. The tests were administered to Jamaican schoolchildren who either suffered or did not suffer from intestinal parasitic infections. After administration of the tests, infected examinees received two doses of Albendazole, which, after several days, eliminated the parasites from their bodies.

The Results

We found that the children showed more deficits on the higher order than on the lower order tests, suggesting that the locus of deficit was more at the higher rather than the lower order of information processing. Moreover, we found that treatment with Albendazole did not remove the difference between the two groups, even after controlling for obvious confounding variables, such as socioeconomic status. Thus, it appears that the deficit is chronic or cumulative, rather than acute. Simply ridding the body of the parasites did not result in an immediate gain in cognitive performance. Rather, a cumulative deficit had built up, which would have to be alleviated by cognitive and educational remediation.

Interestingly, the parasitological and medical personnel involved in our study viewed the results as indicative of a failure. Their expectation was that the medical intervention should result in an immediate cognitive gain. They seemed uninterested in, and even unaware of, the possibility that a cognitive intervention might be needed as well, to follow up on the medical intervention. Thus, we found that the study showed the potential usefulness of psychologists working with medical personnel on such studies. At the same time, we had only partial success in convincing some of these individuals that an immediate cognitive gain was not necessarily to be expected from the medical treatment.

Some Current Testing Projects

We currently have two testing projects under way that we believe are potentially exciting, but for which we do not yet have results. Both of these projects are in collaboration with international teams of investigators. The first project, taking place in Tanzania, is again looking at the effects of parasitic infections on the cognitive functioning of children. In this study with Elena Grigorenko, however, we plan to use dynamic rather than static testing of intellectual abilities. In this testing, examinees will be given test questions but then will be given guided feedback to help them solve the problems (see Brown & Ferrara, 1985; Ferrara, Brown, & Campione, 1986; Feuerstein, 1979; Vygotsky, 1978). The idea is that discrepancies currently in the literature regarding effects of parasitic infections on cognitive functioning in Third World children (see, e.g., Watkins & Pollitt, 1996) may be due to the differential appropriateness of the testing situation for different children taking the tests. In particular, the static testing situation may be strange and uncomfortable for them and, furthermore, may reveal only developed potential and not potential that is on the verge of being developed (the so-called zone of proximal development). Our Tanzania project, therefore, will look at effects through dynamic (as well as static) tests.[1]

In a separate project, in Kenya, Grigorenko and I are looking at the practical intelligence of children in a rural village. It has been shown that such children have a vast storehouse of information regarding medicinal herbs that can be used to treat various kinds of stomach ailments. This knowledge is highly adaptive for the kind of existence they live, and moreover, it is knowledge that is not possessed, even in analogue, by Western children. We are interested in determining whether scores on a test of this largely tacit knowledge will or, as we suspect, will not correlate with scores on conventional tests of intelligence.[1]

Conclusion

The conventional approach to intelligence testing is to construct a single test, which is then used widely for whatever purposes may arise. When the test is used cross-culturally, it may be translated, and occasionally, further adaptations may be made. This chapter has suggested an alternative approach—targeted, theory-based tests that are designed to accomplish specific goals relevant to a given person × task × situation interaction. This form of testing enables one to construct tests that are perhaps more ideal for the constraints of the testing situation at hand. We have used this approach in a large number and wide variety of testing situations, and with some success.

Obviously, there are advantages to the global test strategy that our strategy does not have. When just a single test is used, it is possible to invest more time and effort into perfecting items, developing norms, and creating a nicely published product. But the risk is that the items may be perfected only for measuring limited abilities for some people, relevant only to some tasks and isolated situations. Therefore, the norms that are relevant for one group may not be relevant to other groups; the nicely published product will give an illusion of soundness that the testing procedure, taken as a whole, does not have.

Years ago, when I was working for the summer at a testing organization, I proctored a test that was carefully prepared and standardized, as well as attractively packaged. Indeed, the company was so concerned with standardization that it administered the test via a tape-recording, so that everyone would get exactly the same form of administration of the test. This *controlled administration of standardized tests,* as it was called, was being billed as the ultimate administration technique then available in standardized assessment. However, there was a problem. The individual delivering the test was from Texas and had a very strong Texas accent. The individuals whom I was proctoring, New Yorkers, were having a great deal of difficulty understanding his speech, as was I. No doubt, people in Texas would have found him much easier to understand. But what appeared to be a carefully crafted and standardized test was nothing of the sort; it was largely an illusion.

The problem is not limited to this test. Often, young children take tests, become confused, and start responding in ways that do not correspond to the expectations of the company that produced the examination. The children may not understand the directions, or they may discover, as I once did, that they have misaligned the numbers on the answer sheet, resulting in their getting almost no items correct when the test is scored. As a result, what the teacher will see is a fancy computer printout that makes it appear as though everything is on the up and up and that the scores are as meaningful as any scores could possibly be.

The approach of adapting the test to the circumstances is one that needs to be more carefully considered in the measurement of intelligence. It is not a substitute for the conventional approach, but in many circumstances, it will provide a better option. In our own work, we have found it to be the more useful option, giving us the information we need in given circumstances obtained in ways that fit these circumstances. Often, conventional standardized tests cannot do the same. We need more options in testing to accommodate the wide variety of needs that teachers, employers, and we as psychologists have in order to gain the most useful information possible about those whose intelligence we are testing.

NOTE

1. As this volume was going to press, we found in our Tanzania work that our dynamic tests are only weakly correlated with conventional intelligence tests. We have found in our Kenya research project that our tests of adaptive tacit knowledge are *negatively* correlated with the conventional tests of intelligence.

7 Nontraditional Uses of Traditional Aptitude Tests

JOHN E. LEWIS

Criticisms concerning the use and misuse of standardized tests with respect to ethnically/racially/culturally diverse populations have been historically documented (Samuda, 1975; Samuda, Kong, Cummins, Pascual-Leone, & Lewis, 1989) and are described in the first chapter of this book. Although many critics are adept at pointing out the pitfalls of testing diverse clients using standardized, norm-referenced measures of ability, few have delineated alternatives for using these traditional instruments in nontraditional, culturally appropriate ways. The result of this failure has been that, when diverse clients have been tested, psychometricians have made one of two choices: (a) they have rejected existing standardized instruments, or (b) they have adopted and used them with no regard for the inequities inherent in the instruments and procedures.

Because assessment with culturally diverse populations adds an element of complexity to the testing procedure, it is necessary for examiners to become informed about the appropriate use of existing standardized aptitude tests. Unfortunately, most testers have failed to account for inappropriate test content, inadequate standardization samples, examiner bias, lack of language facility, lack of predictive validity, differing test-taking strategies, and the nonequitable social, educational, and vocational opportunities of the testee.

This chapter examines nontraditional uses of traditional aptitude tests. Preassessment issues that all testing professionals must consider before deciding to use standardized instruments with a culturally different client are examined. Next, the culture-free/culture-fair test movement is reviewed, focusing on the four most commonly used nonverbal instruments from this genre, along with a discussion of the use of translated measures. A delineation of the elements of the System of Multi-cultural Multipluralistic Assessment (SOMPA) is then given. The concept of comprehensive assessment, which describes elements of a multimodal psychometric approach for cross-cultural use, is then examined. Following this is a discussion of the adoption of dynamic approaches to testing by reviewing and adapting test-of-limits procedures with diverse clients. In addition, formal dynamic assessment methods are evaluated by examining the test-train-test via mediation model. Finally, post-assessment issues are reviewed, and specific recommendations for the use of traditional standardized aptitude tests with culturally diverse clients are made.

Preassessment Issues

When planning to conduct an intellectual assessment with a client from a culture outside of the mainstream, the assessor needs to make every effort possible to learn about specific cultures and how each is affected by the use of standardized test procedures. Professional standards and guidelines have been compiled by Prediger (1993) and include the following suggestions:

1. Decide whether the content of the test and the norm or comparison group is appropriate for a linguistically, ethnically, racially, or culturally different client.
2. Evaluate the data available to ascertain whether or not the test performance of a diverse client may be due to culturally biased characteristics of the tests.
3. Determine the reliability and validity of translated and adapted instruments with a non-English speaker and other linguistically different clients.
4. Choose assessment devices that have been developed with the intention of making them as fair as possible, in other words reliable and valid.

With respect to validity, Saunders (1956) used the term *moderator variable* to identify factors that affect the validity of a standardized test. Dana (1993) expanded this definition and stated that a moderator variable is a correction for cultural differences "to obtain a reliable estimate of the potential contribution of cultural variance to an assessment procedure" (p. 113). Moderator variables are now assumed to include demographic classifications (e.g., gender, socioeconomic level), psychological constructs (e.g. interest, motivation), and cultural variables (e.g., acculturation) (Anastasi, 1988; Dana, 1993).

There are two types of moderator variables that are used to identify factors that promote the retention of a client's original culture (Dana, 1993). The first are monolevel variables, which include acculturation, language, customs, values, beliefs, attitudes, and socioeconomic status. The second are bilevel variables, which are used to identify factors that promote the acquisition of mainstream values. They include assimilation and bicultural identity.

The impact of moderator variables needs to be determined, formally or informally, prior to testing a culturally diverse client. By measuring these variables, an assessor can determine the degree to which a testee's performance has been affected by culturally specific variables. Dana (1993) has compiled a list of generic and culture-specific instruments designed to measure the influence of moderator variables on a client's test performance. Assessors should use one or more of these instruments if they have serious concerns about the performance of a culturally different client.

Suzuki and Kugler (1995) have also suggested that examiners need to understand the subtleties of a particular culture and how cultural factors may affect the assessment process. The examiner must explore a client's experience with being assessed, the nature of assessment procedures in the client's culture, and any culturally-specific test-taking styles considered normal in the client's culture. In particular, the examiner should evaluate the impact of cultural difference on the client's familiarity and facility with timed, speeded tests and with tasks requiring analytical and abstract thinking.

Moore (1986) has indicated that ethnic minority clients approach standardized tests differently than clients from mainstream culture. In particular, minority clients often do not respond to the examiner's questions and, if they do, they fail to complete their answers. Moore has also described the presence of a spontaneous elaboration style in many mainstream children that is characterized by an examinee's willingness to elaborate on words and meanings by relating the concepts to personal experiences and verbalizing these relationships. This spontaneity has been considered to be an indicator of how deeply involved the client is in the examination process and how task-focused, motivated, and anxious the client is during testing. Thus, the tester must be in tune with the response style exhibited by the testee and consider nonresponsiveness as a cultural difference rather than a deficit.

The issue of acculturation can also have an impact on the assessment process (Sattler, 1992). Acculturation has been defined as the degree to which culturally different clients accommodate and integrate new cultural patterns into their original cultural patterns (Hood & Johnson, 1997; Panaguia, 1994). It has also been described as a psychosocial adjustment process that occurs as an individual interacts with a new culture (Casas & Casas, 1994).

Over 50 instruments have been developed to assess a client's level of acculturation. These instruments have been comprehensively reviewed and evaluated by Dana (1993) and Ponterotto and Casas (1991). Level of acculturation, or adaptation to the dominant culture, often takes into account the client's age, generational status (i.e., first, second, third generation), monolingual and bilingual facility, and the degree of interaction with the new culture versus social involvement with members of the original culture.

With respect to assessment, the lack of adjustment to the dominant culture is likely to result in test performance that is not reflective of a client's true potential. It is recommended, therefore, to make a formal or informal assessment of the client's level of acculturation prior to testing. It is logical that the greater the level of acculturation into middle-class, mainstream culture, the greater the likelihood the testing situation is equitable or fair.

With respect to preassessment issues, it is obviously apparent that assessors need to combine knowledge of the technical aspects of a test with the cultural background of the client. This combination increases the likelihood that a culturally diverse client will receive a more equitable testing procedure and result. Keeping in mind preassessment issues, the remainder of this chapter will explore various approaches to testing diverse clients.

Culture-Free and Culture-Fair Tests

All standardized tests of aptitude presume that examinees have a common experience of cultural acquisition. This cultural knowledge is learned through education and socialization processes. In other words, the culture of standardized tests is transmitted to the child by parents and other figures in early childhood and then elaborated in the first years of formal schooling through use of the dominant language. Standardized tests, therefore, become measures of how well one has learned the information that has been transmitted in the dominant culture's language.

The movement to use so-called *culture-free* and *culture-fair* tests was begun to counteract, or at least neutralize, the culturally loaded information and language items found in standardized tests. Although no test can be considered culture-free, some can be thought of as culture-reduced instruments. The reduction of the influence of culture has been attempted by decreasing the number of test items with culturally loaded content and by reducing the language components present in the test. The most widely used instruments of this type are Cattell's (1973) Culture Fair Intelligence Test, Raven's (1938) Progressive Matrices, The Leiter (1948) International Performance Scale, and the Goodenough-Harris Drawing Test (Harris, 1963).

The Culture Fair Intelligence Test (Cattell, 1973) is a paper-and-pencil instrument devoid of verbal content. It was developed with the intention of reducing the effects of cultural and educational experience. This multiple-choice test includes four subtests: Series Completion, Classification, Matrices, and Conditions. The test has two parallel forms for each of its three levels. Level 1 is appropriate for children from 4 to 8 years of age and mentally retarded adults; Level 2 for 8 to 14 years of age and average adults; and Level 3 for high school students and college-level adults with above average intelligence. Scores are expressed as deviation IQs with a mean of 100 and a standard deviation 16.

Although the Culture Fair Intelligence Test does remove culturally loaded information items and verbal components, fairly extensive verbal instructions are required in the administration phase, causing difficulty for linguistically different clients. In addition, the subtests are highly speeded. This further reduces the cultural fairness of the instrument, because the emphasis on speed or times can differ cross-culturally. The presence of these differences requires the assessor to explain more fully the nature of the task to the client.

The Raven's (1938) Progressive Matrices Test (RPM) was originally designed to measure Spearman's g factor. It has since gone through many revisions. This test of nonverbal reasoning requires a person to problem-solve using an abstract task. The examinee is given a set of figural matrices, consisting of rows and columns in which one element is missing. The examinee is asked to choose the missing figure from a series of alternatives. The test takes less than one half hour to administer and is not timed. The RPM is available in three forms, each representing a different level of difficulty: Standard Progressive Matrices, Coloured Progressive Matrices, and Advanced Progressive Matrices (Sets I and II).

The Standard Progressive Matrices (SPM; Raven, 1958) consist of 60 black-and-white items designed for children from 6 to 16 years of age and average-intelligence adults. Rudimentary verbal instructions are required. The Coloured Progressive Matrices (CPM; Raven, 1956) consist of 36 colored matrices, and the test is appropriate for children 5 to 11 years of age and for examinees who cannot be adequately examined with the SPM (e.g., children with attention deficit disorder and culturally diverse examinees). The monochromatic Advanced Progressive Matrices (APM) are appropriate for above-average older adolescents and adults. There are 12 items in Set I and 36 items in Set II.

The RPM has a nonverbal construction and nonreliance on an examinee's fluency in English. It has often been used when testers desire a measure of aptitude and ability that is not biased by a client's educational background, ethnic/racial difference, linguistic ability, or cultural deficiencies. The nonspeeded nature of this test is a culturally sensitive feature. Although claims have been that the RPM measures only observation and clear thinking rather than general intelligence (Raven, Court, & Raven, 1983), using this culture-reduced test, in conjunction with other instruments, can produce a more culturally fair assessment procedure.

The Leiter International Performance Scale (LIPS; Leiter, 1948) is a nonverbal performance test that consists of 54 items. This test can be completed by the examinee in 35 to 45 minutes and is appropriate for ages 2 through adulthood. The Arthur Adaptation of the Leiter Performance Scale (Arthur, 1949) is the most often used version of the LIPS with children 3 to 8 years of age. This version was developed in order to lower the inflated norms with this age group on the original instrument. The test requires the testee to select blocks of symbols or pictures and place them in appropriate places. The test comprises (a) colors, shades, and pictures matching, (b) design copying, (c) picture completion, (d) number estimation, (e) series completion and memorization, (f) classification, and (g) spatial relations. Although this instrument has a culturally reduced format by using nonverbal items, its validity across cultures has not been adequately confirmed.

The Goodenough-Harris Drawing Test (Harris, 1963) is a nonverbal test of intelligence suitable for children 3 to 16 years of age, but most often used for ages 3 through 10 years. This instrument has been recommended as a nonbiased test for use with ethnic minority children due to its lack of cultural loading (Oakland & Dowling, 1983). Children are simply asked to draw a person. Evaluation of the completed drawing focuses on the complexity of the child's ability to form concepts. This aptitude includes classification, discrimination, and generalization. The test can be completed in less than 15 minutes, a feature that reduces the time elements of the assessment procedure and removes the stress inherent in timed, speeded tests. The focus on power rather than speed produces more accurate estimates of ability with culturally diverse clients.

The common feature that unites these four instruments is their reliance on a nonverbal format. In addition, three of the instruments remove the time constraints. Although they cannot be considered culture-free or culture-fair, they can be deemed culture-reduced when compared with other verbally predominant, timed instruments. They are only culture-reduced because they still assume that the examinee has been socialized and educated in the culture in which the test originated.

The abilities to classify, serialize, and problem-solve are functions that develop by being socialized and educated in the dominant culture. These culture-specific cognitive abilities are reflected in the underlying structure of standardized tests of ability. As such, they are unfair to non-mainstream clients. Also, the figural and pictorial nature of these instruments may not be culture-fair as claimed because they still require abstract thinking processes and analytical cognitive styles that are not developed in some cultures. In addition, these tests have shown only moderate concurrent validity when correlated with other standardized instruments such as the Wechsler and Binet scales (Anastasi, 1988). Finally, there is little evidence for the predictive validity of these tests with respect to educational achievement or vocational success.

When an English-proficient, yet culturally diverse client is tested, one needs to supplement the assessment procedure with one of the four tests described in this section. Culture-reduced tests appear to be especially useful when combined with traditional standardized measures of intelligence such as the Stanford-Binet: Fourth Edition (Thorndike,

Hagen, & Sattler, 1986). This combination is recommended when the examinee's first language is not English because it provides a verbal and nonverbal indication of the examinee's performance. Using one of the tests without the other is not recommended because both types of tests have basic weaknesses (Sattler, 1992). In particular, most standardized tests are information-based and verbally loaded, whereas culture-reduced tests are not comprehensive and do not demonstrate adequate predictive validity. Using both types of tests can facilitate a more equitable test administration and augment the data obtained from a culturally/linguistically diverse client.

Translated Measures

Language differences have led many clinicians to use instruments that have been translated into, or adapted for, a language other than English. Assessors have also, on occasion, used translators or interpreters during the administration phase of testing to clarify a client's responses for accuracy of communication. Some direct translations of major psychological instruments are available. Most notably, Spanish and French versions of the Wechsler scales and Kaufman Assessment Battery for Children (Kaufman & Kaufman, 1983b) have been developed. Renormed British, Australian, and Dutch adaptations of the original Wechsler scales are also available.

Sattler (1992) and Dana (1993) have outlined difficulties inherent in translated instruments. First, many concepts in one language do not have literal equivalents in another. This dilemma can produce ambiguous instructions and test responses that reduce the test's reliability and validity. Second, translations usually do not take into account national and regional within-group differences. For example, not all Spanish speakers use the same idioms and dialects, and word meanings may be different among Mexican, Cuban, and Puerto Rican clients. Third, translations often produce words with different levels of difficulty and, thus, change the complexity of the original task. This change can affect the meaning of words and result in unanticipated idiosyncratic responses. Sattler (1992) has suggested that translators be well-versed in the language used by the examinee and that language-based tests be avoided when testing a linguistically different client.

Suzuki and Kugler (1995) have also indicated problems inherent in translated instruments. They believe that psychological constructs are not universal but culture-specific and do not translate well on instruments of intellectual assessment. They identify five questions posed by Butcher and Pancheri (1976) to appraise translated tests: (a) Do the constructs exist in the client's culture? (b) Is the test format (e.g., multiple choice) culturally meaningful? (c) Is the test valid in the client's culture? (d) Has the test been translated following appropriate procedures, such as back-translation? and (e) Are the response formats equivalent for all languages used? Suzuki and Kugler have noted that no code of ethics regarding test translations currently exists to guide work in this area. It is, therefore, essential that testers evaluate the translated tests in light of Butcher and Pancheri's questions.

Translating a test of intellectual ability to another language often results in a new instrument that fails to accurately convey the subtleties of meaning or idiosyncratic uses of language. Aiken (1987) has suggested that a *back translation*, rather than literal translation, procedure be used. Back translation occurs when a test is translated into one language by a person, or team of people, and then translated back into English by a different person, or team. This procedure is carried out to maximize the accuracy of the translation and to reduce any cultural bias present in test items.

Anastasi (1988) has described a method for developing translated instruments for use with culturally diverse clients. This method devised by Angoff and Modu (1973) is a two-fold process. First, the assessor selects a group of test items that appear to be appropriate for testees regardless of their culture or language. These items are called anchors and are administered to English speakers in English and non-English speakers in their dominant language. Performance on these items by the different groups allows the assessor to ascertain the level of difficulty and the difference in meaning present for each group. The assessor can accept or reject items based on these two factors in order to assemble anchor items that are suitable for each linguistically different group. Second, the assessor includes the chosen anchor items in a regular assessment of intellect. This method of including items common to each group provides a way of bridging the gap across linguistically different groups.

A crucial problem that exists when using translated or adapted instruments is the comparability of the norms across cultures. Various researchers have examined and renormed translations of the Wechsler scales (Carroll, Herrans, & Rodriguez, 1995; Dai, Ryan, Paolo, & Harrington, 1991; Lopez & Nunez, 1987) and the Kaufman Assessment Battery for Children (Meljac, 1996). These projects have only recently begun and are ongoing. It is hoped that they will prove beneficial in providing valid cross-cultural instruments.

The issue of norm comparability has been examined by Mercer and Lewis (1978). They constructed an instrument designed, in part, to use pluralistic norms for various minority groups. This method of assessment is now examined.

System of Multicultural Pluralistic Assessment (SOMPA)

The SOMPA, developed by Mercer and Lewis (1978), evolved from their concern that culturally and linguistically diverse children were being misclassified as mentally retarded, based on their performance on standardized intelligence tests. The SOMPA is a comprehensive assessment battery suitable for children 5 to 12 years of age. The full assessment can last up to 5 hours and is available in Spanish as well as English. It incorporates three distinct assessment models: medical, social system, and pluralistic.

The medical model presumes that health and perceptual-motor development are related to knowledge acquisition and learning. This model of assessment, therefore, involves six measures: weight by height, visual acuity, auditory acuity, perceptual motor development (as measured by the Bender Visual Motor Gestalt Test, Bender, 1938), physical dexterity, and health history. Assessment involves examiner interaction, medical examination, and parental interview, as well as assessment of whether or not organicity is a factor in the child's learning ability.

The social system model is concerned with the child's ability to adapt and function in social situations. It attempts to measure how well a child meets social expectations at home, at school, and in the community. The Wechsler Intelligence Scale for Children-Revised (WISC-R) or the Wech-

sler Preschool and Primary Scale of Intelligence-Revised (WPPSI-R) are
used to measure the child's social role at school. The score becomes the
School Functioning Level (SFL). The SFL norms are then used to indicate
the level to which the child has inculcated the dominant culture. The
social system also uses two structured parental interviews. One is the
Adaptive Behavior Inventory for Children (ABIC), which has six scales:
Family, Community, Peer Relations, Nonacademic School Roles,
Earner/Consumer and Self-Maintenance. The second is the Sociocultural Scales, which include Family Size, Family Structure, Socioeconomic Status, and Urban Acculturation.

The pluralistic model uses information gathered through the parent
interview to determine the Estimated Learning Potential (ELP) of the
testee. The ELP score is a prediction based on comparisons with children
from the same sociocultural background and has been described as a
WISC-R score partialed out through multiple regression equations for
children from similar backgrounds (Anastasi, 1988; Dana, 1993). This
derived, standard score is computed by taking into consideration the
scores obtained on the Sociocultural Scales. The effect of computing the
ELP in this fashion is a possible elevation of a child's Full Scale IQ in
response to large family size, impoverished background, and limited
urban acculturation. The ELP score is used to predict how much a child
may benefit from an educational program by taking sociocultural factors
into account. The authors have developed pluralistic norms to evaluate
a child's ELP. They provide data on the scores of Anglo, Hispanic, and
African American children. These norms allow the examiner to compare
individual test performance to specific norms as well as dominant culture norms.

Criticisms of the SOMPA have appeared in the *Ninth Mental Measurements Yearbook* (Humphreys, 1985; Reynolds, 1985; Sandoval, 1985).
Sattler (1992) has summarized the main objections to the use of this assessment procedure. First, there are a lack of adequate standardization
samples and an absence of local norms for the ELP score. Second, the
viability of the medical-social system-pluralistic model, with respect to
predictive validity, is questionable because very few validation studies
exist. Third, the conversion of WISC-R to ELP scores, based on sociocultural factors, is controversial because the sociocultural norms developed for the test have not been empirically validated. Fourth, the role of
Bender-Gestalt performance with regard to prediction has been criti-

cized because no separate norms for culturally diverse clients exist. Finally, the assessment procedures do not include an observation of the child at school or an incorporation of current school performance into the final assessment. These criticisms, along with the dearth of validity studies using the SOMPA, have led Sattler (1992) to claim there is "no justification for using the ELP for any clinical or psychoeducational purpose" (p. 354).

Despite these criticisms, the SOMPA represents the first attempt to reduce the stigmatization of minority children and foster multicultural, multilingual programs. In addition, it has helped to further culture-reduced assessment of culturally and linguistically diverse children. Finally, this approach has underscored the need to use a comprehensive approach when assessing the culturally diverse.

Comprehensive Assessment

Assessments that base findings and recommendations on single scores or small numbers of scores do not provide an adequate depiction of a culturally/racially diverse client's intelligence (Samuda & Lewis, 1992; Sattler, 1992). The goal of comprehensive assessment, therefore, is to increase the precision in evaluating an individual's intellectual performance by employing a multimethod approach to assessment. This multifaceted approach is predicated on the notion that single score and single procedure assessments are inappropriate when evaluating clients from diverse educational or cultural backgrounds.

A more equitable approach for a minority client incorporates a wide range of methods to identify the client's level of functioning. A multimodal assessment focuses not only on perceived or inferred intellectual deficits, but also on the assets and strengths a client brings to the testing situation. Such an approach necessitates the use of a team of assessors to gather information about the client. This team needs to consist of psychologists, physicians, counselors, social workers, teachers, administrators, and family members. The team can gather information through testing, observation, and evaluation of archival information. Triangulating the assessment process in such a fashion will lead to diagnosis and remediation based on a consultative process, leading to more beneficial outcomes for clients.

Comprehensive assessment includes a wide range of information: medical information, language dominance, educational level, sensorimotor and perceptual data, developmental information, adaptive behavior indications, personality (including self-report), values, and vocational interests. The assessment of intellect is performed after all of the team's information has been gathered and processed. This procedure allows the aptitude score to be viewed within the context provided by the information already obtained. This approach promotes the placing of test scores into a sociocultural context by considering how an examinee's performance is influenced by acculturation, language proficiency, socioeconomic background, and ethnic/racial identity. It also provides for remedial suggestions and allows the team to carry out and evaluate subsequent intervention strategies.

Comprehensive assessment is a continuous process. As people develop and become more familiar with the dominant culture, their intellectual and achievement profiles change. The monitoring of this evolution emphasizes the importance of helping clients to maximize their strengths and opportunities. This approach requires that the assessor obtain an accurate appraisal of a client's intellectual functioning within the context of his or her cultural, educational, and social background. It focuses on the assets and strengths possessed by the client rather than deficits. Finally, it suggests a program of intervention and remediation for the client. As such, comprehensive assessment has been, and continues to be, a recommended procedure when assessing racially/ethnically diverse children and adults.

Dynamic Assessment Approaches

Dynamic assessment refers to an approach that uses clinical interventions to produce qualitative data about a client. The assessor intentionally changes the traditional static testing situation by going beyond the standardized instructions to uncover hidden potential in the client. Inherent in this approach is the belief that the manifest level of functioning is an inaccurate reflection of an examinee's true ability. The focus on maximal performance, rather than typical performance, and on process, rather than product, is founded on the assumption that examinees have lacked equivalent learning opportunities when compared to clients socialized in the mainstream culture.

Dynamic assessment has been best exemplified by testing-of-limits procedures (Sattler, 1992) and formalized methods of dynamic assessment (Feuerstein, 1979; Gupta & Coxhead, 1988). Testing of limits involves going beyond the standardized instructions and methods to obtain additional information about an examinee. This is done by readministering sections of the test or specific test items using procedures different from those required by the standardized instructions and by changing the role of the assessor during retesting.

A more formal approach to dynamic assessment has been formulated by Feuerstein (1979). This approach postulates that cognitive processes are highly modifiable. Thus, the task of assessment is to measure modifiability rather than the manifest level of functioning as expressed through standardized tests. This approach has spawned a multidimensional instrument, the Learning Potential Assessment Device (LPAD) (Feuerstein, 1979), which is comprehensively described in Chapter 4. Several concepts and procedures have developed from this process-oriented approach and need elucidation in the present chapter.

Testing of Limits

Testing of limits is conducted after the test has been administered in the standardized fashion. Any changes in performance do not affect the overall final score but add vital information concerning the hidden potential of the client to perform the required tasks under nonstandardized conditions. Results obtained from testing-of-limits procedures can be recorded by an examiner after the normal procedures of the test have been followed. The results are then used to further the interpretation of a diverse client's test performance. In particular, scores are likely to indicate greater intellectual potential in a client than is demonstrated by poor performance on a standardized test.

Comprehensive suggestions for testing of limits have been delineated by Sattler (1992). These suggestions, although focused on testing children on the Wechsler scales, could be extended for use with adults assessed on the Wechsler Adult Intelligence Scale—Revised (WAIS-R) and other standardized intellectual assessments.

The first method is the provision of additional cues to the client. Typically, the examiner will first readminister items that have been failed or poorly answered. The examiner asks the client to attempt to discover an alternative solution to the problem. Second, the examiner duplicates the examinee's original response and requests corrections of any mistakes. Third, the examiner provides extra cues by offering the client the first step in solving the problem contained in the test item and provides subsequent steps as necessary. These three procedures give the examiner a clearer picture of how a client benefits from additional cues. The difference in the performance given after these cues more accurately reveals the client's hidden cognitive potential.

The second method is called change of modality. The examiner changes the modality of a test item and readministers it either orally or verbally. If the testee performs poorly on written tasks, one can switch to the oral mode and vice versa. This is especially useful when English-language proficiency is questionable. Allowing clients to operate in their area of strength is intended to enhance performance on certain test items.

The third method is the identification of a client's problem-solving strategies. The examiner readministers items with a view to discovering the cognitive strategies used by the examinee. Because there are many alternative ways to arrive at a solution to a problem, the client is asked to verbalize how he or she arrived at their answer. This procedure allows a glimpse at a client's problem-solving capacities, memory, and organizational ability.

The fourth method, elimination of time limits, is particularly valuable when examining a racially/culturally diverse client. If a client fails to complete a test or subtest within the allotted time, the examiner can readminister the test by removing the time limit, allowing the examinee to finish at his or her own pace. This method helps to ascertain the true level of problem-solving ability.

The fifth method is the use of probing questions. Very often, a diverse client will respond to questions in atypical ways. The examiner can now probe these responses by asking for clarification or elaboration. These probes are intended to facilitate a greater understanding of how the examinee approaches the tasks required by the test.

Sattler (1992) has made other suggestions to incorporate into a testing-of-limits procedure: (a) giving more practice on verbal items and training on the required tasks, (b) rephrasing items that proved particularly difficult, (c) providing positive feedback during this process, (d) allowing the use of paper and pencil on arithmetic items, and (e) restructuring block assembly and picture arrangement items on the Wechsler tests.

Sattler (1992) also recommends testing of limits with the RPM (Raven, 1938). Suggestions include (a) asking clients to reveal their item-solving strategy on items after completing the test, (b) discovering their understanding of principles or rules that underlie specific test items, (c) providing feedback for correct answers and evaluating such feedback on performance, and (d) providing feedback on failed performance by providing correct answers and evaluating the effect of such feedback.

Testing of limits has also been suggested when using the Bender Visual Motor Gestalt Test (Sattler, 1992). Removing time limits and allowing clients to comprehensively compare their drawings with the models provided helps an assessor discover information about a culturally diverse client that may not be revealed in a standardized testing session. Any additional information gleaned during these processes is useful in recommending subsequent intervention strategies.

Measuring Cognitive Modifiability

Rather than focusing on the manifest level of functioning that is expressed by scores on traditional tests, formal dynamic assessment methods have been developed by Feuerstein (1979). These methods go beyond the use of testing-of-limits procedures into the realm of interactive, clinical involvement called *mediation* (Feuerstein, 1979). Mediation is not simply teaching examinees how to solve a problem; it teaches them how to find and use the underlying rules of the task itself. This method proposes use of a test-train-test with mediation procedure. In other words, conventional tests of intelligence are viewed as inventories of present knowledge. As such, conventional tests are static measures, whereas testing-in-the-act-of-learning procedures are considered to be dynamic (Feuerstein, Rand, Jensen, Kaniel, & Tzuriel, 1987).

The uniqueness of mediation is that an examiner is asked to abandon psychometric neutrality and become a teacher-observer who interacts with a learner-performer. The assumption is that a client has not had the same social, educational, or cultural experiences that are presumed by standardized assessment procedures (or methods). The examiner can, through intensive interaction with the client evaluate performance, given his or her background.

This innovative approach originates in the work of Vygotsky (1978), who postulated that each person has a *zone of proximal development* (ZPD) described as "the distance between the actual development level as determined by independent problem solving and the level of potential development as determined through problem solving under adult guidance or in collaboration with more capable peers" (p. 86). The size of this zone is determined by adapting conventional tests of intellectual performance in a test-train-test with mediation methodology. The history of this process-oriented approach to assessment has been well-documented by Lidz (1987), who reveals that nonverbal instruments have most often been used by examiners in the test-train-test model. Feuerstein's (1979) LPAD, outlined in Chapter 4, is the most comprehensive and formalized method of dynamic assessment. It has been used internationally and provides rich qualitative data on diverse clients.

Dynamic assessment via mediation involves testing an individual twice. In the first phase, the examiner provides direct mediation or tutorial guidance to the examinee. Prior to the second phase, the examiner ascertains the client's learning style so the testing material can be presented in the most appropriate fashion. This method can be used with most conventional standardized tests and provides qualitative, prognostic information about the learning potential of the client. A description of this method and its applicability for culturally diverse clients is available in Samuda et al. (1989).

To summarize, the use of dynamic methods through testing of limits, test-train-test, and mediation demand that the examiner go beyond the role of psychometrician and become an active participant in a client's performance during the testing procedure. These process-oriented approaches are not focused on a static score of intellectual ability. Instead, they are concerned with providing a base of qualitative data that take into account the client's ethnic, racial, and cultural background. As such, these approaches are highly recommended for use with diverse clients.

Post-Assessment Considerations

Anastasi (1988) has deemed the interpretations of test scores "by far the most important considerations in the assessment of culturally diverse groups" (p. 66). Misinterpretation of scores with these groups is a grave concern. If low scores are evident with a diverse client, it is necessary to uncover the true reasons for the low level of performance.

During and after assessment, it is incumbent upon the tester to provide information about the testee's performance. These data must include behavioral observations that are embedded within the client's cultural context. Specifically, the examiner should note language facility, familiarity with test procedures, approach to completing the test (i.e., speed vs. power), and noticeable level of anxiety. Any departure from normal standardized procedures must be recorded and any dynamic procedures need to be delineated and recorded in detail. Interpretations that take into account the fairness of the assessment procedure given the client's cultural background are imperative.

Before any recommendations are given, consultation with another professional who comes from the same culture as the client, or who has expert knowledge of the client's culture, is important. This quality check concerning the plausibility of the findings and recommendations provides a more unbiased assessment.

Suzuki and Kugler (1995) have suggested that when used appropriately with attention to culturally sensitive issues, assessments with standardized tests can yield valuable objective data for a culturally different client. Such information benefits the client through interpretations that suggest effective educational, vocational, or clinical interventions.

Recommended Assessment Practices

This chapter has investigated the use of traditional tests of aptitude with culturally diverse clients. Conducting an assessment with a client who is not from mainstream culture requires one to be attuned to the potential strengths and weaknesses of traditional standardized testing. In particular, the assessor must (a) demonstrate awareness and sensitivity regarding a client's cultural background, (b) provide an assessment situation with suitable testing procedures, and (c) generate culturally appropriate interpretations within the larger social context. Precise recommendations in these three areas are offered in the hope that assessments will be as fair as possible for culturally diverse clients.

Awareness and Sensitivity

1. The assessor must learn as much as possible about the client's culture. This knowledge needs to include the values and beliefs of the culture.

2. The assessor must learn about the educational process in the client's culture. In particular, one needs to understand the methods of assessment the client has experienced.

3. One needs to become aware of any stereotypes that are personally held regarding the client and to take steps to minimize the impact of personal biases when testing.

4. The tester must recognize that language issues significantly affect the accuracy of assessment. Using translators or client advocates may improve the fairness of the assessment process when working with limited-English-proficiency clients.

5. The assessor, either formally or informally, needs to assess the client's level of acculturation. The greater the acculturation, the greater the feasibility of comparing the client's score to the published norms of a test.

6. The assessor must be aware of professional and ethical considerations when working with a diverse client. These guidelines are discussed in the last chapter of this book.

Appropriate Assessment Situation and Procedures

1. Assessors must understand that single-score assessment is inappropriate and select only tests that provide a comprehensive picture of the client's abilities. Information should be sampled from a number of areas in order to demonstrate the client's potential, keeping in mind that comprehensive assessment involves triangulation of testing, observation, and archival analysis in addition to a client's educational, social, and cultural history.

2. The examiner needs to use tests of power rather than speed, as many culturally diverse clients are not accustomed to highly speeded tests. This procedure assures their performance is based on their ability, rather than their inability to finish the test.

3. An assessor should use both verbally oriented or nonverbal tests. By using both formats, one can promote a more balanced and, therefore, fair assessment process.

4. Culturally diverse clients exhibit more anxiety during a test situation than mainstream clients, due to the unfamiliarity of the task. To lessen the impact of this anxiety, the assessor must take time, albeit longer than usual, to establish rapport and describe any assessment expectations to the client.

5. Determination of the client's language dominance must be done prior to testing. If the client's dominant language is not English, the tester must consider supplementing the assessment with nonverbal instruments. For this purpose, the Raven matrices or other culture-reduced tests are recommended.

6. If the client's dominant language is not English, the assessor needs to use a test translated or adapted into the client's language, in conjunction with a nonverbal instrument. It is incumbent upon the assessor to evaluate translated and adapted instruments.

7. The assessor needs to ensure that the examinee understands the test directions. This allows the tester to evaluate the viability of using a particular test.

8. An assessor should view nonverbal tests as culture-reduced, rather than culture-free, instruments. The structure of the items and strategies to obtain correct responses have a cultural component and therefore, remain culturally loaded.

9. The SOMPA provides useful adaptive behavior indicators and sociocultural information, but it is not to be used to make clinical or psychoeducational decisions on culturally diverse children because the validity of the ELP score is questionable.

10. Testing-of-limits procedures must be implemented whenever feasible. These procedures need to be used with individual tests of ability, as well as with group measures of aptitude. The client's ability to improve test performance when procedures are modified will help an assessor gain a clearer picture of a client's functioning.

11. Assessors must become skilled at test-train-test via mediation methods. Using a formal dynamic assessment procedure, such as the LPAD, helps the tester identify a client's learning style and ability to profit from tutorial guidance. This shift from product-oriented to process-oriented assessment allows the client to demonstrate learning potential within the context of his or her social and cultural background.

Culturally Appropriate Interpretations

1. The assessor cannot assume that the rules of test interpretation are applicable to the test results of a minority client in the same way they are applied to the test results of a middle-class, mainstream client. Testers need to be flexible when judging cultural factors that are clearly affecting a client's test performance.

2. Acknowledgment of the client's level of acculturation and the effect this level might have on the test result is required. If a lack of acculturation is suspected to have had a role in determining the client's per-

formance, it is necessary to reassess the client when the level acculturation has increased.

3. The assessor needs to use comprehensive assessment data, testing-of-limits results, and other dynamic assessment intervention methods. A qualitative description is needed to outline the strengths and possible deficits of the client.

4. When interpreting scores, the tester must take into account that many traditional tests have not been normed adequately with various cultural groups. They need to be wary of the fact that some examinees are not well-represented by national test norms and make interpretations accordingly.

5. When making recommendations, the examiner must focus on describing strengths rather than weaknesses, potential rather than deficiencies.

6. Recommendations must link assessment to culturally appropriate interventions. These interventions need to focus on helping clients develop their potential.

7. One must never use a single test score to categorize and place a client into a program. A comprehensive approach must always be used.

8. Test results need to eliminate prejudice, racism, and inequities, rather than promote inadequate treatment of culturally diverse clients by providing accurate meaningful scores linked to appropriate intervention strategies.

Conclusion

Given the current emphasis in Western society on test performance for educational, vocational, and clinical purposes, the focus of this chapter has been on using traditional aptitude tests in nontraditional ways to make assessment as fair as possible for culturally diverse clients. Traditional aptitude tests reflect mainstream cultural values and use homogeneous standardization samples. Thus, they predict the ability of mainstream, middle-class clients and are inappropriate for culturally diverse clients. The theme of this chapter has, therefore, been to encourage assessors of the culturally diverse to incorporate nondiscriminatory practices into their testing procedures.

Assessors of the culturally diverse have an ethical and professional obligation to ensure every effort has been made to make the assessment process as culture-free as possible by (a) developing a philosophy that a low score may be attributable to cultural difference rather than a deficit; (b) adopting practices designed to use aptitude tests in such a way as to maximize their validity; (c) realizing that assessment practices require not just sensitivity and knowledge of a client's cultural background, but also the skill to ascertain the impact of this background on test performance; (d) committing to change traditional modes of assessment; and (e) using existing measures of cognitive ability in culturally appropriate ways.

The movement toward culturally skillful assessment is based on the notion that no existing standardized tests are culture-free, but are rather culture-reduced. Any test designed and developed for use by mainstream, middle-class individuals will have information, language, or format biases. These tests may also have structural characteristics that require cognitive processes unfamiliar to some cultures. Thus, several methods for using existing assessment instruments have been suggested in this chapter.

First, it has been advocated that multimodal methods of assessment be used to reduce the discriminatory practice of categorizing and placing cultural diverse clients into programs based on unreliable, single-score assessment. Comprehensive assessment helps reduce the misuse of test scores by identifying the potentialities that exist in a client and contributing to the future development of that client.

Second, innovative approaches have shifted away from a focus solely on quantitative scores to one in which qualitative observations aid in determining the true nature of a client's ability. This approach is based on the notion that ability is not a static product to which a number is assigned, but rather a fluid process that can change, given assessor intervention. Specific recommendations have been given for developing and recording these observations, along with suggestions for the use of these qualitative descriptions when interpreting a client's performance.

In addition, the use of formal dynamic assessment methods has also been discussed with an emphasis on the role of the assessor as mediator.

The approaches recommended in this chapter are based on the notion that testing must have a useful purpose, one that links assessment to effective remediation strategies and culturally appropriate interventions. By adopting nontraditional uses of traditional aptitude tests, assessors are not asked to abandon clinical and psychoeducational assessments with culturally diverse clients. They are, instead, urged to use existing tests, fully aware of their deficiencies, and arm themselves with techniques that can result in equitable assessment.

8 Multicultural Assessment and the Buros Institute of Mental Measurements

On the Cutting Edge of Measurement Concerns

GARGI ROYSIRCAR SODOWSKY
JORGE E. GONZALEZ
PHOEBE Y. KUO-JACKSON

There are three sections in this chapter. Section 1 analyzes the 1993 Buros-Nebraska Symposium on Testing and Measurement: Multicultural Assessment, published as *Multicultural Assessment in Counseling and Clinical Psychology* (Sodowsky & Impara, 1996). Section 2 evaluates popular and recently published ability, achievement, and language tests, available commercially, that have been proposed to have multicultural (MC) relevance. Section 3 evaluates commercial mainstream personality measures that are commonly used with minority populations. Information for Sections 2 and 3 was obtained from recent editions of the *Mental Measurements Yearbook* published by the Buros Institute of Mental Measurements, Department of Educational Psychology, University of Nebraska–Lincoln (1985, 1992, 1995, 1996). Generally associated with classical traditions in measurement, the Buros Institute now finds itself responding to the cutting edge measurement concerns raised by the turn-of-the century dialectics of MC assessment. The first objective of the chapter is to illustrate guidelines for evaluating the MC strengths and weaknesses of assessment measures. The second objective is to provide a resource guide for locating MC instruments.

Section 1: The 1993 Buros-Nebraska
Symposium on Testing and Measurement:
Multicultural Assessment

Scholars currently involved in MC assessment research were invited to the symposium to respond to the lack of MC measures to assess personality. Section 1 consists of three parts. Broad theoretical notions of test bias in the first part lead to specific MC instrumentation in the second and third parts.

Test Bias, MC Assessment Theory,
and MC Instrumentation

Stanley Sue (1996), in "Measurement, Testing, and Ethnic Bias: Can Solutions Be Found?" addresses the nature and extent of bias when one group's regression equation is used as the standard. For instance, a study by Sue and colleagues of predictors of Asian academic achievement showed that a white regression equation both overpredicted and underpredicted the achievements of various Asian groups. In a private communication with the first author (November 1993), Sue emphasized

> that over- or underprediction of GPA involving a difference of .17 is quite substantial, not only to student perceptions but also to admissions to graduate school. As one example, UCLA will not as a rule admit as graduate students undergraduates who have a cumulative GPA of under 3.00. You can imagine how many students receive GPAs between 2.83 and 3.00. . . . Finally, at some universities (such as the University of California, Berkeley), there were attempts to increase the weight of SAT-Verbal over SAT-Math performance in admission. According to our findings, doing so would probably reduce the ability to identify the best Asian American students.

Sue (1996) cites research on misdiagnosis of American ethnic minorities consisting of both over- and underpathologizing. Misdiagnosis in these studies may have resulted from the interaction of client-clinician racial match and mismatch. Sue argues that American minorities are more likely to be misdiagnosed than white Americans. The response biases of Asian American subjects to the Minnesota Multiphasic Personality Inventory-2 (MMPI-2) make Sue question the "metric equivalence" of the MMPI-2. Sue summarizes his coauthored ongoing research on the MMPI-2, showing that diversely acculturated Asian Americans have different profiles. Sue hypothesizes about Asian American personality variables that influence responses to mainstream measures of psychopathology. In this context, Sue suggests using the Asian "loss of face" concept as a validity index—for example, as a "faking good" scale—to understand Asian response sets.

Juris Draguns (1996), in "Multicultural and Cross-Cultural Assessment: Dilemmas and Decisions," draws a distinction between cross-cultural assessment and MC assessment. For instance, it is possible and worthwhile to cross-culturally compare anxiety responses, depression, schizophrenia, or coping responses to catastrophes across political, cultural, and geographic frontiers. Pluralistic localities in the United States provide similar opportunities for investigating the humanly universal conditions of life to which diverse groups respond in culturally variable ways. This is the etic cross-cultural perspective. But in MC assessment, disparities among U.S. racial and ethnic groups, such as the uneven distribution of power and privilege, the complex patterns of acculturation and ethnic identity, and multiple and overlapping group memberships, are studied. These investigations have been taken up by the emic perspective of MC assessment. Draguns also illustrates how to integrate emic-qualitative and etic-quantitative data in order to have a comprehensive understanding of psychopathology across all cultural borders.

Draguns (1996) makes the important point that the concept of culture should generate hypotheses, such as the effects of levels of acculturation or of ethnic identity variations, rather than serve as a convenient source of post hoc explanations. He also suggests solutions to conflicts inherent in assessment assumptions based on the cross-cultural contextualization of psychology. For instance, how does one compare stimuli that are not physically identical (such as schizophrenic symptoms) but are equivalent or that are physically identical (e.g., headaches) but not equivalent. Draguns gives criteria for limiting such stimuli comparisons, such as using caution against artificial matching of individuals from different cultural groups and against comparing samples that are widely divergent in relevant characteristics. To make sure that concepts carry constant meanings, Draguns suggests the systematic collection of empirical data on the equivalence of concepts, use of explicit rules of diagnosis and group assignment, and the employment of multimethods consisting of a series of studies, partial correlations, analysis of covariance, and multivariate analyses.

From the theoretical discourse of Stanley Sue and Juris Draguns, we turn to the presentation of a commercially available MC instrument. Giuseppe Costantino and Robert Malgady (1996), in "Development of the TEMAS [Tell-Me-a-Story], A Multicultural Thematic Apperception Test: Psychometric Properties and Clinical Utility" (Sodowsky & Impara, 1996), present a projective test for Hispanic/Latino and African American children who live in urban pluralistic environments. A nonminority version is also available for urban white children. The authors have done several studies in the 15 years since the development of the TEMAS to study its psychometric properties and its validity. These studies have been conducted in New York as well as in settings in South America.

The primary theoretical difference between the Thematic Apperception Test (TAT) and the TEMAS could be that the TEMAS's basis is in cognitive and ego psychology theories, whereas the TAT seeks to assess interpersonal dynamics related to intrapersonal needs and environmental pressures. The TEMAS assesses three broad functions: cognitive, personality, and affective. The authors have studied the relationships of acculturation, ethnicity, and positive adjustment with TEMAS scores. A useful feature of Costantino and Malgady's (1996) chapter is that it includes samples of TEMAS client protocols and integrated client assessment reports that indicate body-image and self-identity problems, reality-testing problems, relationship difficulties with parental figures, aggression, and sexual molestation tendencies.

Costantino and Malgady (1996) also address psychometric definitions of bias. For example, they argue that even in the absence of compelling empirical evidence, assessment procedures ought not to be routinely generalized to different cultural groups. Thus, MC measures should be increasingly used. They explain that separate norms for mainstream instruments do not remove test bias because mean differences may be valid, and minority norms thus may cause minority populations to be underserved or overstigmatized. Even though classical measurement theory claims that differential validity is rare, mean differences between a minority group and the white majority group suggest that the majority yardstick does not work for minorities. Therefore, emic instruments like the TEMAS are needed.

Costantino and Malgady (1996) request research on face validity. Such research would reveal whether items in mainstream instruments or the *Diagnostic and Statistical Manual* (*DSM-IV*) criteria suspected of cultural bias are concordant or discordant with MC test items or diagnostic criteria considered beyond MC reproach. These authors encourage research that establishes the factor invariance of instruments across racial and ethnic groups because a difference between ethnic groups in number of factors, pattern of factor loadings, percentage of variance explained, or correlations among factors would constitute evidence of test bias.

New Developments in the Theories and Measurement of White and Black Racial Identity

Janet Helms's (1996) "Toward a Methodology for Measuring and Assessing Racial as Distinguished from Ethnic Identity" proposes (a) new theoretical advancements in the black and white racial identity models and (b) a nontraditional psychometric understanding of her instruments.

Helms (1996) introduces a new concept, *sociorace*. Helms says,

> Socioracial groups . . . occupy different positions along the national sociopolitical power hierarchy such that in the U.S., Whites are assumed to define the power group, whereas Blacks are assumed to be their opposite or the inferior, with all other groups of color falling somewhere between the two groups. . . . it is assumed that lower status socioracial groups generally contrast themselves against Whites, whereas Whites generally contrast themselves against Blacks. (p. 154)

Thus, in the case of racial identity, one's race is not defined by one's genes and phenotype, but rather by societal categories, whose internalized consequence is racial identity.

Originally, Helms (1996), who had conceptualized racial identity as a linear, hierarchical developmental process, used the construct of *stages* to describe the respective processes of blacks and whites in the United States who progress from negative and hateful attitudes to positive and healthy attitudes toward both the black and the white racial groups. Helms now suggests that *ego statuses* be used instead of stages. Helms uses a circular diagram to represent the status profile of a person. The circle is used to emphasize that racial identity statuses are not hierarchical, in the sense that the use of one status does not preclude the use of another. According to Helms's revision, a person's racial identity develops along with increasingly more sophisticated differentiation of the ego.

However, the intrapsychic status process cannot be measured. Statuses are hypothetical constructs. Also, different information-processing strategies may underlie each status. Thus, two individuals governed by the same status may actually express themselves through different information-processing strategies. Using this assumption—that there are individual differences in responses to items by test takers operating from the same ego status—Helms argues that each subscale of the Black Racial Identity Attitudes Scale (BRIAS) and White Racial Identity Attitudes Scale (WRIAS) are polifactorial. Therefore, she defends her subscales for not indicating high internal consistency reliabilities. Helms argues that the basic tenets of classical measurement theory regarding measurement error (e.g., items need to be linearly related, as in the case of internal consistency reliability, or interrelationships among items need to indicate the amount of a true score) are not directly applicable to measurement of racial identity responses, which are uniquely ideographic or local.

Racial identity profiles, rather than single scores, should be used to describe individuals. Helms (1996) has used the difference between two subscale scores to determine by how many points subscale raw scores must differ to be significantly different from one another. This method of developing individual profiles is meaningful in comparison to showing group differences. However, Helms does not use standardized scores (e.g., z scores) of the errors of measurement of two subscales scores, as is required by classical measurement theory. Helms includes a table that shows the minimum number of points by which two subscales in a set of a pair of subscales must differ from each other at the .05 level. According to Helms, when paired comparisons are not used, conclusions could be misleading.

Helms (1996) suggests that identity models be considered racial if they describe reaction to racial oppression, and ethnic if the constructs of ethnicity and culture are germane to them. In the latter conceptualization, common cultural socialization is assumed to be the source of interconnectedness among group members. Helms adds that in U.S. society, acknowledgment of ethnicity is largely voluntary, whereas acknowledgment of race is not, and ethnicity typically is permitted by the U.S. white dominant society and by the immigrant group concerned to adapt itself across generations. On the basis of such assumptions, Helms describes her racial identity measures as process measures that, she says, cannot be evaluated by classical measurement theory. On the other hand, she argues that classical measurement theory can be used to construct the content-specific homogeneous constructs of acculturation and ethnic identity measures.

Robert T. Carter (1996), in "Exploring the Complexity of Racial Identity Attitude Measures," examines the scale constructions of the WRIAS and BRIAS and throws light on (a) the underlying dimensions of the various subscales and (b) the use of percentile scores versus raw scores.

Helms and Carter conducted a factor analysis of the WRIAS, a 50-item scale with five subscales, that indicated 11 factors. Carter argues that factor analysis, tests of internal consistency, and interscale correlations focus on items when examining the psychometric aspects. On the other hand, in cluster analysis, distinct dimensions are discernible from scale configurations rather than from item configurations. Then, Carter shows that a two-cluster solution for the five WRIAS subscales represented the best fit in terms of proportion of cases in two clusters. Thus, Helms's white racial identity constructs of *abandoning racism* and *developing a nonracist White identity* may be discernible in the two-cluster solution.

Carter (1996) asks researchers to use transformed percentile scores from norm tables presented in his chapter. To substantiate his recommendation, Carter transformed the two clusters' rank-ordered WRIAS subscale mean raw scores into percentiles, using a newly developed normative table. The percentiles indicate that Cluster 1 is more strongly influenced by Reintegration and Disintegration than by Autonomy, Contact, and Pseudo-Independence. Cluster 2 is more strongly influenced by Pseudo-Independence, Contact, and Autonomy than by Disintegration and Reintegration. When considering the rank-ordered raw scores instead of their matching percentiles, the relative influence of the subscales is less apparent than when using the percentile ranks.

A similar cluster analysis of the BRIAS indicated that a three-cluster solution best fit the data; according to Carter, this suggests three underlying dimensions to the measurement of black racial identity: Pro-White, Racial Confusion, and Racial Pride. At a first glance of the raw scores, the three clusters do not appear to be distinct from each other, with Clusters 2 and 3 having the same rankings of mean subscale scores. However, by using percentiles from a norm table, the rankings change, suggesting distinct profiles within each cluster. Surprisingly, the Pro-White cluster has its strongest influence from Preencounter (anti-black and pro-white attitudes), followed by Immersion-Emersion (pro-black and anti-white attitudes). Carter explains that both these subscales involve stereotypical perspectives of blacks, which might have jointly influenced the cluster.

Sandra Choney and John Behrens (1996), in "Development of the Oklahoma Racial Attitudes Scale-Preliminary Form (ORAS-P)," respond critically to Helms and Carter's conclusion that the WRIAS is factorially complex. According to Choney and Behrens, "the appropriate conclusion is not that the instrument is 'factorially complex' " or that "the constructs are simply more complicated than originally believed" (p. 237). Choney and Behrens argue, "An assent to factorial complexity presumes a level of validity. . . . Such validity is by and large reached by an extensive development process" (p. 237), a process they believe did not occur with the WRIAS. They suggest that Helms revise her instrument rather than her theory. Thus, one of Choney and Behrens's objectives in presenting the ORAS-P is to demonstrate its factor structure is not different from that proposed by their theory.

Calling their own model "pragmatic," Choney and Behrens (1996) say that white racial consciousness is characterized by attitudes regarding the "significance of being White," especially with reference to minorities who do not "share White group membership" (p. 226). The "types" of attitudes that embody the significance of being white reflect ethnocentrism and privilege in white relationships with minorities. Choney and Behrens explain attitude change by using Bandura's social cognitive theory. When there is dissonance between currently held racial attitudes and recent experience, the outcome is a lack of certainty regarding one's attitudes that may lead to changes in types of racial attitudes.

The unique nature of the "dissonant type" is that its experience is available to all types of racial attitudes. The central position of dissonance is indicated by a circumplex diagram, which shows that the four "achieved" types are blocked from each other, except when there is movement through dissonance. The racial consciousness of two "unachieved" types is low because movement between these two type conditions does not require a dissonance experience. This stated assumption about dissonance by Choney and Behrens (1996) makes their understanding about changes in white racial attitudes different from that proposed by Helms (1996), who uses the concepts of ego differentiation and intrapsychic processes.

Choney and Behrens (1996) employed the deductive approach, with items designed to measure seven predetermined constructs. Seven administrations of the ORAS-P over a 3-year period permitted the study of individual item performance, univariate and bivariate distribution of subscale scores, and internal consistency reliabilities. Items were modified, substituted, or newly introduced with each administration and then analyzed.

Although there are relatively few items per type, with only three items in one unachieved type, the internal consistency reliabilities of the subscales are moderately high. Test-retest reliabilities are similar to those of most trait instruments. Confirmatory factor analysis (CFA) results indicate relatively strong loadings for a majority of the items and acceptable goodness-of-fit indexes. Choney and Behrens (1996) agree that future item refinement will need to focus on further distinctions between achieved type subscales because they appear more bipolar than independent. Given the authors' laudable empirical ambitions of "developing" rather than "establishing" the ORAS-P, one expects future refinements of properties that already look promising.

Measurement of the Relationships of Multicultural Counseling Competencies and Counselor Training

Ponterotto et al. (1996), Sodowsky (1996), and Pope-Davis and Neilson (1996), in their respective chapters, pay attention to the nomological net encompassing self-reported multicultural counseling competencies (MCC competency self-reports) for definitional and utilitarian purposes. Ponterotto's self-report Multicultural Counseling Awareness Scale (MCAS) and Sodowsky's self-report Multicultural Counseling Inventory (MCI) are relatively reliable, valid, and pragmatic measures. Sodowsky has published results on her MCI measure in two different articles in the *Journal of Counseling Psychology,* and other authors have published supportive results in the same and other refereed journals. Thus, peer and mainstream recognition is being obtained for an MC instrument used for evaluating multicultural training in professional psychology.

Although the MCAS and MCI assess MC competency self-reports, they differ in their item content and, hence, in their operational definitions of MC knowledge, MC skills, and MC awareness. They have differing numbers of factors. In addition, the item content of their respective factors/subscales indicates that the MCAS focuses on self-reported attitudes and the MCI on self-reported counseling behaviors. Users need to be aware of the two measures' distinctiveness. Nonetheless, one characteristic shared by the measures is their usefulness. After more than a decade of emphasis on practitioners' preparation for MC responsiveness and on relevant theory building for MC training, the MCAS and MCI have made available devices to assess the outcome of such training.

Joseph Ponterotto and his collaborators (1996), in "Development and Initial Validation of the Multicultural Counseling Awareness Scale," show that the MCAS has two subscales, with high internal consistency reliabilities for the Knowledge/Skills subscale and the full scale, a moderate alpha for the Awareness subscale, and moderate high interscale correlations. The longer Knowledge/Skills subscale consistently discriminates among various criterion groups, such as individuals with a higher level of educational preparation in counseling, national multicultural experts, students with supervised minority clinical work, participant race, participant gender, and pretested-posttested students in multicultural counseling classes. However, on the Awareness subscale, score differences are not shown consistently across various groups. Ponterotto and colleagues made strong efforts to recruit participants who were practitioners or graduate students and who represented some diversity with regard to age, race, ethnicity, gender, and state of residence.

Low nonsignificant correlations have been shown between the MCAS subscales and the Crowne-Marlowe Social Desirability Scale. The MCAS Knowledge/Skills subscale and LaFromboise's Cross-Cultural Counseling Inventory-Revised full scale are shown to have a positive, significant, moderate correlation. The MCAS Awareness subscale and Jacobson's New Racism Scale (high score indicating lower white racism toward blacks) have a positive, significant, moderate correlation. The authors state that these correlations provide evidence for the convergent validity of the MCAS.

Sodowsky (1996), in "The Multicultural Counseling Inventory: Validity and Applications in Multicultural Training," first addresses the professional, ethical, and advocacy philosophy of MC training. She then connects MC learning to the empirical need to test whether an MC curriculum leads to MC competency self-reports. This philosophical-psychometric framework is not typical in the measurement literature but is perhaps a turn-of-the-century model that answers the values question, "Why have MC competencies?" and the pragmatic question, "How does one measure such competence?"

Sodowsky (1996; Sodowsky, Taffe, Gutkin, & Wise, 1994) and her collaborators used the following instrument development methods for the MCI: exploratory factor analysis with a large sample of whites from Nebraska; confirmatory factor analysis with a national sample of some diversity to test whether there were one, two, three, or four factors; higher-order CFA to test whether a "general" MC factor accounted for moderate interfactor correlations; estimates of internal consistency reliabilities; tests of factor congruence between the two samples; and qualitative analyses of open-ended responses to develop thematic support for quantitative results. In another validity study, Sodowsky and colleagues (in press) partialed out the effects of race and of their MC Social Desirability Scale, to demonstrate which counselor traits and training variables contribute significantly to MC competency self-reports. Sodowsky (1996) also shows a positive, significant high correlation between the MCI and D'Andrea and Daniel's Multicultural-Awareness-Knowledge-Skills Survey.

Donald Pope-Davis and Deanna Neilson (1996), in "Assessing Multicultural Counseling Competencies Using the Multicultural Counseling Inventory: A Review of the Research," remind readers that a debate continues regarding what should be the content and method of MC training. They suggest that identifying specific factors that may affect the development of MC competency across training modalities would be helpful. Pope-Davis and Nielson review Pope-Davis and his collaborators' survey of various training situations, using Sodowsky's MCI. They provide tables of the internal consistency reliabilities and interscale correlations of the MCI across a variety of studies, demonstrating the strong stability of the MCI. Pope-Davis and Nielson's integrated review provides additional construct validity support for the MCI, in addition to suggesting possible subscale relationships with factors external to the MCI. Examples of predictor variables studied include training in counseling psychology versus clinical psychology, completion of MC seminars/workshops, number of general practica, discussion of MC issues in clinical supervision, work with minority clients, trainees' race, and trainees' white racial identity attitudes, as measured by Helms and Carter's WRIAS. The above and other predictor variables predicted the four MCI factors variously, with MC Awareness being predicted most often, followed by MC Counseling Knowledge, MC Counseling Skills, and MC Counseling Relationship (in that order).

Although Pope-Davis and Neilson (1996) present a configuration of relationships of training variables with MC competency self-reports, they comment that they did not examine the depth or content of MC materials used in training or the theoretical orientation of instructors and supervisors. Their suggestion is that such investigations may eventually point to a theoretical basis for the selection of experiential learning activities that would influence the development of MC competencies.

Section 2: Evaluation of Multicultural Ability, Achievement, and Language Tests

Prototype ability tests, the System of Multicultural Pluralistic Assessment (SOMPA) and the Wechsler Intelligence Scale for Children-Third Edition (WISC-III) are often critiqued with regard to their MC relevance. In this section, evaluations of these two tests are followed by evaluations of recently developed or revised ability, achievement, and language tests purported to have MC validity. Evaluations are guided by the following overarching question: Is it justifiable to use up classroom teaching and learning time to administer a test that is not used to give feedback to the tested student (even though a minor), as well as to develop individualized instructional plans for the tested student? This issue of treatment validity may be of great importance to test consumers, that is, people who are given tests.

System of Multicultural Pluralistic Assessment

The SOMPA, developed by Jane R. Mercer and June F. Lewis in 1978, is published commercially by the Psychological Corporation. It is reviewed in the *Ninth Mental Measurements Yearbook* (Buros Institute, 1985). Designed to be administered to one individual at a time, the SOMPA has unique strengths. The first ability instrument to have MC features, its norming sample included equal size groups of "Hispanics,"[1] blacks, and whites. The SOMPA attempts a systems-oriented assessment of a child, using a medical model, a social systems model that includes parent interviews, and a pluralistic model. The pluralistic model argues for equating a child's IQ score (obtained from the Wechsler Intelligence Scale for Children-Revised [WISC-R] included in the SOMPA battery) with varying sociocultural characteristics, such as family structure and urban acculturation. This derived corrected estimate provides an Estimated Learning Potential (ELP). The SOMPA's Adaptive Behavior Inventory, possessing good inter-observer agreement, is said to be one of the best adaptive behavior measures for children ages 5 to 11. The manuals are complete and well-written.

Among the SOMPA's weaknesses, a question must be raised about its treatment validity, given the enormous investment in time by the examiner to properly administer it and by the examinee to take its several component tests. One asks how is the SOMPA related to remedial interventions and educational outcome? There are other problems, too. Even though the SOMPA is meant to be used with children who may be placed in educational programs for the mentally retarded or the gifted, the validity of the Physical Dexterity Tests has not been established as differentiating at-risk populations. The Health History Inventories show test-retest reliabilities ranging widely, from –.08 to .96. Across demographic groupings, the Trauma Scale has been reported to have varying stability coefficients of .23 and .74 for males and females, respectively. There is weak evidence of construct validity, with .14 reported as the greatest correlation between the Bender Gestalt and the SOMPA Self-Maintenance Scale. No psychometric information is provided in the technical manual for the Sociocultural Scales, nor is interrater agreement between two parents reported. Criterion-related reliability of the ELP has not been established. Finally, the sample was restricted to children in California. Apparently, the SOMPA's intended purposes have not been adequately studied.

Wechsler Intelligence Scale for Children– Third Edition (WISC-III)

The revised WISC-III was published in 1991 by the Psychological Corporation. It is reviewed in the *Twelfth Mental Measurements Yearbook*

(Buros Institute, 1995). Designed to be administered to one individual at a time, the WISC-III's normative sample was large, closely approximating the 1988 U.S. census data for race and ethnicity. Attempts were made to make items sensitive to MC gender concerns. People portrayed on items of Picture Completion and Picture Arrangement come from various racial and ethnic groups. A WISC-III item analysis study eliminated or revised items that functioned differentially, and items were reviewed by a panel of experts. New items were added to address floor and ceiling effects. A co-normed achievement test, the Wechsler Individual Achievement Tests (WIAT), allows for identification of discrepancies between aptitude and achievement. The psychometric properties and enhanced factor structure of the revised measure are adequate. For instance, the internal consistency reliabilities of all subtests, except for the two speeded tests, are in the moderate to excellent range (.61 to .90), and reliabilities of the IQs and Indexes are good to excellent (.80 to .97). Acceptable evidence is provided for convergent validity, divergent validity, academic achievement predictive validity, and theory-expected group difference validity.

Among the WISC-III's weaknesses is the fact that its MC features, although improving its face validity, have failed to radically restructure the test in comparison to the WISC-R, the prototype mainstream intelligence test, which has been considered to have overt cultural bias. Due to large demographic changes projected for the Hispanic and Asian composition of the United States, the WISC-III may need to be renormed by the year 2010. In addition, concerns have been raised about the stability of the subtests and the unclear meaning of the Freedom From Distractibility (FFD) and Processing Speed (PS) factors.

Differential Ability Scales (DAS)

The DAS, developed in 1990 by Colin D. Elliot, is commercially published by the Psychological Corporation. It is reviewed in the *Eleventh Mental Measurement Yearbook* (Buros Institute, 1992). The DAS measures cognitive abilities and achievement. Designed to be administered to one individual at a time, the DAS is for children in preschool from ages 2 years, 6 months, to 3 years, 5 months; and school-age children from 5 to 17 years, 11 months. School achievement tests can be used with children ages 6 years to 17 years, 11 months. The DAS provides a composite measure of both conceptual and reasoning abilities, which is helpful in making diagnostic and placement decisions. Based on Item Response Theory (IRT), mean internal consistency reliabilities range from .70 to .92, .88 to .92, and .90 to .95 for individual subtests, composite scores, and General Conceptual Ability score (GCA), respectively. Mean internal consistency for the Nonverbal Composite is .81 to .94, depending on the age group. Preschool subtest and composite test-retest reliabilities and school age-level test-retest reliabilities are in the adequate range. Standard errors of measurement are reported to be low. Concurrent validity is provided by comparing DAS composites and GCA scores with the Wechsler Preschool and Primary Scale of Intelligence-Revised (WPPSI-R) (.72 to .89); Stanford-Binet Intelligence Test, Fourth Edition (.69 to .77); McCarthy Scales of Children's Abilities (.55 to .84); and Kaufman Assessment Battery for Children (K-ABC) (.63 to .68). The correlations are higher for older children. The DAS was standardized on 3,475 U.S. children. Stratified random sampling, based on the 1988 U.S. census, was used, which included race and ethnicity in the sample. A Bias Review Panel evaluated the test to eliminate racial, ethnic, or cultural factor bias at the item or subtest level. Moreover, expanded samples of black and Hispanic children were collected for the purpose of item bias analysis. The combination of a developmental and educational perspective of the DAS makes it unique and competitive among other tests of cognitive abilities (e.g., WISC-III, K-ABC, WPPSI-R) for children 3 years, 6 months to 6 years old. It is purported to have high sensitivity regarding mild to moderate developmental delays in children. The DAS handbook is comprehensive and exemplary.

Otis-Lennon School Ability Test (OLSAT), Sixth Edition

The developers of the OLSAT are Arthur S. Otis and Roger T. Lennon, and it is published commercially by the Psychological Corporation. The OLSAT is reviewed in the *Eleventh Mental Measurement Yearbook* (Buros Institute, 1992). Designed to be administered to groups of individuals at the same time, the OLSAT is used to measure an examinee's ability to do school learning tasks, as well as to provide information on school placement. Internal consistency reliabilities are reported to be high, in the high .80s and .90s for the total score and in the .80s for the Verbal and Nonverbal scores. The OLSAT was normed on 356,000 students. The sample was stratified, resembling the 1980 U.S. census, according to socio-economic status, urbanicity, region, and ethnicity, which included African Americans, Hispanics, whites, and an "Other" category. Test items were evaluated via qualitative editorial examination by judges from a number of minority groups who have also been well-known outspoken critics of potential biases in tests. Attention was paid to racial, ethnic, and gender balance in the item content. Notable was the attention given to the elimination of stereotypic items as well as items that functioned differentially for blacks, whites, and Hispanics. Among the OLSAT's strengths is the provision of separate scores for Verbal and Non-Verbal School Ability Indexes (SAIs). The manual also includes a discussion of the advantages and limitations of the OLSAT interpretation and uses; however, a more thorough discussion would be desirable.

Among the OLSAT's weaknesses is the absence of test-retest reliability information in the Preliminary Technical Manual, as well as the lack of an alternate form. Validity information for the different uses of the OLSAT is limited, which explains why the OLSAT lacks an integrated and comprehensive discussion of validation procedures and does not clarify what it actually measures. The OLSAT may have little treatment utility.

Peabody Individual Achievement Test-Revised (PIAT-R)

The developer of the PIAT-R is Frederick C. Markwardt, Jr., and its date of revision is 1989. It is commercially published by American Guidance Service. The PIAT-R is reviewed in the *Eleventh Mental Measurement Yearbook* (Buros Institute, 1992). Designed to be administered to one individual at a time, the PIAT-R is a wide-range measure of academic achievement for students ranging in age from 5 years to 18 years, 11 months. It is a screening instrument for academic skill areas. High reliabilities are reported for split-half, Kuder-Richardson, test-retest, and item response theory for the first five tests, with most validity coefficients at or exceeding .94 for both ages and grades. Content validity was provided by employing expert judgment. Construct validity was supported via examination of developmental progression, factor analysis, and correlations ranging from .46 to .97 between the PIAT-R and the PIAT, and

.50 to .72 between the PIAT and the Peabody Picture Vocabulary Test-Revised (PPVT-R). The standardization sample consisted of 1,563 kindergarten through 12th grade students. Geographic, socioeconomic, and ethnic group characteristics were representative of their proportional U.S. distributions. The PIAT-R, the psychometrically strong revision of the PIAT, reflects the developer's intent to address issues surrounding a well-balanced inclusion of racial, cultural, and socioeconomic differences. It is suggested that users acquire appropriate training to score the test properly.

Test of Language Competence-Expanded Edition (TLC-E)

The TLC-E was developed in 1989 by Elisabeth H. Wiig and Wayne Secord, and its commercial publisher is the Psychological Corporation. It is reviewed in the *Eleventh Mental Measurements Yearbook* (Buros Institute, 1992). Designed to be administered to one individual at a time, the TLC-E is used to evaluate delays in emerging linguistic competence, taking also into consideration the use of semantic, syntactic, and pragmatic strategies. It provides a broad-based estimate of language competence. It is typically used to identify students who demonstrate deficits in metalinguistic language competence and to provide a strategy-based approach to the assessment. Detailed data are provided on internal consistency, standard error of measurement, test-retest reliability, and interrater reliability. Evidence is provided of content, criterion-related, predictive, and construct validity. The TLC-E provides evidence of good predictive and construct validity. The norming sample was selected to approximate the U.S. population by geographic region, race, and Spanish origin. In Level 1 of the tests, about 30% of sample students were of black or Spanish origin. The developers suggest that the examiner take variations in dialect into account when scoring and interpreting scores. The authors provide a section on nonstandard dialects, such as black English, Southern white, and Appalachian. The test makes a provision for nonstandard English scoring, as in scoring the responses of a child who speaks black English. Moreover, the developers stress that caution should be taken when interpreting minority scores. The TLC-E is one of few tests that attempt to go beyond discrete point testing by also assessing semantic-syntactic interactions and pragmatics. That is, unlike most language tests that assess vocabulary and syntactic knowledge (discrete point), this test evaluates appropriate expression and the understanding of language as mediated by contextual communication demands. Few language tests are available that provide evidence of criterion-related validity. The TLC-E does.

Test of Nonverbal Intelligence, Second Edition (Toni-II)

In 1990, Linda Brown, Rita J. Sherbenou, and Susan K. Johnson developed the TONI-II. Its commercial publisher is PRO-ED. The TONI-II is reviewed in the *Eleventh Mental Measurements Yearbook* (Buros Institute, 1992). Designed to be administered to one individual at a time, the TONI-II assesses general intelligence via language-free abstract/figural problem-solving items. It is typically used with individuals possessing language and/or motor skill impairments and individuals with poor or different linguistic backgrounds. The test is administered via pantomime and or gesture. As such, the test is not limited by verbal instructions, thereby making it more culture-free than other ability tests. It explicitly considers environmental and respondent conditions that could have some relevance to interpreting test scores. Internal consistency reliabilities exceeded .90 for most ages. Alternate form reliabilities exceeded .80 for all ages. Split-half, immediate test-retest with alternate forms, and delayed test-retest with alternate forms reliabilities have been reported. Moderate to high correlations with other measures of ability and achievement are provided. Thus, this is a well-validated test for assessing populations whose language or motor difficulties would otherwise make them difficult to test with traditional broad-based intelligence tests (e.g., WISC-III, K-ABC).

Among the test's weaknesses are the TONI-II correlations of .74 and .78 for Forms A and B, respectively, with the Language Arts subtest of the SRA. Thus the test may be only apparently free of English language bias. Also claiming the TONI-II is culture-free because of its nonverbal administration format may be an erroneous assumption because the examinee may be relying on internal language dialogue to solve the problems presented. The outdated racial term *Negroid* is used. Finally, the TONI-II may not be an improvement over its previous version.

Language Assessment Scales-Oral (LAS-O)

Developed by Edward A. DeAvila and Sharon E. Duncan, the LAS-O is distributed by CTB Macmillan/McGraw-Hill. It is reviewed in the *Twelfth Mental Measurements Yearbook* (Buros Institute, 1995). Designed to be administered to one individual at a time, the LAS-O is an individually administered instrument reported to assess the degree to which language-minority students possess the oral language skills that are requisite for successful functioning in mainstream academic environments. The LAS-O is purported to measure four major aspects of language: phonology, lexicon, syntax, and pragmatics. It is typically used as a screening device in making placement and reclassification decisions for language-minority students. The LAS-O is reported to possess high concurrent validity. For instance, correlations between Long and Short Forms are reported to be .90 and above, and scores on the LAS-O correlated highly with linguistic proficiency ratings provided by teachers. A strength of the test is that the Story Retelling tasks simulate the use of language in real-life settings, an aspect of utilitarian validity.

Among the LAS-O's weaknesses is its standardization. The manual presents the relevant characteristics of a "tryout" sample composed of both minority and nonminority students. There is, however, no mention of how the tryout sample was collected. The description of the standardization procedures appears insufficient. Thus, the validity of the normal curve equivalent scores used in the manual is questionable.

The LAS-O is laden with scoring difficulties. For example, the Story Retelling subscale is disproportionately weighted; no theoretical rationale is presented for doing this. Another problem with the LAS-O is the inclusion of items in the Minimal Sound Pairs subscale that failed to meet the developers' own criteria for dropping items and whose inclusion the developers do not theoretically justify. A closer examination of the Listening Comprehension subscale reveals that it may measure not only language skills but memory as well, raising concern for construct validity. The manual has typos and makes references to tables that are not there or do not include what the text indicates or are mislabeled or have incomplete data.

Language Assessment Scales, Reading and Writing (LAS R/W)

The developers of the LAS R/W are Sharon E. Duncan and Edward A. DeAvila, its date of development is 1988, and its commercial publisher is CBT Macmillan/McGraw-Hill. The LAS R/W is reviewed in the *Twelfth Mental Measurements Yearbook* (Buros Institute, 1995). Designed to be administered to a group of individuals at a time, the LAS R/W assesses English reading and writing function levels of language-minority students. It is typically used to make entry and exit decisions for students in English as a Second Language (ESL) programs. The LAS R/W is meant to be used in tandem with the LAS-O (see previous evaluation) to arrive at a Language Proficiency Index. When thus used, the strengths of the LAS R/W include its potential usefulness in both predicting success in mainstream classes and making eligibility decisions for ESL classes. The norming sample consisted of 4,000 students in Grades 1 through 12, with twice as many language-minority as language-majority students. Home languages of the norming sample included English, Spanish, Chinese, Vietnamese, Tagalog, Japanese, and Arabic, as well as Native American languages. LAS-R/W Forms A and B correlate adequately with each other, thus providing evidence of alternate-form reliability. Classification of students based on the LAS R/W and the California Tests of Basic Skills yielded correlations between .80 and .90, thus providing some support for concurrent validity.

Among the LAS R/W weaknesses, about half of the subtests possess low internal consistency reliabilities (less than .80), possibly resulting from the small number of items per subtest. In addition, inadequate validity evidence limits the confidence one can place in this instrument.

Receptive One-Word Picture Vocabulary Scale

Developed in 1987 and revised in 1991 by Morrison Gardner, the Receptive One-Word Picture Vocabulary Scale is published commercially by Academic Therapy Publications. It is reviewed in the *Twelfth Mental Measurements Yearbook* (Buros Institute, 1995). Designed to be administered to one individual at a time, this measure assesses receptive single-word vocabulary, and it is used to gather information about individual differences resulting from language impairments, language delays, and bilingualism. Directions include administration and scoring manuals for use with Spanish-speaking children. There is a Spanish-speaking version of the test. Internal consistency reliabilities are adequate, ranging between .81 and .93. Content, criterion-related, and item-level validity are reported as well.

Among the test's weaknesses is the developer's conceptualization that bilingualism falls in the same category as language impairment and delays, reflecting U.S. white society's preference for English monolingualism. In many countries, and within many U.S. ethnic groups, bilingualism and trilingualism are the norm. Even though a moderate correlation is reported between the test and the Vocabulary subtests of the WPPSI and the WISC-R, this may not sufficiently demonstrate convergent validity. Because there is a lack of information on the norming sample, which consisted of a sample of children in San Francisco, it is assumed that the sample was relatively homogeneous. No standardization was undertaken of the Spanish version of the tests, nor was the test administered to any Spanish-speaking children as part of the overall standardization process. The test has little treatment validity in terms of setting up a remedial English program. The test line drawings could be considered crude.

Stanford Achievement Test-Abbreviated Version-8th Edition (SAT)

The developer and commercial publisher of the SAT is the Psychological Corporation, and its date of revision is 1992. The SAT is reviewed in the *Twelfth Mental Measurements Yearbook* (Buros Institute, 1995). Designed to be administered to a group of individuals at a time, the revised SAT, an abbreviated measure of the original SAT, measures student achievement across reading, mathematics, language, spelling, study skills, science, social science, and listening, as well as overall student achievement. Typically, it is used to get descriptive academic achievement information on a student relative to other students, although it may also be used to gather information about group trends. The revised SAT's norms, based on a restandardization sample of 170,000, were stratified with respect to urbanicity, geographic region, socioeconomic status, and ethnicity. Items on the test underwent extensive review by curriculum specialists to ensure freedom from cultural, ethnic, gender, and racial biases with regard to content, style, and vocabulary. Item-level analysis was also conducted to ensure similar item functioning for gender and ethnicity. The abbreviated SAT requires less of a teacher's limited time to administer than the full-length version.

Among the SAT's weaknesses, its internal consistency reliabilities, although excellent, are based on information from the 1988 norms. No reliability information is reported in the new 1991 National Norms Booklet. Similarly, no test-retest reliabilities are reported in the basic manual. The abbreviated SAT version has not been correlated with the original SAT or with other tests of academic achievement. Information about the performance of racial groups, which would aid in establishing convergent validity, is not incorporated. The manual does not provide sufficient information on how the users should use test performance information to address areas of student need or weaknesses and to improve instruction and learning, which are issues of treatment validity.

Aprenda La Prueba De Logros en Español (Aprenda)

The developer and commercial publisher of the Aprenda is the Psychological Corporation, and its date of publication is 1991. The Aprenda is reviewed in the *Supplement to the Twelfth Mental Measurements Yearbook* (Buros Institute, 1996). Designed to be administered to a group of individuals at a time, the Aprenda is an academic achievement test for Spanish-speaking students in kindergarten to Grade 8 who receive instruction in Spanish. From the test, one could develop ideas about classroom instructional improvement. Norms were selected and based on the Spanish-speaking school population by U.S. region, country of origin, and the 1980 census data. Tryout items were reviewed by Spanish-speaking content experts and editors, bilingual education teachers, and measurement specialists. An eight-member bilingual education advisory panel reviewed the tryout items for item bias to include ethnic, class, and regional language differences among Hispanics. Internal consistency reliabilities for all grades for the subtests range from .66 to .97 for the national sample and .70 to .96 with the Spanish-speaking sample. Basic battery internal consistency reliability for all grade levels and groups exceeded .95. Correlations between subtests range between .43 to .86. When the test content is compared with the Aprenda's Index of Instructional Objectives, support for content validity appears to be present. The Aprenda uses the Stanford Achievement Test as a model for test content; yet, unlike many Spanish instruments, which are mere translations of their English counterpoints, the Aprenda is not. Criterion-related validity is asserted by demonstrating progression across benchmarks in instructional sequences, and construct validity by correlating subtests across levels.

Among the Aprenda's weaknesses is a lack of test construction information and supporting evidence for the validity of the test. Alternate form and test-retest reliabilities are not provided. The test is not compared to frequently used textbooks, and test performance is not linked to state-level objectives. The manual does not inform potential users about who participated in the item writing or how test specifications were prepared. For the Spanish-speaking norming sample, it appears the West geographical region was disproportionately represented. For example, although Cubans represent 6% of the U.S. Spanish-speaking population, they were not included in the norms. Although efforts were made to address readability, some vocabulary word meanings have regional differences among Spanish-speaking people and are most consistent with the Mexican American population. Some pictured activities are stereotypic, showing girls as passive and using names that suggest all Spanish-speaking children have names like Lupita and Pepe. The test lacks essential demographic information on the norming sample and does not explain methods used to identify balanced bilinguals (fully and equally proficient in English and Spanish) for the sample.

Comprehensive Scales of Student Abilities: Quantifying Academic Skills and School-Related Behavior Through the Use of Teacher Judgments (CSSA)

Donald D. Hammill and Wayne P. Hresko developed the CSSA in 1994. Its commercial publisher is PRO-ED. The CSSA is reviewed in the *Supplement to the Twelfth Mental Measurements Yearbook* (Buros Institute, 1996). Designed to be administered to one individual at a time, the CSSA was intended to meet the pressing need of teachers to quickly assess via teacher rating a student's ability along a number of taxonomies. It is intended for students ages 6 to 17 in Grades 1 through 11. Typically, the measure is used (a) to identify student strengths and areas of need for intervention designing, (b) to collect prereferral data, (c) to document educational progress, (d) to provide evidence of a need for referral for further assessment, and (e) to do research. The 1990 U.S. census data were used to stratify the norming group for the CSSA. Stratification was conducted by geographical region, gender, race, residence, and ethnicity. High reliabilities are reported, with internal consistency reliabilities ranging between .88 and .99; test-retest reliabilities ranging between .86 and .95; and interrater reliabilities ranging between .92 and .97. The developers are careful to point out that students with cultural differences, such as non-English speakers, may be penalized and receive low scores. As such, the authors provide space on their Profile/Record Form for qualitative information that may affect the score. The developers suggest that results should be treated as a working hypothesis, pending further investigation of numerous factors, before an assessment of a child's ability can be made. Another strength of the CSSA is that it allows teachers to resource others to help score and interpret the measure.

Among the CSSA's weaknesses, the reported high interrater reliability could be considered questionable due to the small sample from which it was derived. Criterion-related validity would be very important for the CSSA because teachers' qualitative judgments would need to be related to student achievement or ability outside teacher analyses; but the claim of criterion-related validity is not convincing. A significant number of items appeared to be inappropriate for students across levels. The manual's advice that one should average interrater, internal consistency, and test-retest reliabilities is not acceptable because each type of reliability relates to a unique source of error. The CSSA may be best limited to experimental purposes.

IDEA Reading and Writing Proficiency Test

Developed in 1993 and commercially published by Ballard and Tighe, the IDEA was created by Beverly A. Amori, Enrique F. Dalton, and Phyllis L. Tighe. The IDEA is reviewed in the *Supplement to the Twelfth Mental Measurements Yearbook* (Buros Institute, 1996). Designed to be administered to a group of individuals at a time, the IDEA consists of sets of tests of reading and writing in English for students whose proficiency in English varies. The IDEA provides broad assessment of initial identification and redesignation of Limited English Proficient (LEP) students for LEP instruction. The manual has detailed information useful for making placement and redesignation decisions. The manual provides an abundance of information on norming sample ages, gender, ethnicity, teacher opinions and expectations, and district language designations. The internal consistency reliabilities for total Reading scores are .95, .91, .90, and .96 for different tests. The internal consistency reliabilities for other multiple-choice subtests are reportedly lower, between .54 and .86. Test-retest and alternate form reliabilities follow similar patterns. Inter-rater reliabilities for the Writing subtests range between .90 and .98. Content validity is supported via the procedure of item-test specifications, which are considered to be exemplary.

Among its weaknesses is the test developers' claim to construct validity through their use of subtest intercorrelations and subtest-total correlations. Criterion-related validity is inadequate. The test lacks a discussion of item discrimination information and a detailed explanation of the standard error of measurement.

In summary, it is interesting to note that, although still very few, an increased number of MC test reviews are appearing in editions of the *Mental Measurements Yearbook,* the gatekeeper of traditional assessment. It is hoped that this section will encourage authors of MC cognitive instruments to investigate their instruments and develop support for their tests' reliability, validity, and treatment utility through instrument refinement. However, because the development of a test could become a never-ending process involving reliability and validity investigations, the authors should make their initially developed instruments available for research and commercial use. Then, they should request reviews in the *Mental Measurements Yearbook.* More MC instruments need to be made public, and their authors must request peer feedback if MC assessment is to be advanced.

Section 3: Evaluation of Select Personality Tests

This section evaluates the multicultural relevance of two mainstream personality tests that are widely used across races, ethnicities, and cultures.

Strong Interest Inventory, Fourth Edition (SVIB or Strong)

The developers of the Strong are Edward K. Strong, David P. Campbell, and Jo-Ida C. Hansen; the date of the Fourth Edition is 1985; and its commercial publisher is Consulting Psychologists Press. The Strong is reviewed in the *Twelfth Mental Measurements Yearbook* (Buros Institute, 1995). Designed to be administered to one individual at a time, the Strong compares a person's interests with interests of people happily employed in a wide variety of occupations. It does not measure aptitude or intelligence. The Strong has been used by counselors for about 60 years, and reviews have appeared in at least seven previous editions of the *Mental Measurements Yearbook*. The inventory has a long, venerable history of use, in part because its authors have responded to social changes during that period.

The major revisions of the 1985 Strong have been the following:

1. The Occupational Scales were extended to reduce the previous overemphasis on professional occupations; there are 34 new scales for vocational-technical occupations.

2. There are 12 new scales for six newly emerging professional occupations.

3. Overall, there are now 207 Occupational Scales, representing 106 occupations, of which 32% have mean educational levels of less than 16 years or do not require a college degree.

4. The older Occupational Scales have been renormed, with all 207 scales reasonably current. The normative sample was expanded for the 1985 edition, testing 142,610 people to get 48,238 sample members.

Scores on the Strong are highly reliable. Even though the Basic Interest Scales range in length from 5 to 24 items, test-retest reliabilities for the same sample over 2 weeks, 30 days, and 3 years were .91, .89, and .87, and coefficient alpha was .92 for males and .91 for females. Concepts of vocational interest on the Strong were initially defined only in empirical terms, but since 1974, they have been linked to Holland's theory of occupational interests. This theoretical grounding helps in understanding and defining the construct of vocational interest and provides a theoretical structure to guide and direct inquiry regarding the construct. It is difficult to imagine a better guide for the counselor or other users than the Strong's user's guide. Extensive attention has been given to help counselors and clients with interpretation.

However, the test manual has no information summarizing the racial composition of the large normative sample. The instrument's items have not been changed since 1974, except for the wording on seven items related to religious activities, so as to make them less specifically Christian. The empirically derived "Special Scales," Academic Comfort and Introversion-Extroversion, continue to face criticism. Although extensive reliability and validity information is given about them, interpretation is difficult because their scale construction, number of items, and the actual items are not disclosed.

The extensive research that culminated in the 1985 revision was largely a result of the women's movement, which focused attention not only on inequities in the job market but also on inequities in the Strong's use of separate Occupational Scales for men and women. This led to the development of the Women-in-General and Men-in-General normative samples for constructing the Occupational Scales, which have both male and female scales. Of the 106 occupations represented, 101 have scales for females and males. The authors conclude that substantial gender differences exist even between men and women in the same occupation. However, they caution that separate scales and separate norms must be used as a means of expanding options and not limiting them. The authors encourage men and women to consider occupations heretofore dominated by the opposite sex.

Minnesota Multiphasic Personality Inventory-2 (MMPI-2)

The MMPI, developed in 1943, was restandardized in 1990 as the MMPI-2. The authors of the MMPI were S. R. Hathaway and J. C. McKinley; for MMPI-2, authorship was expanded to include the restandardization committee: J. C. Butcher, W. G. Dahlstrom, J. R. Graham, A. Tellegen, and Y. Ben-Porath. The MMPI/MMPI-2 is published by University of Minnesota Press and commercially distributed by National Computer Systems. The MMPI-2 is reviewed in the *Eleventh Mental Measurements Yearbook* (Buros Institute, 1992). Designed to be administered to one individual at a time, the MMPI/MMPI-2 is intended to assess a number of major patterns of personality and emotional disorders for ages 18 and over.

The need for the restandardization of the MMPI had been present from the very beginning. The Minnesota normal sample consisted of largely rural, eighth-grade educated, skilled or semiskilled, northern Midwesterners of Scandinavian origins, disparagingly called the "Minnesota farmers" by assessment critics. By making the Minnesota normals a contrast group for the psychiatric criterion groups, as well as the reference group for normative standards, the latter function was compromised. This bias became evident as subsequent normal groups, when plotted on the standard profile form, had scores hovering half a standard deviation above the mean, thus appearing abnormal. In addition, the lack of a nationally representative normative sample became conspicuous as the application of the MMPI expanded outside the psychiatric ward to include general medicine, personnel screening and selection, forensic and child custody evaluations, outpatient psychotherapy, and assessment of disability.

Although the total lengths of the MMPI (566 items) and MMPI-2 (567 items) are almost identical, substantial changes occurred at the item level: 394 unaltered items were carried over to the MMPI-2; 66 items were modified or rewritten; 90 objectionable items were deleted because they were sexist or covered Christian beliefs, bowel and bladder functioning, or sexual adjustment, thus representing potential violations of Equal Employment Opportunity guidelines if included for personnel decisions; 16 duplicate items for the Test-Retest (TR) Index were deleted; and 107 new items were added, some of their phrasings not reflecting the smooth, worn quality of common speech.

Item order was rearranged to permit the three basic validity and nine clinical scales to be scored from the first 370 items, that is, the front side of the answer sheet. Among the new Supplementary Scales are Peterson's Masculine Gender Role (GM) and Feminine Gender Role (GF). These are two independent dimensions tapping sex role differentiation or "rigidity" on the one end (that is, a high score) and "androgyny" or a lack of sex role differentiation on the other end (that is, a low score), College Maladjustment (Mt), and PK (Post Traumatic Stress Disorder; PTSD-Keane) and PS (PTSD-Schlenger). The latter two PTSD Scales share 26 items in common and have an interscale correlation of .90. Because they are experimental, they may have value in epidemiological research but may not be used in clinical work as yet.

The new content scales, developed a priori and tested for internal consistency reliabilities, address anxiety, antisocial attitudes and behavior, anger, low self-esteem, work interference, obsessiveness, health concerns, Type A personality, and negative treatment indicators. However, if used in their own right at this stage of their development, the new content scales have potential for misinterpretation. Because the MMPI-2 content scale items consist of obvious items, the MMPI Weiner and Harmon Subtle-Obvious Subscales have been carried over to the MMPI-2. The availability of the Harris-Lingoes subscales continues, but with some scale items and some subscales being dropped off and some subscales replaced.

The MMPI-2 has added to the MMPI validity scales. The F-b (Back F) occurs in the latter stages of the MMPI-2 booklet, allowing for the identification of random response patterns or endorsement of infrequent responses in the latter portion of the test. The Variable Response Inconsistency Scale (VRIN) and the True Response Inconsistency Scale (TRIN), replacing Greene's Carelessness Scale in the MMPI, evaluate the degree to which a subject has responded to the respective scale items in an inconsistent or contradictory manner.

With so many item and item-order changes, the question that arises is whether the MMPI-2 is measuring the same disorders as the MMPI, a question related to both construct and criterion-related validity. Yet, so far as the three standard validity scales and nine basic clinical scales are concerned, the statistical properties of the MMPI-2 with respect to reliability, validity, and standard error are those of its predecessors, the MMPI, for better or worse.

The provision of the new uniform T-scores for the MMPI-2 is a significant advancement. Previously, the lack of percentile equivalence against the linear T-distributions for the basic clinical scales (although not compromising interpretation from actuarially derived profile types) confounded inferences based on scale-by-scale comparisons because greater elevations did not necessarily correspond to greater statistical deviance. With uniform T-scores, the positive skew of the original MMPI scale distribution is preserved, but a given T-score corresponds to nearly identical percentile values across the scales.

The renorming was based on 2,600 paid volunteer adults (1,138 males and 1,462 females between the ages of 18 and 84), recruited from newspaper advertisements and random mail solicitations and tested under supervision at prearranged sites in seven states: California and Washington (representing the West Coast), Minnesota and Ohio (representing the Midwest), and North Carolina, Pennsylvania, and Virginia (representing the eastern region). Collateral data included biographical information and recent stressful life events. Behavior ratings were collected from 928 couples, with each spouse rating the other.

The sample approximated the 1980 census in terms of age, income ranges, marital status, and select minority groups. There were 19 Asians in the normative data; arbitrarily, a certain percentage of Hispanics were entered as white, and 3% ($N = 73$) were categorized as Hispanics; Native Americans from two federal Indian reservations made up 3% ($N = 77$) of the sample; 12.5% ($N = 314$) were blacks, many of whom were assigned to various military bases. The sample exceeded the 1980 census values for education and occupational status, which is not surprising, given the limited minority sample in the renorming sample. Roughly 50% of males and 42% of females reported an educational level of a bachelor's degree or higher, compared with 20% of males and 13% of females in the 1980 U.S. Census data. In the April 1990 *APA Monitor*, several MMPI experts raised concerns regarding the suitability of the MMPI-2 norms in interpreting tests of respondents from lower socioeconomic status levels. *T*-scores for Scale M/F (5) for men are 11 points lower on the MMPI-2 profile throughout the raw score range. The F validity scale of the MMPI, viewed as elevating too fast, now goes up even faster, partly as a consequence of eliminating high F protocols from the restandardization sample. This effect is especially dramatic for females. In the manual, there are far more negative interpretation descriptors for women who score higher on Masculine Gender Role (GM) or on Feminine Gender Role (GF) than for men who have similarly high scores on either of the scales.

Owing to the marked contrast between the normative samples of the MMPI and MMPI-2, it is not surprising that the response patterns of the MMPI-2 normative sample differed substantially from those of the Minnesota normals of the MMPI. The MMPI-2 clinical scale profiles are typically lower in elevation than the MMPI clinical profiles. This shift is reflected in a reduction of the demarcation point for clinical range elevations from $T > = 70$ on the MMPI to $T > = 65$ on the MMPI-2 profile sheet.

The shortcomings of the MMPI-2 representativeness may compromise the test in multiracial and multiethnic settings. The revision did not go far enough. The nosology of *fin de siècle* psychiatry persists in the clinical scales because the original 1943 criterion groups were retained. The MMPI and MMPI-2 generalizability of findings will vary depending on codetype definition or "crispiness." The generalizability of the MMPI-2 to racial and ethnic minority groups will depend on how it correlates with MC attitude and personality measures, such as those referred to in Section 1.

Mainstream instruments could strive for multicultural relevance only if:

their relationships with minority subjects' identification with their racial or ethnic groups were studied;

their relationships with minority subjects' acculturation were studied;

moderator variables, such as income, education, and English language reading fluency were incorporated; and

culturally relevant validity scales were included along with the traditional faking good and faking bad scales.

Research on mainstream instruments does not address the interaction of specified ethnic or cultural variables with psychopathology or adjustment, thus missing out on the complex psychology of minority individuals. The sampling must be representative of the major racial and ethnic groups in the United States. Mainstream instrumentation has not yet moved beyond the reliance, dictated by circumstance, upon samples of opportunity and convenience, often college-going or college-educated white people.

Conclusion

Multicultural assessment calls for multiple data sets for each individual: quantitative and qualitative, the categorical and the continuous, the personal and the contextual, the individualistic and the group reference point, and the ideographic and the normative. These data points allow for both etic and emic descriptions of minority people living in interracial, interethnic, and intercultural milieus. If such breadth of assessment is attained, then minority-specific, humanly universal, and individualistic facets of a complex human structure can be profiled. How these pieces of person-environment psychology intertwine will gradually be teased out by multicultural assessment.

NOTE

1. Quotation marks are used because the term *Hispanic* does not identify which particular group of Spanish, Latin, or Mexican origin is being discussed.

References

Adler, I. (1968). *Mathematics and mental growth*. New York: John Day.

Aiken, L. R. (1987). *Assessment of intellectual functioning*. Newton, MA: Allyn & Bacon.

American Psychological Association. (1972). *Ethical standards of psychologists*. Washington, DC: Author.

Anastasi, A. A. (1988). *Psychological testing* (6th ed.). New York: Macmillan.

Angoff, W. H., (1956). A note on the estimation of nonspurious correlations. *Psychometrika, 21, 3*.

Angoff, W. H., & Ford, S. F. (1973). Item-race interaction on a test of scholastic aptitude. *Journal of Educational Measurement, 10*, 95-106.

Angoff, W. H., & Modu, C. C. (1973). *Equating the scales of the Prueba de Aptitud Academica and the Scholastic Aptitude Test*. Princeton, NJ: College Entrance Examination Board, Research Report 3.

Applebome, P. (1997, January 3). Prerequisite for better education: Accurate report cards on schools. *New York Times*.

Arthur, G. A. (1930). *A point scale of performance tests: clinical manual* (Vol. 1). New York: Commonwealth Fund.

Arthur, G. (1949). The Arthur Adaptation of the Leiter International Performance Scale. *Journal of Clinical Psychology, 5*, 345-349.

Barnes, M. L., & Sternberg, R. J. (1989). Social intelligence and decoding of nonverbal cues. *Intelligence, 13*, 263-287.

Baughman, E. E., & Dahlstrom, W. G. (1968). *Negro and white children: A psychological study in the rural South*. New York: Academic Press.

Bender, L. (1938). A visual motor gestalt test and its clinical use. *American Orthopsychiatric Association Research Monograph* (3).

Berry, J., Poortinga, Y., Segall, H., & Dasen, P. (1994). *Cross-cultural psychology: Research and applications*. Cambridge, UK: Cambridge University Press.

Binet, A., & Simon, T. (1916). *The development of intelligence in children* (E. S. Kite, Trans.). Baltimore, MD: Williams and Wilkins.

Bogen, J. E. (1969). The other side of the brain: Parts I, II, and III. *Bulletin of the Los Angeles Neurological Society, 34*, 73-105, 135-162, 191-203.

Bogen, J. E., DeZure, R., Tenhouten, N., & Marsh, J. (1972). The other side of the brain: IV. The A/P ratio. *Bulletin of the Los Angeles Neurological Society, 37*, 49-61.

Bracken, B. A. (1985). A critical review of the Kaufman Assessment Battery for Children (K-ABC). *School Psychology Review, 14*, 21-36.

Bransford, J. I., Delclos, V. R., Vye, N. J., Burns, M. S., & Hasselbring, T. S. (1987). State of the art and future directions. In C. S. Lidz (Ed.), *Dynamic assessment: An interactional approach to evaluating learning potential*. New York: Guilford.

Brown, A. L., & Ferrara, R. A. (1985). Diagnosing zones of proximal development. In J. V. Wertsch (Ed.), *Culture, communication, and cognition: Vygotskian perspectives.* New York: Cambridge University Press.

Budoff, M. (1974). *Learning potential and educability among the educable mentally retarded* (Final Report Project No. 312312). Cambridge, MA: Research Institute for Educational Problems, Cambridge Mental Health Association.

Budoff, M. (1987). Measures for assessing learning potential. In C. S. Lidz (Ed.), *Dynamic assessment: An interactional approach to evaluating learning potential.* New York: Guilford.

Buros Institute of Mental Measurements. (1985). *The ninth mental measurements yearbook.* Lincoln, NE: Author.

Buros Institute of Mental Measurements. (1992). *The eleventh mental measurements yearbook.* Lincoln, NE: Author.

Buros Institute of Mental Measurements. (1995). *The twelfth mental measurements yearbook.* Lincoln, NE: Author.

Buros Institute of Mental Measurements. (1996). *The supplement to the twelfth mental measurements yearbook.* Lincoln, NE: Author.

Butcher, J. N., & Pancheri, P. (1976). *A handbook of cross-national MMPI research.* Minneapolis: University of Minnesota Press.

Campione, J. C. (1989). Assisted assessment: A taxonomy of approaches and an outline of strengths and weaknesses. *Journal of Learning Disabilities, 22,* 151-165.

Campione, J. C., & Brown, A. L. (1987) Linking dynamic assessment with school achievement. In C. S. Lidz (Ed.), *Dynamic assessment: An interactional approach to evaluating learning potential.* New York: Guilford.

Carlson, J. S., & Wiedl, J. H. (1978) Use of testing-the-limits procedures in the assessment of intellectual capabilities in children with learning difficulties. *American Journal of Mental Deficiency, 82,* 559-564.

Carlson, J. S., & Wiedl, J. H. (1979) Toward a differential testing approach: Testing-the-limits employing the Raven matrices. *Intelligence, 3,* 323-344.

Carroll, J. F., Herrans, L. L., & Rodriguez, J. M. (1995, July). *Factor Analysis of the Puerto Rican WISC-R (EIWN-R de Puerto Rico) at 11 age levels between 6 and 16 years.* Paper presented at the Interamerican Congress of Psychology, San Juan, Puerto Rico.

Carter, R. (1996). Exploring the complexity of racial identity attitude measures. In G. R. Sodowsky & J. C. Impara (Eds.), *Multicultural assessment in counseling and clinical psychology* (pp. 193-224). Lincoln, NE: Buros Institute of Mental Measurements.

Casas, J. M., & Casas, A. (1994). *Acculturation: Theory, models, and implications.* Santa Cruz, CA: Network.

Cattell, R. B. (1963). Theory of fluid and crystallized intelligence: A critical experiment. *Journal of Educational Psychology, 18,* 165-244.

Cattell, R. B. (1973). *Technical supplement for the Culture Fair Intelligence tests Scales 2 and 3.* Champaign, IL: Institute for Personality and Ability Testing.

Choney, S. K., & Behrens, J. (1996). Development of the Oklahoma Racial Attitudes Scale-Preliminary Form (ORAS-P). In G. R. Sodowsky & J. C. Impara (Eds.), *Multicultural assessment in counseling and clinical psychology* (pp. 225-240). Lincoln, NE: Buros Institute of Mental Measurements.

Cleary, T. A. (1968). Test bias: Prediction of grades of Negro and white students in integrated colleges. *Journal of Educational Measurement, 5,* 115-123.

Cleary, T. A., Humphreys, G. L., Kendrick, S. A., & Westman, A. (1975). Educational uses of tests with disadvantaged students. *American Psychologist, 30,* 15-31.

Cole, M., Gay, J., Glick, J., & Sharp, D. W. (1971). *The cultural context of learning and thinking.* New York: Basic Books.

Comprehensive Tests of Basic Skills. Level Cal Form S: Examiner's manual and technical bulletin No. 1. (1974). Monterey, CA: CTB/McGraw-Hill.

Cordary, P. M. (1996). *Cross-cultural validity of the Kaufman Assessment Battery for Children: A literature review.* Unpublished manuscript, Nova Southeastern University.

Costantino, G., & Malgady, R. (1996). Development of the TEMAS, a multicultural thematic apperception test: Psychometric properties and clinical utility. In G. R. Sodowsky & J. C. Impara (Eds.), *Multicultural assessment in counseling and clinical psychology* (pp. 85-136). Lincoln, NE: Buros Institute of Mental Measurements.

Dai, X., Ryan, J. J., Paolo, A. M., & Harrington, R. G. (1991). Sex differences on the Wechsler Adult Intelligence Scale-Revised for China. *Psychological Assessment, 3,* 282-284.

Dana, R. H. (1993). *Multicultural assessment perspectives for professional psychology.* Boston: Allyn & Bacon.

Das, J. P. (1973). Structure of cognitive abilities: Evidence for simultaneous and successive processing. *Journal of Educational Psychology, 65,* 103-108.

Das, J. P., Kirby, J. R., & Jarman, R. F. (1975). Simultaneous and successive synthesis: An alternative model for cognitive abilities. *Psychological Bulletin, 82,* 87-103.

Das, J. P., Kirby, J. R., & Jarman, R. F. (1979). *Simultaneous and successive cognitive processes.* New York: Academic Press.

Davidson, K. L. (1992). A comparison of Native American and White students' cognitive strengths as measured by the Kaufman Assessment Battery for Children. *Roeper Review, 14,* 111-115.

Davidson, J. E., & Sternberg, R. J. (1984). The role of insight in intellectual giftedness. *Gifted Child Quarterly, 28,* 58-64.

Davis, F. (1974). *Standards for educational and psychological tests.* Washington, DC: American Psychological Association.

Devet, C. V., & MacLean, K. (1958). *Second game.* New York: Street & Smith.

Draguns, J. C. (1996). Multicultural and cross-cultural assessment: Dilemmas and decisions. In G. R. Sodowsky & J. C. Impara (Eds.), *Multicultural assessment in counseling and clinical psychology* (pp. 37-84). Lincoln, NE: Buros Institute of Mental Measurements.

Dranesfield, E. (1953). *Administration of enrichment to superior children.* New York: Teachers College Press.

Dunn, L. M., & Dunn, L. M. (1981). *Peabody Picture Vocabulary Test-Revised* (PPVT-R) Circle Pines, MN: American Guidance Service.

Dunn, L. M., & Markwardt, F. C. (1970). *Peabody Individual Achievement Test.* Circle Pines, MN: American Guidance Service.

Eisner, E. W. (1994). *Cognition and curriculum reconsidered* (2nd ed.). New York: Teachers College Press.

Ferrara, R. A., Brown, A. L., & Campione, J. C. (1986). Children's learning and transfer of inductive reasoning rules: Studies of proximal development. *Child Development, 57,* 1087-1099.

Feuerstein, R. (1979). *The dynamic assessment of retarded performers: The Learning Potential Assessment Device, theory, instruments, and techniques.* Baltimore, MD: University Park.

Feuerstein, R. (1980). *Instrumental enrichment: An intervention program for cognitive modifiability.* Baltimore, MD: University Park.

Feuerstein, R. (1986). *Learning Potential Assessment Device manual.* Jerusalem, Israel: Hadassah-WIZO-Canada Research Institute.

Feuerstein, R. (1995). *Revised LPAD examiner's manual.* Jerusalem, Israel: International Center for the Enhancement of Learning Potential.

Feuerstein, R., & Feuerstein, S. (1991). Mediated learning theory: A theoretical review. In R. Feuerstein, P. S. Klein, & A. J. Tannenbaum (Eds.), *Mediated learning experience: Theoretical, psychosocial, and learning implications.* London: Freund.

Feuerstein, R., Feuerstein, R., & Gross, S. (1996). The Learning Potential Assessment Device: History, theory, applications, and results. In D. P. Flanagan, J. L. Genshaft, & P. L. Harrison (Eds.), *Beyond traditional intellectual assessment: Contemporary and emerging theories, tests and issues.* New York: Guilford.

Feuerstein, R., Feuerstein, R., & Shur, Y. (in press). Process as content in regular education and in particular in education of the low functioning retarded performer. In A. L. Costa & R. M. Liebmann (Eds.), *If process were content: Sustaining the spirit of learning.* Thousand Oaks, CA.: Corwin.

Feuerstein, R., Rand, Y., Jensen, M., Kaniel, S., & Tzuriel, D. (1987). Prerequisites for assessment of learning potential: The LPAD model. In C. S. Lidz (Ed.), *Dynamic assessment.* New York: Guilford.

Flaugher, R. L. (1978). The many definitions of test bias. *American Psychologist, 33,* 671-679.

Fourqurean, J. M. (1987). A K-ABC and WISC-R comparison for Latino learning-disabled children of limited English proficiency. *Journal of School Psychology, 25,* 15-21.

Gardner, H. (1993). *Multiple intelligences: The theory in practice.* New York: Basic Books.

Gerken, K. C. (1978). Performance of Mexican American children on intelligence tests. *Exceptional Children, 44,* 438-443.

Gladwin, T. (1970). *East is a big bird.* Cambridge, MA: Harvard University Press.

Glutting, J. J. (1986). Potthoff bias analyses of the K-ABC MPC and Nonverbal Scale IQ's among Anglo Black and Puerto Rican kindergarten children. *Professional School Psychology, l,* 223-247.

Goleman, D. (1995). *Emotional intelligence.* New York: Bantam Books.

Goodman, N. (1955). *Fact, fiction, and forecast.* Cambridge, MA: Harvard University Press.

Greenfield, P. (1977). Testing in collectivistic cultures. *American Psychologist, 52,* 1115-1124.

Gupta, R. M., & Coxhead, P. (Eds.). (1988). *Cultural diversity and learning efficiency: Recent developments in assessment.* New York: St. Martin's.

Guthke, J. (1992). Learning tests—The concept, main research findings, problems, and trends. *Learning and Individual Differences, 4,* 213-233.

Guthke, J., & Stein, H. (1996). Are learning tests the better version of intelligence tests? *European Journal of Psychological Assessment, 12,* 1-13.

Guyote, M. J., & Sternberg, R. J. (1981). A transitive-chain theory of syllogistic reasoning. *Cognitive Psychology, 13,* 461-525.

Hamers, J. H. M., Sijtsma, K., & Ruijssenaars, A. J. J. M. (Eds.). (1993). *Learning potential assessment.* Lisse: Swets & Zeitlinger.

Harris, D. B. (1963). *Children's drawings as measures of intellectual maturity: A revision and extension of the Goodenough Draw-a-Man Test.* San Diego, CA: Harcourt, Brace & Jovanovich.

Haywood, H. C., & Tzuriel, D. (Eds.). (1992). *Interactive assessment.* New York: Springer-Verlag.

Helms, J. (1996). Toward a methodology for measuring and assessing racial as distinguished from ethnic identity. In G. R. Sodowsky & J. C. Impara (Eds.), *Multicultural assessment in counseling and clinical psychology* (pp. 143-192). Lincoln, NE: Buros Institute of Mental Measurements.

Herrnstein, R. J., & Murray, C. (1994). *The bell curve: Intelligence and class structure in American life*. New York: Free Press.

Hilliard, A. (1982, March). *The Learning Potential Assessment Device and Instrumental Enrichment as a paradigm shift*. Speech to the Symposium on Feuerstein LPAD/IE at the American Educational Research Association Annual Meeting, New York.

Hood, A. B., & Johnson, R. W. (1997). *Assessment in counseling* (2nd ed.). Alexandria, VA: American Counseling Association.

Humphreys, L. G. (1985). Review of the system of multicultural pluralistic assessment. In J. V. Mitchell (Ed.), *The ninth mental measurement yearbook* (pp. 1517-1519). Lincoln: University of Nebraska Press.

Hunt, J. McV. (1961). *Intelligence and experience*. New York: Ronald Press.

Jensen, A. R. (1969). How much can we boost IQ and scholastic achievement? *Harvard Educational Review, 39*, 1-123.

Jensen, A. R. (1973). *Educability and group differences*. New York: Harper & Row.

Jensen, A. R. (1980). *Bias in mental testing*. New York: Free Press.

Jensen, A. R. (1984). The black-white difference on the K-ABC: Implications for future tests. *The Journal of Special Education, 18*, 377-408.

Jensen, A. R., & Figueroa, R. A., (1975). Forward and backward digit span interaction with race and I.Q. *Journal of Educational Psychology, 67*, 882-893.

Jitendra, A. K., & Kameenui, E. J. (1993). Dynamic assessment as a compensatory assessment approach: A description and analysis. *Remedial and Special Education, 14*(5), 6-18.

Jones, B. F. (1994). Cognitive designs in education. In *Encyclopedia of education research* (6th ed.). New York: Macmillan.

Joyce, B., & Showers, B. (1988). *Student achievement through staff development*. New York: Longman.

Kamin, L. (1976). Heredity, intelligence, politics, and psychology: II. In N. Block & G Dworkin (Eds.), *The IQ controversy* (pp. 374-382). New York: Pantheon Books.

Kamphaus, R. W., Beres, K. A., Kaufman, A. S., & Kaufman, N. L. (1995). The Kaufman Assessment Battery for Children (K-ABC). In C. S. Newmark (Ed.), *Major psychological assessment instruments* (2nd ed.). Boston: Allyn & Bacon.

Kamphaus, R. W., & Kaufman, A. S. (1986). Factor analysis of the Kaufman Assessment Battery for Children (K-ABC) for separate groups of boys and girls. *Journal of Clinical Child Psychology, 15*, 210-213.

Kamphaus, R. W., & Reynolds, C. R. (1987). *Clinical and research applications of the K-ABC*. Circle Pines, MN: American Guidance Service.

Kaufman, A. S. (1973). Comparison of the performance of matched groups of black children and white children on the Wechsler Preschool and Primary Scale of Intelligence. *Journal of Consulting and Clinical Psychology, 41*, 186-191.

Kaufman, A. S. (1979). *Intelligent testing with the WISC-R*. New York: Wiley-Interscience.

Kaufman, A. S. (1984). K-ABC and controversy. *The Journal of Special Education, 18*, 409-444.

Kaufman, A. S., & Doppelt, J. E. (1976). Analysis of WISC-R standardization data in terms of the stratification variables. *Child Development, 47*, 165-171.

Kaufman, A. S., & Kamphaus, R. W. (1984). Factor analysis of the Kaufman Assessment Battery for Children (K-ABC) for ages 2 1/2 through 12 1/2. *Journal of Educational Psychology, 76*, 623-637.

Kaufman, A. S., & Kaufman, N. L. (1973). Black-white differences at ages 2 1/2-8 1/2 on the McCarthy Scales of Children's Abilities. *Journal of School Psychology, 11*, 196-206.

Kaufman, A. S., & Kaufman, N. L. (1983a). *Interpretive manual for the K-ABC assessment battery for children*. Circle Pines, MN: American Guidance Service.

Kaufman, A. S., & Kaufman, N. L. (1983b). *K-ABC: Kaufman Assessment Battery for Children.* Circle Pines, MN: American Guidance Service.

Kaufman, A. S., O'Neal, M. R., Avant, A. H., & Long, S. W. (1987). Introduction to the Kaufman Assessment Battery for Children (K-ABC) for pediatric neuroclinicans. *Journal of Child Neurology, 2,* 3-16.

Kazdin, A. E. (Ed.). (1992). *Methodological issues and strategies in clinical research.* Washington, DC: American Psychological Association.

Kearins, J. M. (1981). Visual spatial memory in Australian aboriginal children of the desert regions. *Cognitive Psychology, 13,* 434-460.

Keith, T. Z., & Dunbar, S. B. (1984). Hierarchical factor analysis of the K-ABC: Testing alternate models. *Journal of Special Education, 18,* 367-375.

Kinsbourne, M. (Ed.). (1978). *Asymmetrical function of the brain.* Cambridge, MA: Cambridge University Press.

Krohn, E. J., & Lamp, R. E. (1989). Concurrent validity of the Stanford-Binet Fourth Edition and K-ABC for Head Start children. *Journal of School Psychology, 27,* 59-67.

Krohn, E. J., Lamp, R. E., & Phelps, C. G. (1988). Validity of the K-ABC for a black preschool population. *Psychology in the Schools, 25,* 15-21.

Labov, W. (1970). The logic of nonstandard English. In F. Williams (Ed.), *Language and poverty.* Chicago: Markham.

Lamp, R. E., & Krohn, E. J. (1990). Stability of the Stanford-Binet Fourth Edition and the K-ABC for young black and white children from low income families. *Journal of Psychoeducational Assessment, 8,* 139-149.

Leiter, R. G. (1948). *Leiter International Performance Scale.* Chicago: Stoelting.

Levy, J., & Trevarthen, C. (1976). Metacontrol of hemispheric function in human split-brain patients. *Journal of Experimental Psychology: Human Perception and Performance, 2,* 299-312.

Lidz, C. S. (Ed.). (1987). *Dynamic assessment: An international approach to evaluating learning potential.* New York: Guilford.

Lopez, S., & Nunez, J. A. (1987). Cultural factors considered in selected diagnostic criteria and interview schedules. *Journal of Abnormal Psychology, 96,* 270-272.

Lubart, T. I., & Sternberg, R. J. (1995). An investment approach to creativity: Theory and data. In S. M. Smith, T. B. Ward, & R. A. Finke (Eds.), *The creative cognition approach* (pp. 269-302). Cambridge: MIT Press.

Luria, A. R. (1966). *Higher cortical functions in man.* New York: Basic Books.

Luria, A. R. (1973). *The working brain: An introduction to neuropsychology.* London: Penguin.

Luria, A. R. (1980). *Higher cortical functions in man* (2nd ed.). New York: Basic Books.

McCallum, R. S., & Merritt, F. M. (1983). Simultaneous-successive processing among college students. *Journal of Psychoeducational Assessment, 1,* 85-93.

McCarthy, D. (1972). *Manual of the McCarthy Scales of Children's Abilities.* New York: The Psychological Corporation.

Meljac, C. (1996, August). *Cross-cultural validation of the Kaufman Assessment Battery for Children in France.* Paper presented at the International Association of Cross-cultural Psychology Conference, Montreal, Canada.

Mercer, J. R. (1979). *System of Multicultural Pluralistic Assessment (SOMPA): Technical manual.* New York: The Psychological Corporation.

Mercer, J. R., & Lewis J. F. (1978). *System of Multicultural Pluralistic Assessment.* San Antonio, TX: The Psychological Corporation.

Merz, W. R. (1985). Test review of Kaufman Assessment Battery for Children. In D. J. Keyser & R. C. Sweetland (Eds.), *Test overviews* (pp. 393-405). Kansas City, MO: Test Corporation of America.

Messick, S. (1980). Test validity and the ethics of assessment. *American Psychologist, 35,* 1012-1027.

Miller, G. A., Galanter, E., & Pribram, H. H. (1960). *Plans and the structure of behavior.* New York: Holt, Rinehart & Winston.

Miller, T. L., & Reynolds, C. R. (1984). Special issue . . . The K-ABC. *Journal of Special Education, 8,* 207-448.

Moore, E. G. J. (1986). Family socialization and the IQ test performance of traditionally and transracially adopted black children. *Developmental Psychology, 22,* 317-326.

Naglieri, J. A. (1984). Concurrent and predictive validity of the Kaufman Assessment Battery for Children with a Navajo sample. *Journal of School Psychology, 22,* 373-380.

Naglieri, J. A., & Das, J. P. (1988). Planning-Arousal-Simultaneous-Successive (PASS): A model for assessment. *Journal of School Psychology, 26,* 35-48.

Naglieri, J. A., & Das, J. P. (1990). Planning, attention, simultaneous, and successive cognitive processes and a model for intelligence. *Journal of Psychoeducational Assessment, 8,* 303-337.

Naglieri, J. A. & Hill, D. S. (1986a). Comparison of WISC-R and K-ABC regression lines for academic prediction with Black and White children. *Journal of Clinical Child Psychology, 15,* 352-355.

Naglieri, J. A., & Hill, D. S. (1986b). WISC-R and K-ABC comparison for matched samples of Black and White children. *Journal of School Psychology, 24,* 81-88.

Naglieri, J. A., & Jensen, A. R. (1987). Comparison of black-white differences on the WISC-R and the K-ABC: Spearman's hypothesis. *Intelligence, 11,* 21-43.

Narrol, H., Silverman, H., & Waksman, M. (1982). Developing cognitive potential in vocational high school students. *Journal of Educational Research.*

Neisser, U., Boodoo, G., Bouchard T. J., Jr., Boykin, A. W., Brody, N., Ceci, S. J., Halpern, D. S., Loehlin, J. C., Perloff, R., Sternberg, R. J., & Urbina, F. (1996, February) Intelligence: Knowns and unknowns. *American Psychologist, 51*(2), 77-101.

Nolan, R. F., Watlington, D. K., & Willson, V. L. (1989). Gifted and nongifted race and gender effects on item functioning on the Kaufman Assessment Battery for Children. *Journal of Clinical Psychology, 45,* 645-650.

Oakland, T. D., & Dowling, L. (1983). The Draw-a-Person test: Validity properties for nonbiased assessment. *Learning Disability Quarterly, 6,* 526-534.

Obringer, S. J. (1988, November). *A survey of perceptions by school psychologists of the Stanford-Binet IV.* Paper presented at the meeting of the Mid-South Educational Research Association, Louisville, KY.

Okagaki, L., & Sternberg, R. J. (1993). Parental beliefs and children's school performance. *Child Development, 64,* 36-56.

Osterreith, P. A. (1945). Copie d'une figure complexe. *Archives de Psychologie,* 205-353.

Panaguia, F. A. (1994). *Assessing and treating culturally diverse clients.* Thousand Oaks, CA: Sage.

Perkins, D. N. (1995). *Outsmarting IQ: The emerging science of learnable intelligence.* New York: Free Press.

Perlman, M. D. (1986). *Toward an integration of a cognitive-dynamic view of personality: The relationship between defense mechanisms, cognitive style, attentional focus, and neuropsychological processing.* Unpublished doctoral dissertation, California School of Professional Psychology-San Diego.

Ponterotto, J. G., & Casas, J. M. (1991). *Handbook of ethnic/racial minority counseling research.* Springfield, IL: Charles C Thomas.

Ponterotto, J. G., Rieger, B. P., Barrett, A., Harris, G., Sparks, R., Sanchez, C. M., & Magids, D. (1996). Development and initial validation of the Multicultural Counseling Awareness Scale. In G. R. Sodowsky & J. C. Impara (Eds.), *Multicultural assessment in counseling and clinical psychology* (pp. 247-282). Lincoln, NE: Buros Institute of Mental Measurements.

Pope-Davis, D. B., & Neilson, D. (1996). Assessing multicultural counseling competencies using the Multicultural Counseling Inventory: A review of the research. In G. R. Sodowsky & J. C. Impara (Eds.), *Multicultural assessment in counseling and clinical psychology* (pp. 325-343). Lincoln, NE: Buros Institute of Mental Measurements.

Potthoff, R. F. (1966). *Statistical aspects of the problem of biases in psychological tests* (Institute of Statistics Mimeo Series No. 479). Chapel Hill: University of North Carolina, Department of Statistics.

Prediger, D. J. (Ed.). (1993). *Multicultural assessment standards: A compilation for counselors.* Alexandria, VA: American Counseling Association.

Ramey, C., & MacPhee, D. (1981). A new paradigm in intellectual assessment? *Contemporary Psychology, 26*(7), 507-509.

Rand, Y., Tannenbaum, A., & Feuerstein, R. (1979). Effects of IE on the psychoeducational development of low functioning adolescents. *Journal of Educational Psychology, 71,* 751-763.

Rasch, G. (1966). An item analysis which takes individual differences into account. *British Journal of Mathematics and Statistical Psychology, 19,* 49-57.

Raven, J. C. (1938). *Progressive matrices.* London: Lewis.

Raven, J. C. (1947). *Progressive matrices, sets I and II.* Dumfries: The Crichton Royal.

Raven, J. C. (1956). *Coloured progressive matrices, Sets A, Ah, and B.* London: H. K. Lewis.

Raven, J. C. (1958). *Standard progressive matrices, Sets A, B, C, D, F.* London: H. K. Lewis.

Raven, J. C., Court, J. H., & Raven, J. (1983). *Manual for Raven's Progressive Matrices and Vocabulary Scales.* San Antonio, TX: Psychological Corporation.

Raven, J., Summer, B., Birchfield, M., Brosier, G., Burciaga, L., & Byrkit, B. (1986). *Manual for Raven's Progressive Matrices and Vocabulary Scales: Research supplement No. 3.* London: Lewis.

Rey, A. (1959). *Test de copie d'use figure complexe* (Manual). Paris: Centre de Psychologie Appliquée.

Reynolds, C. R. (1982). The problem of bias in psychological assessment. In C. R. Reynolds & T. B. Gutkin (Eds.), *The handbook of school psychology.* New York: John Wiley.

Reynolds, C. R. (1985). Review of the System of Multicultural Pluralistic Assessment. In J. V. Mitchell (Ed.), *The ninth mental measurements yearbook* (pp. 1519-1521). Lincoln: University of Nebraska Press.

Reynolds, C. R., Chatman, S., & Willson, V. L. (1983, March). *Relationships between age and raw score increases on the K-ABC.* Paper presented at the meeting of the National Association of School Psychologists, Detroit, MI.

Reynolds, C. R., & Willson, V. L. (1984). *Factorial consistency of simultaneous and sequential cognitive processing for whites and blacks ages 3 to 12 1/2.* Paper presented at the meeting of the National Council on Measurement in Education, New Orleans, LA.

Reynolds, C. R., Willson, V. L., & Chatman, S. (1983, August). *Differential validity of the K-ABC for whites, blacks and Hispanics.* Paper presented at the meeting of the American Psychological Association, Anaheim, CA.

Samuda, R. J. (1975). *Psychological testing of American minorities.* New York: Harper & Row.

Samuda, R. J., Kong, S. L., Cummins, J., Pascual-Leone, J., & Lewis, J. (1989). *Assessment and placement of minority students.* Lewiston, NY: Hogrefe/ISSP.

Samuda, R. J., & Lewis, J. (1992). Evaluation practices for the multicultural classroom. In C. Diaz (Ed.), *Multicultural education for the 21st century.* Washington DC: National Education Association.

Sandoval, J. (1985). Review of the System of Multicultural Pluralistic Assessment. In J. V. Mitchell (Ed.), *The ninth mental measurements yearbook* (pp. 1521-1526). Lincoln: University of Nebraska Press.

Sattler, J. (1988). *Assessment of children's intelligence and other special abilities* (3rd ed.). San Diego, CA: Author.

Sattler, J. M. (1992). *Assessment of children* (revised and updated 3rd ed.). San Diego, CA: Author.

Saunders, D. R. (1956). Moderator variables in prediction. *Educational and Psychological Measurement, 16,* 209-222.

Scarr, S. (1977). Testing minority children: Why, how, and with what effects? In R. Bossone & M. Weiner (Eds.), *Proceedings of the national conference on testing: Major issues* (pp. 71-101). New York: The Graduate School and University Center of the City University of New York.

Shuey, A. M. (1966). *The testing of Negro intelligence* (2nd ed.). New York: Social Science Press.

Sodowksy, G. R. (1996). The Multicultural Counseling Inventory: Validity and applications in multicultural training. In G. R. Sodowsky & J. C. Impara (Eds.), *Multicultural assessment in counseling and clinical psychology* (pp. 283-324). Lincoln, NE: Buros Institute of Mental Measurements.

Sodowsky, G. R., & Impara, J. C. (Eds.). (1996). *Multicultural assessment in counseling and clinical psychology.* Lincoln, NE: Buros Institute of Mental Measurements.

Sodowsky, G. R., Kuo-Jackson, P. Y., Richardson, M. F., Corey, A. T. (in press). Correlates of self-reported multicultural competencies: Counselor multicultural social desirability, race, social inadequacy, locus of control racial ideology, and multicultural training. *Journal of Counseling Psychology.*

Sodowsky, G. R., Taffe, R. C., Gutkin, T. B., & Wise, S. (1994). Development of the Multicultural Counseling Inventory (MCI): A self-report measure of multicultural competencies. *Journal of Counseling Psychology, 41,* 137-148.

Sperry, R. W. (1968). Hemisphere deconnection and unity in conscious awareness. *American Psychologist, 23,* 723-733.

Sperry, R. W. (1974). Lateral specialization in the surgically separated hemispheres. In F. O. Schmitt & F. G. Worden (Eds.), *The neurosciences: Third study program.* Cambridge: MIT Press.

Sternberg, R. J. (1977). *Intelligence, information processing, and analogical reasoning: The componential analysis of human abilities.* Hillsdale, NJ: Lawrence Erlbaum.

Sternberg, R. J. (1980). Sketch of a componential subtheory of intelligence. *Behavioral and Brain Sciences, 3,* 573-584.

Sternberg, R. J. (1981). Intelligence and nonentrenchment. *Journal of Educational Psychology, 73,* 1-16.

Sternberg, R. J. (1982). Natural, unnatural, and supernatural concepts. *Cognitive Psychology, 14,* 451-488.

Sternberg, R. J. (1983). Components of human intelligence. *Cognition, 15,* 1-48.

Sternberg, R. J. (1984). The Kaufman Assessment Battery for Children: An information-processing analysis and critique. *The Journal of Special Education, 18,* 269-279.

Sternberg, R. (1985a). *Beyond IQ: A triarchic theory of human intelligence.* New York: Cambridge University Press.

Sternberg, R. J. (1985b). Implicit theories of intelligence, creativity, and wisdom. *Journal of Personality and Social Psychology, 47,* 607-627.

Sternberg, R. J. (1988). Mental self-government: A theory of intellectual styles and their development. *Human Development, 31,* 197-224.

Sternberg, R. J. (1991). Death, taxes, and bad intelligence tests. *Intelligence, 15,* 257-269.

Sternberg, R. J. (1993). *Sternberg Triarchic Abilities Test.* Unpublished test.

Sternberg, R. J. (1997). *Thinking styles.* New York: Cambridge University Press.

Sternberg, R. J., Conway, B. E., Ketron, J. L., & Bernstein, M. (1981). People's conceptions of intelligence. *Journal of Personality and Social Psychology, 41,* 37-55.

Sternberg, R. J., & Davidson, J. E. (1982, June). The mind of the puzzler. *Psychology Today, 16,* 37-44.

Sternberg, R. J., & Davidson, J. E. (1983). Insight in the gifted. *Educational Psychologist, 18,* 51-57.

Sternberg, R. J., Dennis, M., & Beatty, P. (1996). *Construction of a battery of survey-based instruments to assess cognitive abilities.* Unpublished manuscript.

Sternberg, R. J., Ferrari, M., Clinkenbeard, P. R., & Grigorenko, E. L. (1996). Identification, instruction, and assessment of gifted children: A construct validation of a triarchic model. *Gifted Child Quarterly, 40,* 129-137.

Sternberg, R. J., & Gardner, M. K. (1983). Unities in inductive reasoning. *Journal of Experimental Psychology: General, 112,* 80-116.

Sternberg, R. J., & Gastel, J. (1989a). Coping with novelty in human intelligence: An empirical investigation. *Intelligence, 13,* 187-197.

Sternberg, R. J., & Gastel, J. (1989b). If dancers ate their shoes: Inductive reasoning with factual and counterfactual premises. *Memory and Cognition, 17,* 1-10.

Sternberg, R. J., Powell, C., McGrane, P., & Grantham-McGregor, S. (1995). *Effects of a parasitic infection on cognitive functioning.* Manuscript submitted for publication.

Sternberg, R. J., & Lubart, T. I. (1995). *Defying the crowd: Cultivating creativity in a culture of conformity.* New York: Free Press.

Sternberg, R. J., & Lubart, T. I. (1996). Investing in creativity. *American Psychologist, 51,* 677-688.

Sternberg, R. J., Smith, C. (1985). Social intelligence and decoding skills in nonverbal communication. *Social Cognition, 2,* 168-192.

Sternberg, R. J., & Wagner, R. K. (1993). The *g*-ocentric view of intelligence and job performance is wrong. *Current Directions in Psychological Science, 2,* 1-5.

Sternberg, R. J., Wagner, R. K., Williams, W. M., & Horvath, J. A. (1995). Testing common sense. *American Psychologist, 50,* 912-927.

Sternberg, R. J., & Weil, E. M. (1980). An aptitude-strategy interaction in linear syllogistic reasoning. *Journal of Education Psychology, 72,* 226-234.

Stricker, L. J. (1982). Identifying test items that perform differently in population subgroups: A partial correlation index. *Applied Psychological Measurement, 6,* 261-273.

Sue, S. (1996). Measurement, testing, and ethnic bias: Can solutions be found? In G. R. Sodowsky & J. C. Impara (Eds.), *Multicultural assessment in counseling and clinical psychology* (pp. 7-36). Lincoln, NE: Buros Institute of Mental Measurements.

Sundberg, N. D., & Gonzales, N. R. (1981). Cross-cultural and cross-ethnic assessment: Overview and issues. In P. McReynolds (Ed.), *Advances in psychological assessment* (Vol. 5, pp. 460-541). San Francisco: Jossey-Bass.

Suzuki, L. A., & Kugler, J. F. (1995). Intelligence and personality assessment: Multicultural perspectives. In J. Ponterotto, J. Casas, L. Suzuki, & C. Alexander (Eds.), *Handbook of multicultural counseling* (pp. 493-515). Thousand Oaks, CA: Sage.

Terman, L. M. (1916). *The measurement of intelligence.* Boston: Houghton-Mifflin.

Terman, L. M. (1917). Feeble-minded children in the schools of California. *School and Society, 5,* 161-165.

Thorndike, R. L., Hagen, E. P., & Sattler, J. M. (1986). *Technical manual Stanford-Binet Intelligence Scale: Fourth Edition.* Chicago: Riverside.

Turnbull, W. (1975). Foreword. In R. J. Samuda, *Psychological testing of American minorities.* New York: Harper & Row.

U.S. Department of Education, National Center for Education Statistics. (1980a). *The condition of education* (Table 2.7). Washington, DC: Government Printing Office.

U.S. Department of Education. (1980b). *Report on education of the disadvantaged, 15*(21).

U.S. Department of Health, Education, and Welfare, Office for Civil Rights. (1972). *Elimination of discrimination in the assignment of children to special educational classes for the mentally retarded* (Mimeo to the state and local education agencies). Washington, DC: Author.

U.S. Office for Civil Rights. (1980). *State, regional, and national summaries of data from the 1978 Child Rights Survey of Elementary and Secondary Schools.* Alexandria, VA: Killalea Associates.

Valencia, R. R. (1984). Concurrent validity of the Kaufman Assessment Battery for Children in a sample of Mexican American children. *Educational and Psychological Measurement, 44,* 365-372.

Valencia, R. R. (1985). Stability of the Kaufman Assessment Battery for Children for a sample of Mexican American children. *Journal of School Psychology, 23,* 189-193.

Valencia, R. R., & Rankin, R. (1986). Factor analysis of the K-ABC for groups of Anglo and Mexican-American children. *Journal of Educational Measurement, 23,* 209-219.

Valencia, R. R., & Rankin, R. (1988). Evidence of bias in predictive validity on the Kaufman Assessment Battery for children in samples of Anglo and Mexican American children. *Psychology in the Schools, 25,* 257-263.

Vincent, K. R. (1991). Black/white IQ differences: Does age make the difference? *Journal of Clinical Psychology, 47,* 266-270.

Vincent, K. R., & Cox, J. A. (1974). A re-evaluation of Raven's Standard Progressive Matrices. *Journal of Psychology, 88,* 299-303.

Vygotsky, L. (1978). *Mind in society: The development of higher psychological processes.* Cambridge, MA. Harvard University Press.

Wada, J., Clarke, R., & Hamm, A. (1975). Cerebral hemisphere asymmetry in humans. *Archives of Neurology, 37,* 234-246.

Wagner, D. A. (1978). Memories of Morocco: The influence of age, schooling, and environment on memory. *Cognitive Psychology, 10,* 1-28.

Wagner, R. K., & Sternberg, R. J. (1985). Practical intelligence in real-world pursuits: The role of tacit knowledge. *Journal of Personality and Social Psychology, 49,* 436-458.

Wagner, R. K., & Sternberg, R. J. (1986). Tacit knowledge and intelligence in the everyday world. In R. J. Sternberg & R. K. Wagner (Eds.), *Practical intelligence: Nature and origins of competence in the everyday world* (pp. 51-83). New York: Cambridge University Press.

Watkins, W. E., & Pollitt, E. (1996). "Stupidity of worms": Do intestinal worms impair mental performance? *Psychological Bulletin, 121,* 171-191.

Wechsler, D. (1958). *The measurement and appraisal of adult intelligence* (4th ed.). Baltimore, MD: Williams & Wilkins.

Wechsler, D. (1967). *Manual for the Wechsler Preschool and Primary Scale of Intelligence (WPPSI)*. New York: Psychological Corporation.

Wechsler, D. (1974). *Manual for the Wechsler Intelligence Scale for Children-Revised (WISC-R)*. San Antonio, TX: Psychological Corporation.

Whiteworth, R. H., & Chrisman, S. M. (1987). Validation of the Kaufman Assessment Battery for Children comparing Anglo and Mexican American preschoolers. *Educational and Psychological Measurement, 47*, 695-702.

Willson, V. L., Nolan, R. F., Reynolds, C. R., & Kamphaus, R. W. (1989). Race and gender effects on item functioning on the Kaufman Assessment Battery for Children. *Journal of School Psychology, 27*, 289-296.

Woodcock, R. Q., & Johnson, M. B. (1977). *Woodcock-Johnson Psycho-Educational Battery: Technical report*. Allen, TX: DLM Teaching Resources.

Zazzo, R. (1964). *Le test de deuz barrages*. Neuchatel: Delachaux et Niestle.

Index

ABIC. *See* Adaptive Behavior Inventory
for Children
Academic skills, assessment of, 264-265
Acculturation levels, 221, 236, 238-239
Achievement tests:
concurrent validity of K-ABC and
other tests, 95-99
in Spanish, 263-264
Kaufman Test of Educational
Achievement—Comprehensive
Form (K-TEA), 49-50
Adaptability, intelligence as, 11
Adaptive behavior:
differences across cultures, 197-198, 199
tacit knowledge, 209-211
tests of, 36-37, 228, 254
Adaptive Behavior Inventory for
Children (ABIC), 228
ADD. *See* Attention Deficit Disorder
ADHD. *See* Attention Deficit
Hyperactivity Disorder
Adults, intelligence tests, 10, 59
Advanced Progressive Matrices (APM),
223
Affective-energetic factors, 108, 114-115,
158-159
African Americans:
highest socioeconomic group, 63-64
Instrumental Enrichment mathematics
program, 191-194
intelligence test scores, 58-60, 81-83
K-ABC scores, 58-65, 76-78, 81-83,
95-99
nonstandard English speakers, 258
predictive validity of K-ABC, 89-91,
92-94
racial identity, 246, 247, 248-249
tests designed for, 245

See also Minority students
American Psychological Association, 57
Analytical intelligence, tests of,
204-205
Analytic Perception instrument, in
Instrumental Enrichment (IE), 174
Angoff, W. H., 226
APM. *See* Advanced Progressive
Matrices
Aprenda La Prueba De Logros en
Español, 263-264
Aptitude tests, 7, 10
Armed Service Vocational Aptitude
Battery (ASVAB), 210
Arthur, G., 223
Asian groups:
conceptions of intelligence, 198
test bias and, 243
See also Minority students
Assessment:
cognitive maps, 111-115, 137, 146
comprehensive, 229-230, 237,
272-273
interpretation of results, 5-6, 235,
238-239
medical model, 227
need for, 1-2
new approaches, 11, 195-196
of learning potential, 11, 100-102,
159-160, 228, 254
purpose in educational system, 8
qualitative aspects, 139-140, 142, 240
social system model, 227-228
targeted, 216-217
See also Cross-cultural assessment;
Dynamic assessment; Intelligence
tests
Assisted Learning for Transfer, 101

287

Association of Black Psychologists, 57
Associative Recall instrument, in LPAD, 120-121, 150
ASVAB (Armed Service Vocational Aptitude Battery), 210
Atlanta (Georgia, Instrumental Enrichment mathematics project, 190-194
At-risk students, 162
Attention Deficit Disorder (ADD), 40
Attention Deficit Hyperactivity Disorder (ADHD), 39-41, 51, 55
Avant, A. H., 64

Back translation, 226
Barnes, M. L., 211
Beatty, P., 203
Behrens, J., 249-250
The Bell Curve (Herrnstein and Murray), 2-3
Bender Visual Motor Gestalt Test, 233
Bernstein, M., 200
Bias, test, 56-57
    analysis of K-ABC items, 71-75
    attempts to reduce, 254-255
    definitions, 57-58, 245
    differences in predictive validity of K-ABC, 86-94
    gender, 71-72, 73-75, 255
    in standardized tests, 243-245, 246
    item selection, 70-71, 256
    racial, 71-73
    relative lack of in K-ABC, 99
Bilingual individuals, 25, 262, 264
Binet tests, 11, 20
Black Racial Identity Attitudes Scale (BRIAS), 247, 248-249
BRIAS. *See* Black Racial Identity Attitudes Scale
Buros Institute of Mental Measurements, 242
Buros Nebraska Symposium on Testing and Measurement (1993), 17-18, 243-253

Career interest tests, 210, 267-268
Carter, R. T., 248-249

Categorization instrument, in Instrumental Enrichment (IE), 172-173
Cattell, R. B., 11, 222
Center for Creative Leadership, 210
Chatman, S., 96-97
Choney, S. K., 249-250
Chrisman, S. M., 69, 84-85
Class. *See* Socioeconomic status
Cleary, T. A., 57-58
Cognitive development, 103-104
    baseline data for LPAD, 141, 143-146
    deficiencies, 107-111, 146, 163
    enhancing with Instrumental Enrichment (IE), 165, 190-194, 195
    See also Mental acts
Cognitive maps, 111-115, 137, 146
Coloured Progressive Matrices (CPM), 122-123, 223
Comparisons instrument, in Instrumental Enrichment (IE), 170-172
Complex Figure Drawing Test, in LPAD, 118-119, 150
Comprehensive assessment, 229-230, 237, 272-273
Comprehensive Scales of Student Abilities (CSSA), 264-265
Comprehensive Tests of Basic Skills (CTBS), 87-91
Conceptual projection, 206
Continuum of Assessment Model, 101
Convergent tests, 206-208
Conway, B. E., 200
Costantino, G., 245-246
Counseling, multicultural competencies, 250-253
CPM. *See* Coloured Progressive Matrices
Creative intelligence, assessment of, 202-203, 206-208
Cross-cultural assessment, 239-241
    acculturation levels, 221, 236, 238-239
    culture-fair tests, 17, 221-225
    culture-free tests, 221-225, 259-260
    culture-reduced tests, 222, 224, 238
    distinction from multicultural assessment, 244-245
    federal government guidelines, 57
    interpretation of results, 235, 238-239
    issues, 3-7, 8, 56-58

non-timed tests, 224, 232, 237
personality tests, 267-272
pluralistic norms, 227-229, 253-254
preassessment issues, 219-221
problems with standardized tests, 10,
    218
recommended practices, 235-239
test reviews, 266
test-taking styles, 220-221
translated tests, 225-227, 237
See also Bias, test; Dynamic assessment
Cross-Cultural Counseling
    Inventory-Revised, 251
Crow Indians, 67
    See also Native Americans
Crowne-Marlowe Social Desirability
    Scale, 251
CSSA (Comprehensive Scales of Student
    Abilities), 264-265
CTBS (Comprehensive Tests of Basic
    Skills), 87-91
Culture Fair Intelligence Test, 222
Culture-fair tests, 17, 221-225
Culture-free tests, 221-225, 259-260

Dana, R. H., 219, 220
DAS. *See* Differential Ability Scales
Das, J. P., 22, 23
Davidson, J. E., 207
Davidson, K. L., 67-68
Dennis, M., 203
Developing countries:
    effects of illness on children, 213-214,
        215
    practical intelligence, 215
    use of dynamic assessment, 157, 160,
        215
Devet, C. V., 197
Diagnostic and Statistical Manual
    (*DSM-IV*), 246
Differential Ability Scales (DAS), 255-256
Differential Aptitude Battery, 10
Diffuse Attention Test, in LPAD, 121-122,
    150
Divergent tests, 207, 208
Diverse population. *See* Cross-cultural
    assessment
Draguns, J. C., 244-245

Dunbar, S. B., 28
Dynamic assessment, 100-101
    approaches, 101, 230-231
    changes produced, 152-153
    cognitive maps, 111-115, 137
    criteria, 129-130
    examiner roles, 140-141
    future applications, 157
    goals, 14-15, 136-138
    of groups, 146-150
    process orientation, 136-138, 152,
        234
    relationship to academic content,
        156-157
    testing of limits, 231-233, 234-235, 238
    use in developing countries, 157, 160,
        215
    value of, 160-161, 238
    See also LPAD; Mediation

Educational system:
    focus on middle-class values, 6
    purpose of assessment in, 8
Efficiency, mental, 114-115
Ego statuses, 246-247
Elaborational phase, of mental acts,
    109-110, 112-113
ELP. *See* Estimated Learning Potential
English as a Second Language (ESL)
    programs, 261
English language:
    Limited English Proficient (LEP)
        students, 265-266
    nonstandard, 258
Equal opportunity, 3-4
ESL. *See* English as a Second Language
Estimated Learning Potential (ELP), 228,
    254
Ethnicity, 247-248

Face validity, 246
Factor analysis, of K-ABC construct
    validity, 75-80
Family Relations instrument, in
    Instrumental Enrichment (IE), 176
Feedback, 134-135
    See also Mediation

Feuerstein, Rafi, 152
Feuerstein, Reuven, 13-16, 100, 103, 107,
        116, 138, 146, 148, 152, 154, 157,
        163, 196, 231, 233
Feuerstein, S., 107
Fourqurean, J. M., 85-86
French language, tests in, 225

g (intelligence), 9, 10, 22
Galton, Sir Francis, 9
Gardner, M. K., 204
Gastel, J., 207
Gender:
    differences in sequential and
        simultaneous information
        processing, 76
    sex role differentiation, 269
Gender bias:
    attempts to reduce, 255
    in K-ABC test items, 71-72, 73-75
    in MMPI-2, 271
General Aptitude Test Battery, 10

Gifted students, identifying, 192,
        194-195
Glutting, J. I., 92-94
Goodenough-Harris Drawing Test, 224
Grades. See Predictive validity
Groups, LPAD assessment of, 146-150
Gutkin, T. B., 252
Guyote, M. J., 204

Harris, D. B., 224
Helms, J., 246-248, 250
Hemingway, E., 2
Herrnstein, R. J., 2-3
Hill, D. S., 59, 60, 89-91
Hispanics:
    assessment with K-ABC, 25, 95-99
    conceptions of intelligence, 198
    K-ABC score differences with Whites,
        68-70, 78-79, 83-86
    predictive validity of K-ABC, 87-89,
        92-94
    tests designed for, 245, 263-264
    See also Minority students
Horvath, J. A., 209

IDEA Reading and Writing Proficiency
        Test, 265-266
IE. See Instrumental Enrichment
Illness, effects on cognitive processes,
        213-214, 215
Illustrations instrument, Instrumental
        Enrichment (IE), 183-185
Immigrants:
    acculturation levels, 221, 236, 238-239
    conceptions of intelligence, 198
    ethnic identities, 248
    performance on standardized tests, 3
    See also Minority students
Information processing:
    components of intelligence, 204-205,
        208
    sequential and simultaneous, 21-23,
        67-68, 75-76, 79, 81-82
Input phase, of mental acts, 108-109,
        112-113
Instructions instrument, in Instrumental
        Enrichment (IE), 181-183
Instrumental Enrichment (IE), 15-16, 100,
        148, 163-164
    Atlanta Project, 190-194
    bridging instruments to content,
        188-189
    cognitive functions developed in, 165,
        195
    cumulative effects, 193
    goals, 190
    link to LPAD, 164
    mathematics program, 191-194
    success factors, 194, 195
    teacher's role, 133, 164-165, 195
Instrumental Enrichment (IE)
        instruments, 164, 165-190
    Analytic Perception, 174
    Categorization, 172-173
    Comparisons, 170-172
    Family Relations, 176
    Illustrations, 183-185
    Instructions, 181-183
    Numerical Progressions, 178-181
    Organization of Dots, 165-166
    Orientation in Space, 166-170
    Representational Stencil Design
        (RSD), 188
    Syllogisms, 185-188

Temporal Relations, 176-178
Transitive Relations, 185
Intelligence:
    crystallized, 11
    definitions, 7-8, 9-10, 11, 14, 127,
        198-199
    distinction between skills and factual
        knowledge, 24
    dynamic view of, 14, 159-160
    fixed and variable aspects, 199
    fluid, 11, 12, 127
    g, 9, 10, 22
    measuring. *See* Intelligence tests
    multifactorial theory, 10
    nature/nurture debate, 2-3, 14
    Sequential and Simultaneous
        information processing theory,
        21-23, 67-68
    structural cognitive modifiability
        (SCM) theory, 100, 103, 151-152,
        159-160, 163
    triarchic theory, 16, 199, 202-205, 208
Intelligence tests:
    academic content, 24
    analytical skills measured in,
        204-205
    based on middle-class culture, 6-7
    constructing, 199-200
    creativity assessed in, 206-208
    criticisms, 8, 10
    differences between African American
        and White scores, 58-60
    issues, 2-3, 8
    levels-of-processing, 213-214
    most widely used, 10-12, 20
    performance of minority children, 3,
        4-5, 6, 58-60, 65, 81-83
    practical abilities, 209-211
    predictive validity, 4, 127
    procedures of conventional tests, 131,
        132-133, 134-135
    prototype-based, 200-202
    reliability, 26, 127
    social competence, 211-212
    standardization samples, 10
    survey, 212-213
    targeted for specific goals, 216-217
    uses, 1-2, 4, 11-12
    See also specific tests

Intermediate Visual and Auditory
    Continuous Performance Test
    (IVA), 51
Intestinal parasites, 213-214, 215
IQ (intelligence quotient), 10, 228
IVA. *See* Intermediate Visual and Auditory
    Continuous Performance Test

Jamaica, 214
Jarman, R. F., 22, 23
Jensen, A. R., 57, 62, 63, 64-65, 81

K-ABC. *See* Kaufman Assessment Battery
    for Children
Kamin, L., 5
Kamphaus, R. W., 71-72, 76, 77
Kaufman, A. S., 20, 21, 22, 23, 24, 25, 26,
    28, 59, 60, 62, 63, 64, 65, 68, 70, 71,
    75, 76, 81, 83, 85, 86, 87, 95, 96, 97-99
Kaufman Assessment Battery for
    Children (K-ABC), 12-13, 20
    Achievement Scale, 76, 77-78, 79, 81,
        86-87
    administering in Spanish, 25
    African American–white differences,
        58-65, 76-78, 81-83
    assessment of minority children, 13,
        24-26, 28
    assessment of potential learning
        disabilities, 39-55
    assessment of verbal development
        delays, 29-39
    case study: John V., 29-39
    case study: Roberto G., 39-55
    concurrent validity, 95-99
    construct validity, 75-86
    content validity, 70-75
    controversial aspects, 20-21, 24
    correlation with other tests, 80-86
    correlation with WISC-R results, 27,
        67, 69, 81-83, 85-86
    gender and race bias in specific items,
        71-75
    gender differences, 76
    goals, 21, 56
    Hispanic–White differences, 68-70,
        78-79, 83-86, 87-89

interpretation of results, 28-29
item selection, 25
Mental Processing Scales, 24-25, 59, 65, 69, 76, 81, 87, 91
Native American-White group differences, 65-68, 86
norms by race and socioeconomic status, 26, 63-64
predictive validity, 86-94
relative lack of bias, 99
reliability, 26
standardization sample, 25-26, 63-64, 68, 76
teaching items, 24-25
theoretical framework, 21-24
translated versions, 225, 227
use of, 20, 28
validity, 26-27, 70-94, 95-99
Kaufman Assessment Battery for Children (K-ABC) instruments:
Face Recognition, 62
Gestalt Closure, 25, 62, 68, 71, 73, 78
Hand Movements, 23, 73, 76
Magic Window, 25, 78
Number Recall, 23, 25, 62-63, 67, 73
Photo Series, 73
Riddles, 67, 78
Selecting, 62-63
Spatial Memory, 68, 73
Triangles, 23, 68, 73
Word Order, 23, 63, 67
Kaufman, N. L., 20, 21, 22, 23, 24, 25, 26, 28, 29, 59, 60, 62, 64, 65, 68, 70, 71, 75, 76, 81, 83, 85, 86, 87, 95, 96, 97-99
Kaufman Survey of Early Academic and Language Skills (K-SEALS), 35
Kaufman Test of Educational Achievement—Comprehensive Form (K-TEA), 49-50
Keith, T. Z., 28
Kenya, 215
Ketron, J. L., 200
KeyMath Diagnostic Arithmetic Test, 95-97
Kirby, J. R., 22, 23
Krohn, E. J., 59, 60, 83
K-SEALS. See Kaufman Survey of Early Academic and Language Skills
K-TEA. See Kaufman Test of Educational Achievement

Lamp, R. E., 59, 60, 83
Language:
assessment of verbal development delays, 29-39
bilingual individuals, 25, 262, 264
English as a Second Language (ESL) programs, 261
Limited English Proficient (LEP) students, 265-266
nonstandard English, 258
oral skills, 260
reducing role in assessment, 25
tests in Spanish, 25, 225, 262, 263-264
translated tests, 225-227, 237
vocabulary, 261-262
Language Assessment Scales-Oral (LAS-O), 260
Language Assessment Scales, Reading and Writing (LAS R/W), 261
LAS-O. See Language Assessment Scales-Oral
LAS R/W. See Language Assessment Scales, Reading and Writing
Learning disabilities, assessment of, 39-55, 85-86
Learning Potential Assessment Device. See LPAD
Learning Potential system, 101
Learning process, 158
See also Mediation
Learning Propensity Assessment Device. See LPAD
Learning Tests, 101
Leiter International Performance Scale (LIPS), 223-224
Leiter, R. G., 223
LEP. See Limited English Proficient (LEP) students
Levels-of-processing intelligence test, 213-214
Lewis, J. F., 227
Lichtenberger, E., 29
Limited English Proficient (LEP) students, 265-266
LIPS. See Leiter International Performance Scale
Long, S. W., 64
LPAD (Learning Propensity Assessment Device), 13-15, 231

baseline data, 141, 143-146
cognitive maps, 111-115, 137, 146
comparison to other dynamic
    assessment methods, 150-157
evaluation of changes, 153-155
examiner-examinee relationship,
    131-136, 139, 140-141, 156
focus on higher-order mental
    processing skills, 156-157
goals, 115-116, 152-153, 160-161,
    163
group assessment, 146-150
interpretation of results, 141-146
mediation process, 103-108, 136,
    155
modifiability profile, 107, 137-140, 142,
    158
ongoing development, 157-159, 160
process orientation, 152-153, 234
skills needed by examiners, 140-141,
    156, 160
structure, 126-131, 156
testing situation, 131-136
theoretical background, 100-103,
    151-152
validity, 159
See also Instrumental Enrichment
LPAD instruments, 116-126, 156-157
    Associative Recall, 120-121, 150
    Complex Figure Drawing Test,
        118-119, 150
    Diffuse Attention Test, 121-122, 150
    expansion of, 157-158
    for group assessment, 150
    Matrices, 122-123, 150
    Numerical Progressions, 125, 150
    Organization of Dots, 116-117, 150
    Organizer, 125-126, 150
    Plateaux Test, 119-120
    Positional Learning Test, 119, 150
    Representational Organization of
        Complex Figures, 118-119
    Representational Stencil Design Test
        (RSDT), 123-125, 130, 150
    Set Variations, 123, 150
    16-Word Memory Test, 121, 150
    structure, 127-131
Lubart, T. I., 206, 207
Luria, A. R., 22, 23

MacLean, K., 197
Malgady, R., 245-246
Mathematics:
    Instrumental Enrichment (IE)
        program, 191-194
    K-ABC Arithmetic subtest, 76
    KeyMath Diagnostic Arithmetic Test,
        95-97
Matrices instruments:
    Advanced Progressive Matrices
        (APM), 223
    Coloured Progressive Matrices (CPM),
        122-123, 223
    in LPAD, 122-123, 150
    Raven's Progressive Matrices (RPM),
        59, 122-123, 127, 222-223, 233
    Standard Progressive Matrices (SPM),
        122-123, 223
MC (multicultural) assessment, 244-245,
    272-273
    See also Cross-cultural assessment
MCAS (Multicultural Counseling
    Awareness Scale), 250-251
MCC (multicultural counseling
    competencies), 250-253
McCarthy, D., 60
MCI (Multicultural Counseling
    Inventory), 250-251, 252-253
Mediated Learning Experience (MLE),
    100, 102, 104-107, 130, 163
    as part of LPAD, 136, 140, 153
    inadequate, 107
    in groups, 148-149
    research on, 158
    See also Instrumental Enrichment (IE)
Mediation, 104-107, 233-234, 238
    processes, 164, 190
    purpose of interventions, 111, 114, 136,
        155
Medical model of assessment, 227
Memory:
    K-ABC instruments, 68, 73
    LPAD instruments, 119-122, 150
Mental acts:
    complexity, 113-114
    contents, 111-112
    elaborational phase, 109-110, 112-113
    input phase, 108-109, 112-113
    level of abstraction, 114

level of efficiency, 114-115
operations, 113
output phase, 110, 112-113
Mercer, J. R., 227
Merrill, M., 11
Mexican Americans, 78-79, 83-86, 87-89, 198
See also Hispanics
Minnesota Multiphasic Personality
Inventory-2 (MMPI-2), 243-244,
268-272
Minority students:
bilingual, 25, 262, 264
case studies of K-ABC use, 29-55
middle-class, 6
parents' views of intelligence, 198
performance on standardized tests, 3,
4-5, 6
test bias and, 56-58, 71-75, 243-244
tests designed for, 245
value of K-ABC for assessing, 13,
24-26, 28, 99
See also African Americans;
Cross-cultural assessment;
Hispanics; Native Americans
MLE. *See* Mediated Learning Experience
MMPI-2. *See* Minnesota Multiphasic
Personality Inventory-2
Moderator variables, 219-220
Modifiability profile, 107, 137-140, 142,
158
Modu, C. C., 226
Motivation, of examinee, 131-136, 158-159
Multicultural (MC) assessment, 244-245,
272-273
See also Cross-cultural assessment
Multicultural Counseling Awareness
Scale (MCAS), 250-251
Multicultural counseling competencies
(MCC), 250-253
Multicultural Counseling Inventory
(MCI), 250-251, 252-253
Multifactorial theory of intelligence, 10
Murray, C., 2-3

Naglieri, J. A., 22, 59, 60, 64-65, 81, 86,
89-92
NASM. *See* Needs Assessment Survey
Mathematics

NASR. *See* Needs Assessment Survey
Reading
Native Americans:
intelligence test scores, 65
K-ABC score differences from whites,
65-68, 86
predictive validity of K-ABC, 91-92
Nature/nurture debate, 2-3, 14
Navajo children, 65, 86, 91-92
See also Native Americans
Needs Assessment Survey Mathematics
(NASM), 92-94
Needs Assessment Survey Reading
(NASR), 92-94
Neilson, D., 250, 252-253
Neuropsychological processing models,
22-23
New Racism Scale, 251
Nolan, R. F., 71-75
Numerical Progressions instrument:
in Instrumental Enrichment (IE),
178-181
in LPAD, 125, 150

Occupational interests tests, 210, 267-268
Okagaki, L., 198, 201
Oklahoma Racial Attitudes
Scale-Preliminary Form (ORAS-P),
249, 250
OLSAT. *See* Otis-Lennon School Ability Test
O'Neal, M. R., 64
ORAS-P. *See* Oklahoma Racial Attitudes
Scale-Preliminary Form
Organization of Dots instrument:
in Instrumental Enrichment (IE),
165-166
in LPAD, 116-117, 150
Organizer instrument, in LPAD, 125-126,
150
Orientation in Space instruments, in
Instrumental Enrichment (IE),
166-170
Otis-Lennon School Ability Test (OLSAT),
256-257
Output phase, of mental acts, 110, 112-113

Parasitic infections, 213-214, 215

Parents:
  conceptions of intelligence, 198
  interview instruments, 228
Peabody Individual Achievement Test
  (PIAT), 92, 95
Peabody Individual Achievement
  Test-Revised (PIAT-R), 257-258
Peabody Picture Vocabulary
  Test—Revised (PPVT-R), 35-36, 48
  African American–white score
  differences, 64
  concurrent validity with K-ABC, 95,
  97-99
Perceptual organization, LPAD
  instruments, 116-119
Personality tests:
  Minnesota Multiphasic Personality
  Inventory-2 (MMPI-2), 243-244,
  268-272
  multicultural relevance, 267-272
  Strong Interest Inventory, Fourth
  Edition (SVIB), 267-268
Phelps, C. G., 83
PIAT. *See* Peabody Individual
  Achievement Test (PIAT)
PIAT-R. *See* Peabody Individual
  Achievement Test-Revised
Plateaux Test, in LPAD, 119-120
Pluralistic norms, 227-229, 253-254
Ponterotto, J. G., 250, 251
Pope-Davis, D. B., 250, 252-253
Positional Learning Test, in LPAD, 119, 150
Post traumatic stress disorder (PTSD),
  269-270
Potthoff technique, 89-90
PPVT-R. *See* Peabody Picture Vocabulary
  Test—Revised
Practical intelligence:
  assessment of, 202-203, 209-211
  of children in developing countries,
  215
Predictive validity:
  of intelligence tests, 4, 127
  of K-ABC, 86-94
  of LPAD, 159
  of WISC-R, 89-91, 92
Preschool children. *See* Wechsler
  Preschool and Primary Scale of
  Intelligence (WPPSI)

Problem solving skills, 201, 232
Professionals, differing conceptions of
  intelligence, 198-199
Propensity, learning, 102
  See also LPAD
Prototype-based intelligence tests,
  200-202
Psychology, multicultural counseling
  competencies (MCC), 250-253
PTSD. *See* Post traumatic stress disorder
Puerto Rican students, 92-94
  See also Hispanics

Race:
  bias in K-ABC items, 71-73, 74
  ego statuses, 246-247
  K-ABC norms by, 26
  perceived differences based on test
  scores, 5-6
  See also African Americans; Minority
  students
Racial identity, 246, 247, 248-250
Rankin, R., 78-79, 87
Raven, J. C., 122, 222, 223, 233
Raven's Progressive Matrices (RPM), 59,
  122-123, 127, 150, 222-223, 233
Receptive One-Word Picture Vocabulary
  Scale, 261-262
Representational Organization of
  Complex Figures instrument, in
  LPAD, 118-119
Representational Stencil Design Test
  (RSDT):
  in Instrumental Enrichment (IE), 188
  in LPAD, 123-125, 130, 150
Retarded individuals, 110, 144
Reynolds, C. R., 71-72, 76-77, 78, 96-97
RPM. *See* Raven's Progressive Matrices
RSDT. *See* Representational Stencil Design
  Test

SAT. *See* Stanford Achievement Test
Sattler, J. M., 231, 233
School Functioning Level (SFL), 228
Schools:
  Title I, 190-191
  use of tests, 1-2

See also Educational system
SCM. *See* Structural cognitive
    modifiability
Sequential and simultaneous information
    processing, 21-23, 67-68, 75-76
    gender differences, 76
    racial differences, 67-68, 75-76, 79,
    81-82
Set Variations instrument, in LPAD, 123,
    150
SFL. *See* School Functioning Level
Simultaneous information processing. *See*
    Sequential and Simultaneous
    information processing
Sioux children, 65, 86
    See also Native Americans
16-Word Memory Test, in LPAD, 121, 150
Smith, C., 211
Social intelligence:
    assessment of, 201, 211-212, 227-228
    School Functioning Level (SFL), 228
Social system model of assessment,
    227-228
Sociocultural Scales, 228
Socioeconomic status:
    adjusting IQ scores for, 228
    Instrumental Enrichment as remedial
    program, 190-194
    K-ABC norms by race and, 26, 63-64
    middle class, 4-5, 6-7, 221-222
    schools in poor districts, 190-191
Sociorace concept, 246
Sodowsky, G. R., 242, 250, 251-252
SOMPA. *See* System of Multicultural
    Pluralistic Assessment
Spanish language, tests in, 25, 225, 262,
    263-264
Sperry, R. W., 22
SPM. *See* Standard Progressive Matrices
Standardized tests:
    based on middle-class culture, 4-5, 6-7,
    221-222
    combining with culture-reduced tests,
    224-225
    controlled administration of, 216
    criticisms, 162, 218
    performance of minority children, 3,
    4-5, 6
    procedures, 131, 132-133, 134-135

test bias, 243-245, 246
use with diverse populations, 219-221
validity and moderator variables,
    219-220
Standard Progressive Matrices (SPM),
    122-123, 223
Stanford Achievement Test (SAT),
    262-263, 264
Stanford-Binet Intelligence Scale (SB-LM),
    83
Stanford-Binet test, 10, 11, 20, 58, 59, 224-225
Stanford Diagnostic Reading Test, 95
Sternberg, R. J., 16, 63, 198, 199, 200, 201,
    202, 203, 204, 206, 207, 208, 209,
    211, 212, 213
Sternberg Triarchic intelligence test,
    202-204
Strong Interest Inventory, Fourth Edition
    (SVIB), 267-268
Structural cognitive modifiability (SCM)
    theory, 100, 103, 151-152, 159-160,
    163, 233-235
    as basis of LPAD, 102, 130-131, 152-155
    modifiability profile, 107, 137-140, 158
Students. *See* Minority students; White
    students
Sue, S., 243-244
SVIB. *See* Strong Interest Inventory,
    Fourth Edition
Syllogisms instrument, in Instrumental
    Enrichment (IE), 185-188
System of Multicultural Pluralistic
    Assessment (SOMPA), 227-229,
    238, 253-254

Tacit knowledge, 209-211
Taffe, R. C., 252
Tanzania, 215
TAT. *See* Thematic Apperception Test
Teachers:
    conceptions of intelligence, 198
    mediation roles, 133, 164-165, 195
    roles in Instrumental Enrichment,
    164-165, 188-189
TEMAS test, 245
Temporal Relations instrument, in
    Instrumental Enrichment (IE),
    176-178

Terman, L. M., 5-6, 11
Test bias. *See* Bias, test
Testing of limits methods, 231-233,
    234-235, 238
Testing the Limits system, 101
Test of Language Competence-Expanded
    Edition (TLC-E), 258-259
Test of Nonverbal Intelligence, Second
    Edition (Toni-II), 259-260
Tests. *See* Aptitude tests; Assessment;
    Intelligence tests; Standardized
    tests; *and specific tests*
Thematic Apperception Test (TAT), 245
Third World. *See* Developing countries
Tic disorders, 40-42, 53
TLC-E. *See* Test of Language
    Competence-Expanded Edition
Toni-II. *See* Test of Nonverbal Intelligence,
    Second Edition
TOTE (Test-Operate-Test-Exit) model, 134
Tourette's syndrome, 40-42, 53
Transitive Relations instrument, in
    Instrumental Enrichment (IE), 185
Translated tests, 225-227, 237
Triarchic theory of intelligence
    (Sternberg), 16, 199, 202
    information processing components,
        204-205, 208
    test based on, 202-204

U.S. Department of Labor, 10
U.S. government, assessment guidelines, 57

Valencia, R. R., 78-79, 84, 87
Validity, 58
    concurrent, of K-ABC, 95-99
    construct, of K-ABC, 75-86
    content, of K-ABC, 70-75
    face, 246
    moderator variables, 219-220
    of LPAD, 159
    See also Bias, test; Predictive validity
Vincent, K. R., 59-60, 64
Vineland Adaptive Behavior Scales, 36-37
Visual-motor skills, LPAD instruments,
    116-119
Vocational interests tests, 210, 267-268

Vygotsky, L., 8, 14, 151, 234

Wagner, R. K., 209
WAIS. See Wechsler Adult Intelligence
    Scale
WAIS-R. *See* Wechsler Adult Intelligence
    Scale-Revised
Watlington, D. K., 72-75
Wechsler Adult Intelligence Scale (WAIS),
    10
Wechsler Adult Intelligence Scale-Revised
    (WAIS-R), 10, 59
Wechsler, D., 12
Wechsler Individual Achievement Tests
    (WIAT), 255
Wechsler Intelligence Scale for Children
    (WISC), 10
Wechsler Intelligence Scale for
    Children-Revised (WISC-R), 10, 20
    bias in, 255
    correlation with K-ABC results, 27, 67,
        69, 81-83, 85-86
    differences in African American and
        white scores, 58, 64-65
    differences in Hispanic and white
        scores, 69, 83
    differences in Native American and
        white scores, 67, 86
    predictive validity, 89-91, 92
    scores of African Americans, 81-83
    social roles assessed by, 227-228
Wechsler Intelligence Scale for
    Children-Third Edition (WISC-III),
    254-255
Wechsler Intelligence Scales, 10, 11-12, 20
    theoretical framework, 22
    translated versions, 225, 227
    Verbal Scale, 24
    See also specific tests
Wechsler Preschool and Primary Scale of
    Intelligence (WPPSI), 10
    correlation with K-ABC, 83, 84-85
    differences in African American and
        White scores, 60
    differences in Mexican American and
        White scores, 69, 84-85
    social roles assessed by, 227-228
Weil, E. M., 204

White Racial Identity Attitudes Scale (WRIAS), 247, 248-249
White students:
  intelligence test scores, 58-60
  K-ABC concurrent validity, 95-99
  K-ABC predictive validity compared to minorities, 87-91, 92-94
  K-ABC score differences with African Americans, 58-65, 76-78, 81-83
  K-ABC score differences with Hispanics, 68-70, 78-79, 83-86
  K-ABC score differences with Native Americans, 65-68, 86
  racial identity, 246, 247, 248-250
  test bias against, 74
Whiteworth, R. H., 69, 84-85
WIAT. See Wechsler Individual Achievement Tests
Wide Range Achievement Test (WRAT), 95
Williams, W. M., 209
Willson, V. L., 71-75, 76-77, 78, 96-97
WISC. See Wechsler Intelligence Scale for Children

WISC-III. See Wechsler Intelligence Scale for Children-Third Edition
WISC-R. See Wechsler Intelligence Scale for Children-Revised
Wise, S., 252
Woodcock Reading Mastery Tests (WRMT), 95-97
Word Memory Test, in LPAD, 121, 150
WPPSI. See Wechsler Preschool and Primary Scale of Intelligence
WRAT. See Wide Range Achievement Test
WRIAS. See White Racial Identity Attitudes Scale
WRMT. See Woodcock Reading Mastery Tests

Yonkers (New York), 190-191

Zone of proximal development, 8, 14, 151, 234

About the Authors

Louis H. Falik has worked for 10 years with Reuven Feuerstein at the International Center for the Enhancement of Learning Potential, providing training and consultation in the applied systems of the structural cognitive modifiability theory. He has worked with children, adolescents, and adults, and he has trained and consulted with practitioners in the United States, Canada, Europe, and Asia. He has been on the faculty of San Francisco State University for over 30 years, teaching in the areas of marriage, family, and child counseling; learning development and disability; and psychoeducational assessment. He is the coauthor with Professor Feuerstein and others of numerous scholarly papers related to these activities.

Rafi Feuerstein is Director of the Benehev Center for the Learning Potential Assessment Device and Dynamic Assessment at the International Center for the Enhancement of Learning Potential, Jerusalem, Israel. He is also a scholar in Jewish Studies and an ordained rabbi at Kibbutz Ein Tsurim. He is known for his pioneering work and his teaching in the didactics of Jewish studies, philosophy, and cognitive psychology. He has completed studies in philosophy and cognitive psychology at Bar Ilan University and the Hebrew University.

Reuven Feuerstein is an eminent cognitive psychologist, known for his seminal work in cognitive psychology. He is founder and director of the Hadassah-Wizo-Canada Research Institute and the International Center for the Enhancement of Learning Potential, Jerusalem, Israel. He has developed the theory of Structural Cognitive Modifiability and the related theory of Mediated Learning Experience while working with culturally deprived, developmentally disabled, and low-performing children and adolescents. He has established the principle that all individuals can learn, throughout all of their lives. He has established applied systems in assessment (the Learning Potential Assessment Device), intervention (the Instrumental Enrichment program), and the shaping of modifying environments. He has written extensively, and his work has generated a directly related literature in excess of 2,000 entries.

Jorge E. Gonzalez is a doctoral student in the School of Psychology Program and a research assistant with the Buros Institute in the Department of Educational Psychology, University Nebraska–Lincoln (UNL). He received his MA in school psychology from the University of Texas–Pan American, where he did research on psychological and linguistic influences on psychological assessment and multiple-group factor invariance of measures of self-concept.

Yvette Jackson is Director of Instructional Services for the National Urban Alliance at Teachers College, Columbia University in New York City, where she works with school districts to deliver a systematic program of integrated instruction geared for expanding student learning and literacy at all levels. The philosophical and methodological basis for her research was derived from the work of Professor Reuven Feuerstein, with whom she has collaborated for several years. She previously served as executive director for instruction and professional development for the New York public school system. Her applied research in gifted education and cognitive mediation theory served as the basis for the Gifted Programs as well as the Comprehensive Education Plan of the New York City Public Schools. She serves as a member of Professor Feuerstein's International Center for the Enhancement of Learning Potential in Jerusalem.

Alan S. Kaufman is Clinical Professor of Psychology at the Yale University School of Medicine, coeditor of the journal, *Research in the Schools,* and editor of a book series, *Assessment Made Simple.* With his wife, Nadeen, he coauthored the Kaufman Assessment Battery for Children (K-ABC), the Kaufman Test of Educational Achievement (K-TEA), the Kaufman Adolescent and Adult Intelligence Test (KAIT), and five other psychological tests, and is also author or coauthor of several books. He is a fellow of four divisions of the American Psychological Association. He and his colleagues have won four awards for outstanding research, including the Mid-South Educational Research Association Outstanding Research Award in 1988 and 1993 and the Mensa Education and Research Foundation Award for Excellence in 1989.

Nadeen L. Kaufman is Lecturer at the Yale University School of Medicine, supervisor of psychoeducational assessment services at the California School of Professional Psychology (San Diego), and associate editor of the book series *Assessment Made Simple*. With her husband, Alan, she has coauthored eight tests, including the K-ABC, K-TEA, and KAIT. A fellow of the American Psychological Assocation and the American Psychological Society and former associate editor of *School Psychology Review*, she is certified as both a teacher and a school psychologist and has founded and directed several clinics for the psychoeducational assessment of children and adults.

Phoebe Y. Kuo-Jackson is a doctoral candidate in the Counseling Psychology Program, Department of Educational Psychology, University of Nebraska–Lincoln (UNL). At UNL's Health Center, she is a clinical assistant providing counseling services to American racial and ethnic minority and international students. Her research interests include ethnic and racial identity formation; bicultural identity and competence; racial consciousness; and stress of second-generation Asian American youth and adolescents.

John E. Lewis is Associate Director of the Southeast Institute for Cross-Cultural Counseling and Psychotherapy and a member of the faculty at Nova Southeastern University. He is a certified Instrumental Enrichment trainer, having received training and experience in Canada and Israel. He has carried out cross-cultural research in penitentiary settings and schools and used Instrumental Enrichment with maximum security prisoners. His current focus is on cross-cultural assessment and psychotherapy training at the graduate level and supervising cross-cultural research. He has written extensively on cross-cultural assessment and intercultural clinical interventions and has presented on cross-cultural assessment issues, both nationally and internationally.

Elizabeth O. Lichtenberger is a research scientist at the Salk Institute's Laboratory for Cognitive Neuroscience and an adjunct faculty member of the California School of Professional Psychology (San Diego). As associate director of Psychoeducational Assessment Services in San Diego, she has worked closely with Drs. Alan and Nadeen Kaufman. She has also coauthored many chapters on intellectual assessment with Alan Kaufman.

Ronald J. Samuda is Professor in the Center for Psychological Studies and Director of the Institute for Cross-Cultural Counseling and Psychotherapy at Nova Southeastern University, where he has served on the faculty since 1988. Born in Jamaica and educated in England and Canada, he received his Ph.D. in the Department of Psychology and Education from the University of Ottawa in 1966. In 1971, he was asked to create an Institute for the Assessment of Minorities at the Educational Testing Service. In 1972, he became Associate Professor in the Department of Human Development at Teachers College, Columbia University, where he also served as Assistant Dean for Minority Affairs and Director of the Center for Ethnic Studies. From 1972 to 1975, he continued at ETS as Associate and Consultant to President Turnbull and Vice President Belvin Williams, helping to organize the first National Conference on Testing in Employment and Education at Hampton Institute in Virginia.

He was chosen as Professor and Chairman of the Counseling Department of Queen's University at Kingston, Canada, in 1975. He has initiated and published several research projects focused on the testing and counseling of students in Canadian high schools. In 1988, he was elected Professor Emeritus of Queen's University. He has written or edited several books in the area of minority counseling and assessment. He has served as North American delegate for the International Association for Cross-cultural Psychology. He is a Registered Psychologist in the provinces of Ontario and British Columbia and a fellow of the Canadian Psychological Association, and he has been nominated as a fellow in Division 45 of the American Psychological Association.

Gargi Roysircar Sodowsky is Associate Professor and Training Director in the Counseling Psychology Program of the Department of Educational Psychology, University of Nebraska–Lincoln. A first-generation immigrant from India, she does research on acculturation attitudes, ethnic identity, and acculturative stress of immigrants in the United States; worldview differences; multicultural counseling competencies and multicultural training in professional psychology; and multicultural instrument development. She is coeditor of *Multicultural Assessment in Counseling and Clinical Psychology.* Her instrument, the Multicultural Counseling Inventory, is being widely used to assess the multicultural competence of psychologists and trainees. Recently she implemented a program that offers psychoeducational services to immigrant middle-school students in English as a Second Language programs.

Robert Sternberg is IBM Professor of Psychology and Education in the Department of Psychology at Yale University. He is a fellow of the American Academy of Arts and Sciences, American Association for the Advancement of Science, American Psychological Association, and American Psychological Society. He is past editor of *Psychological Bulletin* and incoming editor of *Contemporary Psychology.* He is the author of about 600 publications in the field of psychology.